TC

Tom Carroll

TC

Tom Carroll

Nick Carroll

EBURY PRESS

An Ebury Press book
Published by Random House Australia Pty Ltd
Level 3, 100 Pacific Highway, North Sydney NSW 2060
www.randomhouse.com.au

First published by Ebury Press in 2013
This edition published in 2014

Addresses for companies within the Random House Group can be found at
www.randomhouse.com.au/offices

National Library of Australia
Cataloguing-in-Publication Entry

Carroll, Tom, 1961– author.
Tom Carroll autobiography/Tom Carroll and Nick Carroll.

Carroll, Tom, author.
TC/Tom Carroll & Nick Carroll.

ISBN 978 0 85798 705 1 (paperback)

Carroll, Tom, 1961.
Surfers – Biography.
Surfing.
Other Authors/Contributors: Carroll, Nick, author.

797.32092

Internal design and typesetting by Peter Guo/LetterSpaced Typesetting
Printed in Australia by Griffin Press, an accredited ISO AS/NZS 14001:2004
Environmental Management System printer

Random House Australia uses papers that are natural, renewable and
recyclable products and made from wood grown in sustainable forests. The
logging and manufacturing processes are expected to conform to the
environmental regulations of the country of origin.

For our children, our parents and our partners

CONTENTS

PROLOGUE

Hawaii, December 2011

'You're gonna trip out on this,' Tom tells me.

He half-chortles at some private thought, then swings the wheel, pulling the big clumsy rental car off the Kamehameha Highway and into the churchyard above Waimea Bay.

For a moment it feels oddly familiar: this old grassy car park, lined with low lava rock walls, framed by tangled old trees under which, together or separately, we've wedged other vehicles a hundred or more times over the years – arriving dustily in cars loaded with 9'6" guns and laughing mates on twenty-foot days, sneaking a parking spot under the trees so the wax in the cars wouldn't melt as the hours passed and we fell out of the sky on crazy Bay bombs, screeching, joking, paddling for our lives, shaking off wipeouts, enveloped in warm water and enormous fizzing waves, leaving the world behind. The whole magnificent impossible idiocy of charging big surf.

This is sacred ground, I think, *but I've never even been in the church.*

Then the familiar moment is gone, because now it's after sunset, yet the car park is half full and the famous old church is lit softly from within, and people not dressed in boardshorts are sitting on the low rock walls, talking quietly, waiting for the meeting to begin.

Ever since he completed addiction rehabilitation treatment in February 2007, Tom has attended Narcotics Anonymous meetings, regularly and consistently, wherever he's been in the world. On the road he will look for NA but go to AA – he's not fussy. Now, years down the track, I'm attending one of these meetings for the first time in support of my little brother.

We're both nervous. I am, and I know Tom is, because he is suddenly forgetful.

'Shit, the car keys,' he mutters, and dashes back, leaving me to say hello to the people on the low rock walls.

The walls line a narrow passage past the old church's entry and around to a slightly newer building that can't quite be seen from the highway. Just outside the door is the local chapter leader, an excellent surfer, highly accomplished at Pipeline in his prime. He greets me with a huge laugh.

'You're here to make sure he keeps his story straight!' he jokes.

As if. I've been trying to avoid that job all my life.

Inside, the room is unadorned. You can make tea or coffee or take a cookie or jellybean from a table near the entrance. People are milling around the table, smiling. Some in their late fifties, older than us. A couple of big strong tattooed late-teens who look caught between glowering at everyone and falling to bits.

But there's a structure here and a sense of ritual, and the rules of the meeting as laid down by the chapter leader are clear and unequivocal. Everyone here has a lot on the line. I mean, everyone always has a lot on the line, it's just that these people know it.

Tom walks up the aisle and steps up onto the stage, and again there's that odd familiarity. I think of all the other stages my little brother's strode, strutted even. The first pro junior surfing contest in history, waving a giant cheque for the unheard of sum of $500. The Coca-Cola contest at Narrabeen, and a much bigger cheque, and thousands of people knowing they were looking at someone who'd soon be a world champion. The world championship night of nights itself at some flashy Sydney hotel and the big silver cup toward which all the best surfers had bent their will, and little Tommy Carroll holding it up, standing on all their shoulders, claiming it. The Pipeline Masters finals days, the Samurai helmets and Oakley sunglasses and impenetrable winner's smile. The retirement banquet and the Prime Minister's handshake, the endless flow of praise.

I wonder, *Is he thinking of those stages too?* But he shows no sign of it. He is just Tom, a short man, not quite 5'6", balding, scarred. None of that old winner's glamour is about him, but he is quite calm. He takes out a pair of reading glasses, briefly studies his notes, though this is a story he has told too often now to forget a word.

He looks up and faces his audience, and begins.

Part one

Youth

'I did quite well at school before surfing,' Tom said. 'But then I put so much energy into surfing that there wasn't much left over for school ...

'Surfing was so real. If I had been surfing in the morning and had caught some incredible wave or faced a life and death situation like nearly drowning or something, it was pretty hard to pay attention to what a teacher was writing on a blackboard.'

—*The Sydney Morning Herald*, 1990

Part One

Youth

SIR THOMAS TOM

I just love travel. It's like every cell in my body is meant to move. I'm a traveller through and through, and it feels right for me to get up and go, to learn and understand more about myself. And join in on different cultures. I was always stimulated by languages, and by the way other people lived. Alan French, my first real surfing mate, we were down at the surf club one morning, and he said, Tom, we're going to travel together one day and we're gonna surf around the world!

I hadn't even thought of that. Wow! Are we? How? That's a big idea, you know? It sparked something in me.

I looked at Alan and said, We're going to travel the world together! But funnily enough it turned out that I was the mover. Al was the one who stayed home. But he planted the seed.

It was evident from the outset that there was a restlessness in me. Growing up on Sydney's Northern Beaches, Newport was never enough. I had to go around the corner and see what was there, or walk to Bungan, or around the rocks to Bilgola, always looking. There was a restlessness about the search for a different wave or a change of some kind. Bilgola might have a good sandbank, so I'd go around there and get stuck there for days. Or I'd hop on the bus or hitch a ride to Little Avalon. When I got a pushbike it became all about riding all the way to Palm Beach. Not with boards – just riding, going up to see what's there. A day's adventure but we got there. It was travelling under my own steam too, by foot or bike or hitching, which I liked. It was a natural thing for me to get up and go. Up in the morning first thing, before light if possible, before the sun came up.

I notice whenever I go somewhere I haven't been before that it's always super stimulating, even when it's not a place I'm really up for. It always sparked an interest in me – what the people are doing there, how they behave, how they do things – and it was always really nice reading up and stimulating that inquisitive part of me before going.

It takes a lot of energy, though, to keep moving. I'd say even today I'm travelling at least six or seven months of the year, interstate or overseas, half of every month. It adds up to a pretty restless soul. The movement stirs the inner being. It stirs the soul. Sometimes coming back home can be a really big adjustment. The soul doesn't want to settle, and the reality of that is very confronting.

The thing about travel is that it's dreamy for me; it creates a dream. When I've read books by travellers, Bruce Chatwin and people like that, they always feel dreamy, these journeys full of dreams. When I'm in a foreign country and I don't understand the language, I'm in my head a lot, and life becomes a little bit smaller in some ways. Sometimes I can sink into myself, and that's another kind of travel. That's a journey in itself.

You've always been a traveller, little brother. Maybe it's genetic. Both our parents are travellers, in their different ways.

Thomas Victor Carroll, youngest of three children, born 26 November 1961 to Janet Middleton Carroll and Victor Joseph Carroll, soon to be of 209 Barrenjoey Road, Newport Beach, Australia. 'Sir Thomas Tom', as Dad calls you.

He recites A. A. Milne as you scamper down the hallway, a tiny freckled goblin in a singlet:

> *Of all the Knights in Appledore*
> *The wisest was Sir Thomas Tom ...*
> *No other Knight in all the land*
> *Could do the things which he could do.*

Victor is a country boy, born in Mackay, Queensland, to Flora, a schoolteacher, and George Johnston Carroll, whose father had come out from Ireland to follow the Ballarat gold rush and who'd eventually married a nice Irish Melburnian girl, Annie O'Keefe.

Flora is the third daughter of the Hatfields of Mackay, a clan of cane farmers and businesspeople. Vic and his big brother George grow up surrounded by Hatfields but knowing almost nothing of their father's early years and family. Vic wonders later if he's found one reason for his dad's reticence when he discovers the mode and timing of George Johnston's own dad's death after a long stay in hospital: 'delusional melancholia', they called it. G. J. senior had been ill for eighteen months, slowly eroding in front of his five-year-old son.

After his father's death in 1888, young George appears to have lived with his mum and two older sisters at various Melbourne addresses. He then shows up in Western Australia in 1901, before signing up to the 8th Battalion Horse and heading to South Africa for the Boer War. By 1911 he is in Mackay, working at a local sawmill, then a sugar mill near the Hatfields' farm, 'The Barrie'. This is where he gets to know Flora and her sisters.

In February 1915 he enlists for the Great War, thinking he's thirty years old – in fact, he's thirty-one. He serves with the 25th Battalion infantry in Gallipoli and France with considerable distinction; wounded three times, he is eventually promoted to Captain and awarded the Military Cross, probably for his actions during the Battle of Pozières on the Western Front in 1916. After marrying Flora he buys a shop, then a furniture business, then a pub, where the family weathers the Depression years. Later, as a retirement business, they own a newsagency in the middle of town.

Dad is given a bike when he is ten and rides it to school and down to the river to swim. The ocean beaches near Mackay don't have surf, but they have fish.

Uncle George, tall and gregarious, turns out to be a community man, a joiner. He takes over the newsagency and Carroll's Newsagency becomes a Mackay landmark. He chairs the local RSL, helps found a local building society, runs for council, sits on various committees. He is chairman of the nursing home in which Flora eventually dies in 1973, aged eighty-four.

Dad himself avoids committees wherever possible. He sees war service in the 2nd AIF in New Guinea and Borneo, goes to the University of Queensland, studies economics and plays rugby, knocking out footy hero Rex Mossop in a tackle. He respects his parents and loves his brother, but he is inclined to solitude and likes the idea of wandering and observing. When he makes some money on the stockmarket in the early 1950s wool boom, he splurges on a grand tour of Europe, including a visit to his father's old battlefields, and spends a total of eight months overseas before boarding the P&O liner *Oronsay* in mid-1955 for the trip home.

Aboard *Oronsay*, sailing out of Naples, he is seated for dinner. And there she is at his table, 'small and beautifully formed', as Vic tells it: the ship's nursing sister, RN Janet White, only daughter of Dr Syer Barrington White and Ada Madeleine White of 23 Hilltop Road, Reigate, Surrey, England. The country boy with the wonderful observant mind and the stylish experienced Englishwoman from the St Bartholomew's Hospital mobile midwifery team. They spend the voyage together, meet again in November, and at their next meeting in January 1956, Vic proposes marriage. Janet is flying back to Sydney the next day to rejoin *Oronsay*; the ceremony takes place within three hours and ten minutes of his proposal. They don't know it, but Janet is already pregnant with our big sister, Jo.

Janet comes back out to Brisbane, a ten-pound Pom. While she is on the boat, Syer White dies of pancreatic cancer, so Vic never gets to meet his father-in-law. Later, he does get to know Ada Madeleine very well. When I come along three years after Josephine, Vic is thrilled at his first-born son: 'It's a bottler!' he shouts, to the onlookers' amusement.

At the suggestion of an old schoolmate's dad, Vic turns his hand to journalism. In 1960 he takes a job with the *Sun-Herald* in Sydney as finance editor. The family moves south, first to a Fairfax-owned flat in Neutral Bay, then to a house on the main road just opposite Bungan Beach.

A beach, just across the dusty gutterless two-lane Barrenjoey Road, a road so quiet we wait five minutes to see one car go past.

Then you come along. You're like a little monkey. You'd been wriggling around in the womb so much you'd got the umbilical cord tangled around your neck and the doctors have to perform an emergency caesarean section. Family legend later credits this to your attempting pre-birth backhand re-entries. With the brood complete, Dad relaxes into a very jolly father figure, full of bonhomie, and puts on a fair bit of weight. His best mate, Col Erickson, has a house at Clareville on the Pittwater side of Avalon. Col and another mate, Norman Glen, meet Dad down at the Newport Arms for a beer every Saturday afternoon.

And there are the three of us: serious, beautiful, warm-hearted Josephine Jane; you the scampering freckly goblin who always wakes up before everyone; and me in the middle, the observer, always watching and listening – learning from Jo, worrying about you.

Ada Madeleine, now a widow, comes to Australia and takes a flat overlooking Bungan, where we stay as a treat on Friday nights while Dad and Mum go out or do whatever adults get up to when the kids aren't around. Somehow we compress the word 'grandmother' down to just 'Nam'.

On summer weekend mornings Dad drives us down to Newport for a swim and watches us from the beach, his big straw hat on his head, while we go out, wrestle around, try to bodysurf, listen half-fearfully for the shark alarm to blow. He swims out with us while we squabble over the surfoplane. When a big set of waves comes, we yell and hand him the surfoplane to hang on to and dive as deep as we can, eyes shut tight while the wave's energy throws us around.

On the way home he stops and gets us a 'bottle of pop' – usually Schweppes lemonade. 'Want a bottle of pop?' he says, pulling over to the Box O' Birds takeaway fish-and-chip shop, grinning. Or we beat him to it: 'Let's get a bottle of pop!'

We stretch out on our wet towels on the back verandah and soak up the sun before lunch, when we'll get our bottle of pop.

I was the youngest and always treated as the cute little guy. At the same time there were two sides to that: I got amazing support for being the last child in the family, felt really supported, but on the other side, I didn't feel heard. So when I'd make a suggestion I'd often shrink down into myself, because what I was saying wouldn't be picked up on. Sometimes it'd even be laughed at. Being sensitive to that, I would withdraw and just shut up.

Nick and Jo would do really well at school and I just didn't get it. My energy, being kinda irrepressible, came out in other ways. I had to find these other ways to express myself. I'd wake up before everyone on summer mornings at 4 am, before daylight saving, and go outside by myself, climb the tree in the front yard and watch the sun rise, feeling the day begin, with the birds and the cicadas starting up. I'd play around in the dirt and the bush near our house, anything to be out in nature. I was in my own little world.

I felt that big father figure with Dad. He was always pretty firm; I always felt his firm hand. I must have caused him a lot of worry because I was so active, running around and falling over and always carrying on. I'll never forget him saying to me, Slow and steady wins the race, Tom. He said that a lot. I felt a distant warmth from him. He never expressed his love directly – it was never really spoken about – but he showed it through genuine support. He was there. Well, he was not always there but he was there. I always felt he had an honesty and a practical nature that was a little at odds with me. I was always more out there somewhere, up a tree, outside all the time.

I remember the smell of the zinc he would rub all over the top of his head on summer mornings before we went to the beach, a smell that would get me excited. I remember wishing he was around more when I was a kid, wishing I could kick a ball around the oval and play more games with him. I wished that a lot at some points.

We used to take walks on the beach with Dad in winter after a storm. I remember being in wonder at the beach, seeing what had happened to the sand, and the things that had washed up. There was joy in it for me. It woke something in me, running on the beach, checking things out. There was a strong sense of adventure.

I can't remember clearly my first experiences of water. The photos of us at Clareville seem pretty distant, when we would go down and play around there with Mum. I only remember bits of that vaguely. It just seemed so natural to be in the water. It never occurred to me that it might be any other way.

There's a few moments when I felt myself tested. At Tate's swimming pool on Saturday mornings at Mona Vale, during swimming lessons, I had to do two laps of the pool for my sixth birthday – which is quite a lot, huh, at that age. I only did one and a half, and I remember being pretty upset that I hadn't made it. I had to eventually do my two laps to prove that I could get a surfboard.

My memories of Mum are fleeting. There're ones with quite a bit of sadness, and there're ones with a nice soft warm feeling. I remember the hair on her face, little baby soft hairs on her cheeks. I remember her saying, Oooh, Tom, and I wasn't quite sure what she was saying, but there was a sadness in her voice, and she'd give me a cuddle. I connect with that memory now, maybe as a message that she knew something was wrong with her, something was happening to her. There might have been enough time for her to know what was happening with the cancer.

She died in 1969, so I was just seven. She'd been in hospital for about a year on and off, longer maybe. I was probably five or six when my memories of her being at home are based, her picking me up and cuddling me. They are such early memories.

I remember being at the back kitchen door and asking her how old I was, and she said: You're going to be four in three months.

I thought, Four and three! It was cool.

There's a photo of me in that back door against the sunlight, looking up at Mum while she washed dishes in the sink, and asking her that. That's a really strong memory. It was probably one of my first memories, I can't remember much before that.

I remember Mum's skin – her dry skin, all the dead skin peeling off on the bed. I saw that stuff and wondered what was going on. That's when I got that Coolite board for Christmas. It was under the bed, Mum's bed, and I dragged it out. It was grey with a yellow racing stripe. I thought Nick was supposed to get one, he was older, but I guess Mum and Dad knew I'd be overwhelmed. And I was – I was in shock.

In the ocean we used to use the surfoplane a bit, but even that's vague to me. It was nice being pushed along, but my first memory of really being propelled by a wave – really getting hooked into it – was on that foam Coolite. And it became clearer to me then why it set a spark inside me: the Coolite had been given to me. It was mine. I never thought of the surfoplane as mine – Nick was bigger than me, and Jo was there to boot. I was the outside chance of getting it, so I was pretty much left swimming. But once I got my hands on that Coolite my memories become much clearer and more vivid.

Once I got hold of that thing, it was all day every day as far as I was concerned. I'd hound Dad, harass him hard. He'd be so toasted on a Saturday after a week at the newspaper, he'd just want to have his afternoon kip, and I'd be at him, every fifteen, twenty minutes: Dad! Dad! Let's go to the beach! Dad! That's all that was on my mind: get me down to the beach so I can ride this board.

Dad must have thought, God, why did I get him this surfboard? He'd mow the lawn – this huge lawn – and we'd have to rake it up, and as soon as we'd finish I'd say, Let's go to the beach!

He'd say, No, Tom, I'm having a snooze. And he'd sit back on the garden bench, have a snooze, and I'd have to wait. Sometimes I'd sit there just watching him, thinking, *He's gotta wake up! He's gotta wake up!*

I couldn't carry the board. It was a pretty thick Coolite and I couldn't put my arm round it. I'd get a towel and put it on my head, like the guy I watched who would walk up the path beside the house from the street below. He would go all the way to Bungan Beach in the morning and come back in the afternoon, longboard on his head with a towel in between head and board. I used to wonder, Where's he going? What's he doing with that board? Then I'd see them riding their boards near the front of the surf club when we'd go swimming between the flags, and I kind of put those two things together: that's what he's doing.

There were all these little learning steps to figure out what to do with the board. I slipped off it all the time at first, so we went to the Ampol station on the way home and got some of their surfboard wax. Then we had to figure out how to actually get the wax on the board, trying to melt it and drip it on somehow.

At the same time I'd begun observing what kind of wave was better than others, what sort of wave I was looking for. That was at Newport on those semi-low-tide days when there was a bit of a slope of clean water underneath the whitewater, so I could get just in front of it and ride along. I wanted to get to that slope. I remember really observing it and thinking, That's where I want to be. I could really feel how deep the water needed to be, and I could note that sort of slope and the whitewater on top of it, so I could get down the slope and feel the board. Ultimately, if I could get to the corner of the wave, just to the green where the slope was biggest, I'd be really happy – extremely happy. But those first few runs, getting pushed along by the ocean …

I remember Dad pulling me out of the water on numerous occasions because I didn't know what I was doing – I was just going out. He'd be there saying, You're too far out! You're stuck in the rip! You're getting sucked out to sea!

Treading water next to me, really angry.

And I'd be: Really?

Mum erodes slowly, over years. Nobody seems to know what's wrong with her. She goes to hospital for weeks, comes back home, and never gets better. I hear words spoken by adults –

diabetes, dermatitis, and other more complex words – and try solemnly to associate them with what's happening to our mother. We go on hospital visits and are sent out to the broad lawns behind Royal Prince Alfred, overlooking the university football ground, and listen to the distant yells and whistles of the game, wondering what we're doing there.

Nam takes charge of the house. She stands about five feet tall, and she's full of starch and optimism. She's been through two world wars, a depression and the death of a husband. She doesn't understand her nervy, intelligent daughter. As the illness wears on, they explode in blazing, furious rows, Nam baffled, Mum screaming in rage. *Why is she so angry?*

We just block it out; we hear it but we don't. None of it seems real next to the summer days, the incredible sunburns, the bleeding rashes we develop from the Coolite and the Ampol wax, the sensation of the waves.

We don't deal with Mum's death at all. The funeral happens without us. It's an adult thing. We spend the day being looked after by neighbours. I remember Jo crying, you standing there looking uncertain, me thinking coldly, *Well, that's happened. That's that. Better look after each other now.*

We visit the crematorium a few years running, but it feels too much like the hospital visits. It remains a kind of mystery, a clouded remote experience, slowly dissolving into the past.

Dad doesn't deal with it either. He loses weight and rarely smiles. For a while he catches glimpses of Mum in the street, thinks to walk up to her, looks again and it's a trick of the light or some shift of shape; Mum's there and then she's gone, replaced by a stranger with a similar hairdo.

He never cracks, though. He's not uncrackable, but he doesn't crack. He goes to work instead and becomes a great journalist, one of Australia's greatest ever journalists. They call him 'The Cobra' because of the way he'll look at an errant journo from underneath his eyebrows, fixing the poor human with his stare, saying as little as possible – the look does it all. He drives home every evening with a map of all the phone boxes in the Northern Beaches in his head, stopping at each one to get a report on how the paper's coming through the press. At home, the paper now beyond his reach, he eats his dinner, drinks a glass of wine and falls asleep at the table. In the mornings he goes down to the beach for a run and a swim, 6.30 pretty much on the dot, and if we're up – you're always up, Sir Thomas Tom, awake at the crack of dawn – we get a ride down with our boards. He has to toot the car horn to get us out of the water.

Every year he takes two weeks off and goes up to Fraser Island, tailor fishing with his mates. The way he packs for those trips, the way he visibly relaxes as he stuffs his fishing gear, old shorts and T-shirts and other bits and pieces into bags, leaves a memory with me sitting now next to the memories of you packing for surf trips – the same sense of declension into the present, away from the remove of the everyday, the anticipation of fun.

Once I see him packing a couple of rolls of toilet paper. He sees me watching.

'Just in case you need to nap a crap in the sandhills,' he says, smiling.

I'm warmed by this, that he sees me as grown-up enough to parse a half-rude word.

That's as close as we get to Dad for many years. People a long time later say things about you, like, 'Surfing's in his blood.' Surfing isn't in our blood. We don't have the faintest clue what we're getting into. We fall into it, away from the emptiness, the cloudy mystery of our childhood. By the time we're in our teens we're gone.

I can't remember the exact moment when I moved on from the idea of that little slope in the wave. I wanted to ride, I guess, the waves I was seeing in the magazines and in the book we had at home, *A Pictorial History of Surfing*. I didn't read a word of that book. Just looked at the pictures, gazed at them and dreamed. There were guys surfing Sunset Beach, these shots pulled back, and there'd be these guys all standing in line coming down the wave – a long strip of wave – and you'd see the trails, the wakes coming off the boards. How the wake came off the board was a really big thing for me. I used to love looking at that, and I began looking behind me at the track my board was making.

It was so raw. I remember being told to go in at Mona Vale Basin. Dad took us down there one day, I can't remember why, and I had the Coolite. I paddled out there in my sluggos – I didn't have any boardies – and I wanted to get a few of the little rights that looked like fun. I'd heard about it at school or somewhere, this little wave.

I was paddling out, and this guy said, What are you doing in those sluggos? Surfers don't wear those! Get out of here.

Just kicked me out of the Basin … for wearing sluggos! I was so upset! It was so wrong. I stood on the beach watching, thinking, I can't go out! That was the start of my drive to get a pair of boardshorts, and I think it helped Dad to realise I needed them too. I was probably eight years old. What sort of bloke's kicking an eight-year-old out for wearing sluggos?

There was fear in it. I was worried that I was never going to be able to ride a wave, or be able to get back out if I did. I had to push myself into situations I didn't like. There was a hell of a lot of poundings, lost boards, swimming, understanding rips, getting pounded again, losing boards on rocks and dinging things. But one day I got out next to the Peak, got out the back. There were a few of the older guys out there, and they said, What are you doing out here?

I was scared but I wanted to catch one of those waves. It was a classic offshore day, where the wave faces were dark because of the wind and sun being over to the west. It looked like those photos from the book. I wouldn't say I was out to ride big waves, but that was where it was taking me. I wanted to ride what those other guys were riding. I remember standing on the beach, thinking, I'm not going to get out here. I'm scared. But I'm going to give it a go.

I had a borrowed board. No legropes. It was all about rolling the board, not being able to hang on, swimming in. But there was a lull that day and I just sprinted out, and I was out there with those older guys, them saying, What are you doing out here, grommet?

I thought, I'm not allowed out here. But this is me, this is the spot. I can take care of myself in this place.

I've always been the best at everything: higher marks at school, better swimmer, better tennis player. I can't let you get too far ahead of me. The summer after the Coolite I wangle Dad into buying me a top-of-the-line super Coolite, a Midget Farrelly Pro Champ model. It's so special it has a rubber fin set in a box on the tail. It's practically a real board. I'm the king for three and a half weeks until the Midget Farrelly Pro Champ snaps in half in the Newport shorebreak. You get hold of the rubber fin and with the help of Wayne Ramsay's dad, stick it into your Coolite.

I start looking for a real board, a 'fibo', a fibreglass surfboard with which I can get the edge back. More than an edge. A fibo will put me way out in front. A bloke at school, Nigel Savage, offers to sell me his little semi-kneeboard for $22, only slightly damaged – half the tail has broken off and been replaced.

I have some money, borrow the rest from Dad and bring home the fibo. But by this time it's autumn, competition tennis time, and it feels too cold to surf. You and your new mate Michael Twemlow make a habit of borrowing the fibo.

One Saturday afternoon I come home from tennis and there's a furtive rustling and whispering from the garage. There's you and Twemlow, looking panicked. There's the fibo, with the half-tail repair broken clean off again and smeared with the polyester resin you've tried to use to fix it, but failed because none of us have ever heard of resin needing catalyst.

I'm never letting you guys use the fibo again. But it doesn't stop you. Soon you've found your own fibo. You borrow $25 from Dad for a Ron Wade pop-out with a huge blue fin, and you surf all through the winter on it, no wetsuit, relying on the fires that guys light along the beachfront on cold afternoons. You come home literally blue but grinning, freckles sticking out like paint splatters.

As the warm days return and I start talking about coming with you, you look at me and say, 'You're really going to hate it. You'd better get ready. Because I'm a lot better than you now.'

You say it again, a couple of times, looking at me, meaning it.

I think, *Something just changed here. But what, I don't know.*

TWEMLOW

Then there was an array of little friendships that popped up and dissipated, like bubbles that come to the surface, some lasting longer than others. Adam Milgate, he rings a bell. I'd go round to his place after school and get invited to his birthday parties. He was a play buddy. At school there was Sandy Fraser then Wayne Ramsey. Wayne and I had good fun together; our friendship was action-oriented. I used to stay at his house and his mother took a liking to me. Kevin Long and I were close at that time, too. I would occasionally sleep at his house over the weekend. That was around fifth class, when I was about ten years old. We did stuff, laughed together a lot and had a good boyish relationship.

I couldn't be inside or at home for very long. That was a requirement of being friends with me, running around outside, crawling around in the undergrowth, climbing trees, digging, exploring. Getting dirty was a good thing for me.

There were some girl friendships early on. Michelle Cooper was a good friend at primary school. We seemed to get on really well and enjoyed each other's company, we had the same sort of sparky thing and were open with each other, which was kinda nice when I look back on it. Until, of course, it all implodes down the track, when the hormones start kicking and you begin looking at each other completely differently. And you wonder, *Well, why can't I just do you?* But that wouldn't be appropriate right then.

Alan French. Alan who I hung out and surfed with – that was a much more water-based friendship. He was a good surfer and had a fibreglass surfboard, and he had older brothers who surfed. He had a lot of assets, things that I wanted. I wanted his board, I wanted to know how to surf like him. That was when we started hanging down the beach, down in front of the surf club, surfing a lot.

Then this bloke came out of nowhere and set up camp with his family in a unit across the road from the beach. Twemlow! That was a way more intense relationship.

I was already hanging out with this guy at school, Tim Martinus. I was already being attracted to a more intense sort of person, someone outside the square. I was exploring, I think. Risk-taking. I found myself acting as a mediator between Tim and Twemlow in the school playground, because they had heavy conflicts. They were fighting every lunchtime, physically, to the death. To the fucken death. It'd start off as some pathetic argument about something, and they'd just tick each other off and it'd be on.

How fucken dare you! Bash.

Something was going on with those two. I'd actually be the fuel to the fire. Something would happen between me and Twemlow, and Twemlow would try to hit me. He was unpredictable – he'd be your best friend one minute and be really nasty the next. And Tim would take offence to that and say, Don't you hit my little mate! And it'd be on again. It was pretty insane.

But we'd surf together.

It was funny hanging out with Twemlow. He was one guy who I knew would be there for the early morning session. I'd come down to the beach on my bike, pre-sunrise, and all the lights would be on. The Twemlow household would be on fire, there'd be stuff flying everywhere. He'd be sliding some sort of sly, cheeky remark at his sister as he slid out the door, and she'd throw something. He'd just get out the door and mutter, Stupid bitch!

It was such a contrast to our house, which was quiet and subdued and organised and spacious. Twemlow's was a small box and it was foaming at the mouth.

I might have left my board in his garage, because boards were pretty dangerous to carry on a bike. I remember losing it early one morning at the bottom of the driveway, hitting the gutter and flying over the handlebars with my board, going over into the grass and totalling myself. I crawled back on my bike and down to the surf. We ended up leaving the boards at the surf club, joining the club and leaving them there.

The Government decides it's going to widen Barrenjoey Road, so it buys half our front yard. Dad, perhaps a bit relieved at the chance, sells the house opposite Bungan, buys a block of land on Nullaburra Road a couple of streets back from Newport shops and builds a big new brick house on the block. Just like that we're within a five-minute bike ride of Newport Beach.

We've been going there all our lives in the back of Dad's car, yet now, on our own, it suddenly feels different. It looks different. We ride down and prop our bikes against the surf club steps and look at the beach through our half-formed surfer's eyes. A long arc of sand, broken some way along by a concrete stormwater outlet, framed to the north by a crumbling cliff and a short rock platform, and to the south by a taller cliff and a hill and a long exposed reef.

We'd always just thought it was a beach. Now, from other grommets and from what we can overhear of the older surfers' talk, we learn the beach's hidden identities. The Cove, off that north rock shelf. The Point, just across from it. The Peak, which breaks all summer over a jumble of submerged rock and sand. The Pool, the south end's reef break, which breaks in winter. And the reef itself, clouded in foam, the Path, which we hear breaks when a southerly change hits in summer.

Nobody but the surfers know these names, or can even see the places named by them. We're too scared to surf the Peak because of the good older surfers who kick us out whenever we try, and we're too scared to surf the Pool because it's too big. They're out of our reach. They seem magical places, waiting for us, somewhere in our futures.

We watch the older surfers. The Miller boys, sons of the famous cricketer who lives up our street now but who is never there; you never see the famous man, just his boys with their motorcycles and the dangerous glitter in their eyes, and his wife, who has an American accent and smiles at us every day as she walks past. The Windshuttles. Wilbur – can it really be his name? Can somebody really be called Wilbur? Richard Feathers, who according to rumour makes surfboards in a shed in his parents' backyard. Billy Wawn, who invites Josephine to the school fancy-dress dance and shows up at the door dressed as Wee Willie Winkie.

Who are they? What do they know?

We watch them, we look at the surfing magazines, we listen to the surf movie soundtracks on Nam's stereo. We grovel around in the sandbank waves near the surf club, imagining we're bigger than we are.

~~~

This was when we began coming into contact with early morning surfing. Real early morning surfs. Once we finally had the freedom of getting ourselves down to the beach, we ran down or rode pushbikes from the house in Nullaburra. That was a really cool time. You could get there right on daybreak and there would be the other hardcore guys, lighting fires under the earthen cliffs along the sand in the freezing cold offshores. Different types of days, there'd be big days and small days, but always better conditions early in the morning.

And it'd give you that backlit Crystal Cylinders look, like the shots of Hawaii we were seeing in the magazines. Looking at lefts in the winter morning sun was a lot like how the Pipeline shots looked. So I was keenly observing all the changes in the light as well.

There was that energy in and under the wave, that feeling of being pushed along for the first time, all of a sudden being alive and understanding that energy. When there's a bump here and a bump there, and you're feeling it, sensing it, without having to look. I'll always remember surfing those north-east windswells that had such a short period between them, surfing them so often and loving them so much that I knew when the waves were coming, even though I couldn't see them. Through the chaotic madness I'd built up a pattern in my head of the wave train. It was like my mind had already organised it. Chaotic but there was order in it.

We had a regular surfing group: Steven Seiler, who we called Sam, and Twemlow, Hunter and Robert Hale. I remember that as a really stable time. Going surfing with Sam, he tended to neutralise Twemlow a bit. We'd get Sam from his house on Palm Road and Glen Stokes had a house on Palm Road too. Haley and I developed a kind of language of our own – we were next door neighbours, and our relationship extended beyond surfing and into hanging out on our bikes, doing whatever we could to entertain each other, because there wasn't always surf.

I think we all joined in on the feeling of surfing, the sensation and the stories we used to share. We had the stories about the older local guys, the legends like Dave Jones and Jeff Crowe, of them surfing the bigger waves out the Path. We really wanted those stories to be true. It helped create this fantasy of surfing, that we could make what we wanted of it, and it was perfect for the young male mind, to learn this rite of passage in the waves and to watch our surfing just beginning to happen.

Surfing was it. There wasn't much else. When I was ten or eleven years old there were guitar lessons, and that was something that felt really organic and nice. I was doing it with Jo's friend, Janet Carroll. How's that? That was her name; it was crazy. Janet Carroll teaching me guitar. She was really cool. But my relationships with people who surfed were much easier to navigate – they were my tribe and it felt right. I guess I was pretty myopic in that sense, but it just felt normal. That's all that mattered: the surfboard, the surf and who was doing better than the other.

There were some really funny things going on around here then though – guys who surfed but obviously weren't well. Guys who didn't make any sense. I wasn't quite sure about them. Heroin was big, and there'd been this group of guys who rode motorbikes and surfed from time to time. There was no example of rebellion in our home, no disregard for authority; there was always a strong respect for elders and what they did. I was always looking up to older guys for guidance, so it was confusing to watch this crew who were wild and looked strange. It was odd to see them vomiting in the street. Later on it all clicked for me – they were smoking and shooting heroin; they'd taken it a step further. They rode motorbikes real fast, doing wheelstands along the car park.

I was trying to get a gauge on how to behave from them. It was confusing. Then they started disappearing. There was James Chandler, who was a really good surfer when I started. He had a motorbike accident and became a quadriplegic.

Then you had the Grots. The Grots had their own language, they had a nasal, sneering tone of speech, *nyyyerrr, nyahhhh*. They were all a bit slovenly, more prone to smoking pot and being lazy about the surf prospects. They weren't looking outward or upward. I guess if anything they just looked low energy, they were down, and I was looking for the up energy all the time.

The message from them was to stay clear. Like the time Mad Linda came down to the surf club on her horse. She came around the corner pretty quickly and lost it, coming off and knocking herself unconscious on the grassy verge. We were all hanging under the stairs nearby, and me and Alan didn't know what to do. The Grots were a bit older than us and got hold of her. They laid her down in the dressing sheds, not knowing what the hell to do either, but then things got weird. They saw an opportunity to look at her. They took her pants off. It was heavy. Me and Alan left – we didn't like the idea of what was going on. I don't think they did anything, and eventually she woke up and left. The horse was wandering around on the beach. It all felt wrong.

Probably the ultimate Grot was Cookie. He used to do all sorts of weird stuff. He tried to break into Charlie's surf shop and disarm the alarm with a fork. Then he got busted trying to break into the Box O' Birds with a knife. He'd always get himself into trouble. The Grots weren't necessarily junkies, but some of them became addicts later, and Cookie was the one who made me realise heroin was around. I remember seeing him on the nod, standing on the footpath outside the Westpac bank. He's on heroin, I thought. That's what it looks like when you're on heroin. He wasn't doing anything, just standing there, asleep. As if he wasn't there.

Twemlow went to Barrenjoey High and I went to Pittwater. I'd be up front in woodwork, doing these dovetail joints, getting them all schmick, then this group of guys turned up at the back of the class. Kev was there, and so was Glen Stokes, who we called Boj, right in the middle of it.

Those guys were making really bad work, and I was thinking, *Those guys! They can't do anything right!* But they seemed to be having a good time down the back, laughing and carrying on. So over about three years I drifted to the back of the class.

I was still trying to keep up my work. Boj would be laughing and doing something cheeky. Mr Blackman, the woodwork teacher, somehow never managed to learn Boj's name, so he couldn't really bust him. It'd be like: Hey, you blokes down the back – what are you doing! Long, Carroll, and … Long, Carroll! Out the front now! Boj was the one screaming and yelling, laughing and carrying on, breaking guys' stuff, but he'd never get busted. Me and Kevin would get pulled out: Carroll, you are gonna end up in the gutter!

It's a big contrast. Kev does beautiful work now, but back then he didn't look like he had that in him.

Me and Boj would meet up down the beach. Paul Lindley was in another class, but he'd be there too. But I was closer with Twemlow. We were pretty thick and kind of looked alike – blond hair, white zinc on our lips. We used to catch a bus up to Palm Beach on the weekends, and we bonded on those trips. We were doing stupid shit: egging people, like the pedophile Philip Bell. We'd see him in Newport and say, There he is! There he is! Get half a dozen eggs, quick! We'd raid Twemlow's mother's fridge: Is he still there in the car park?

We didn't know what he was all about at the time – we just knew we had to egg him. He was creepy. You don't see people like him around surfing anymore. The scene was a haven for pedophilia. There used to be a lot of vulnerable little boys without parents in sight. Not anymore – there's too much parental support around now, too many adults.

But there were no adults around then. It was all youth. All the parents I knew were busy, off doing other stuff. There wasn't one who came and hung out, at all, ever. The idea of a parent hanging out didn't make sense anyway – it wasn't part of the culture. We wouldn't have got it. I fully understand when kids these days look at you like, What are YOU doing here? I don't feel out of place among kids in surfing today though. We've got a much better connection with young kids; I think they're much more open to us now. There's just a lot more humans doing the same thing.

We were definitely on different pages back then. The oldest surfer I knew of was Harry the Hat. Then you had the Old Madman of the Sea, Ron Ware. There was Mr Gorman, too, Rory's dad, Terry, he used to surf. But Harry the Hat! You'd hear the word go around: Harry the Hat's out the Pool! Check him out! It was like observing another life form really.

There was only us. That was it.

RECOGNITION

I can always remember storms. I'll never forget the May 1974 storm and the crazy evening that preceded it. It was a wild wind that night. Haley had been up the back earlier, yelling from his balcony. That was how we used to communicate. All of a sudden there was this crazy blue flash. I saw it out of my bedroom window and he saw it out of his. Not lightning – something else.

Did you see the blue flash?

Yes! I saw the blue flash!

Early in the morning we got our bikes and went down to the beach to see what had happened. It was carnage. There was still a lot of rain and wind. Thick layers of sand had been washed up over the northern end of the car park, and the waves had come along the old drain and into the low part of the main road, running into the houses along the back. We were riding around, just loving it because everything had changed. You could slide the tail of your bike out over the sand in the car park, and look at all the carnage and the damage. It was the perfect age for something like that to happen, because we weren't responsible for any of it. We hadn't been hurt, and we didn't have to fix anything. It's all happening to other people, so we got to be these great observers and have fun with it all.

I remember looking at the ocean. The whole front of the surf club had been gouged out, and there was a big cliff with all these rocks exposed. Everything that had been hidden before was being exposed. Everywhere we thought water would have gone, we went. Underneath the units on the beach waves had broken in and washed sand in. The big pine trees at the south end – all their roots had been exposed. It was a smorgasbord of change in a very brief moment. Not only was there the blue flash – whatever that was – lots of stuff had changed. There was now a left-hander going into the Pool, coming from a deep spot between the bombies outside, and it was barrelling, like Pipeline, spitting, this big left. Then there was another current and a bigger left outside that. It looked massive, untouchable for us. There were a lot of concerned residents at work in front of the surf club, trying to prop up the cement and the path. The earthen cliff that was in front of the club had gone and it never came back. There's still only sand there now.

The Peak just disappeared. Because the whole beach had been eroded, there was a big trough between the beach and the outside banks, so everything was a shorebreak. Me and Twemlow were really big on the left-hander shorebreak that appeared in front of the Peak. There was a bunch of rocks inside there, causing it to form, and we used to call it the Peak

Shorebreak. It was a little bowly kinda thing. We were really enthusiastic about that wave. All the sand had been taken and deposited well outside the Peak area, and it didn't come back for a long time. Seemed like forever, back then.

The Peak Shorebreak was ours. We were very enthusiastic shorebreak surfers, so the fact that everything turned into a shorebreak was fantastic to us. But what we used to know as the beach was gone. By the time the Peak came back a year or so later, I was a different surfer.

We're all different surfers. We're growing.

The May storm has washed away the barriers between us and Newport's scary magic places. It's even made a new spot, down near the stormwater outlet, a little wedgy right breaking across the remains of a storm sandbar. Most of the older guys have given up or gone away; it's up to us to name this spot. With grommetty imagination we call it The Pipes.

In the same way, we begin to name each other. Nicknames flourish like weeds among the juvenile delinquents who've laid claim to the Elysian fields of the resurgent Peak. Peter Stephens is 'Knob' – I still don't know where that came from. Mark Hayward is 'Weevil'. Haley nicknames Derek Hynd 'Pinchest' because of DH's adolescent pigeon chest, which he refuses to expose to light – he changes in and out of his wetsuit with the towel almost wrapped around his neck. Scott Beggs is 'Scrotum'. Stuart Cooper is 'Stretch' because he just keeps getting taller. Dougall Walker is 'Hips' or 'Swivel', because he surfs like a hula dancer. Hunter is just Hunter. Peter Phelps is just Phelpsy. Glen Stokes is 'Boj' because his board has a 'B' and a 'J' in the logo and what looks like an 'o' in the middle. Paul Lindley is 'Squeak' because he has a hilarious high giggle.

You have a ready-made nickname thanks to one of my schoolmates, Todd More, who calls you a 'grotesque little goblin', which given your leprechaun face, cleanly segues into 'Gobbo'. Somehow, thanks to my black hair and developing monobrow, I become 'Woggo'. Everyone knows wogs don't surf!

Gobbo and Woggo. You're a goofy-foot, right foot forward. I'm the opposite, a natural-foot. We wonder if it makes a difference.

It turns out Wilbur's name is a nickname; his real name is Robert Fowler. Wilbur now says hello to us. 'These guys are surfing good!' he tells the two or three older surfers who are left. We feel as if we've been knighted.

There are brothers, arrays of brothers: the Hynds, the Haywards, the Gormans, the Walkers, the Carrolls, the Lindleys, the Kings, the Longs, the Bales, the Nowanes. Brothers gnawing and fighting among themselves, brothers already growing apart, brothers like us, trying to look after each other and kill each other at the same time.

Richard Feathers suggests he make you a surfboard. Older, more cautious, I trail along, watch the process from a distance. Your board comes back a glowing yellow, like Gerry Lopez's Pipeline surfboards in *Five Summer Stories*, with a little rounded-off tail and a nose curving up dramatically, like a dried gumleaf.

Richard has glassed his trademark – a real seagull feather – under the deck. Later you use a paint spray can to fit a neat little red lightning bolt up near that gumleaf-curved nose. In your mind you're Gerry Lopez, and the little backlit waves out the Cove are the vast barrels of the Pipeline.

Summer approaches. The council sweeps the May storm sands out of the car park in time for the crowds, the panel vans with the P-plates and forty-five-degree roof racks, the awkward eighteen-year-olds who drive down from the north shore and the western suburbs, hoping to be surfers too. From Parramatta and the like. 'Parras!' we yell derisively from behind the Norfolk pines. 'Rubbernecks!'

We paddle from shorebreak to shorebreak, trying to outdo each other, harassing the Parras, yapping like little dogs. And just as we're beginning to feel ourselves expand, to begin to occupy our little territory between the headlands, something odd happens to the new shop up on the corner of Coles Parade and Foamcrest Avenue. A guy we've never seen before, an older guy in his twenties, is painting a mural along one wall, an airbrushed mural of a perfect blue wave. Another guy is there too, long straight blond hair, corduroy flares and Crystal Cylinders button-down shirt and Beachcomber Bills thongs, and a big grin that he flashes easily at everyone.

Hunter, the social animal, is first to corner him, and soon the word is out. The guy's name is Charlie. Charlie from Newcastle or somewhere. Charlie Ryan. He's living in a unit upstairs with his girlfriend, Dale, and he's starting a surf shop.

A real surf shop! In Newport! We can't believe it.

There was no world champion in surfing when we began. It was just this semi-hippie, really strange scene, and then Charlie showed up with his surf shop and we began building a life around surfing as a primal source, a spirit.

I'd received recognition already. I'll never forget, we were leaving our boards in the surf club – we had a deal with Big Al Walker that we could keep our boards there – and I was in the back of the shed when Squeak and a few of the boys filtered in after a surf, and I heard Squeak say, How good a surfer is Tom now – that's crazy, how amazing is he!

I had no idea I was having that effect on people. When I heard that kind of natural statement in the shed that day, it was really strong feedback for where I was at with my surfing. Squeak, and he's the same today, is not the sort of person who will come out with any idle compliments. So for him to say that was pretty cool. I thought, Maybe I'm not too bad.

All of it was a build-up to the feeling that I'm special, that I had something. And it served me on some level. It helped me concentrate on what I loved doing.

Charlie Ryan was the first one to give me recognition from completely outside our group. I was riding that yellow board from Richard Feathers, the banana-looking thing, six-footer round-tail. Charlie had just come to town. I was surfing out off the point and he said, Man, you're good! I'll get you a sponsored board!

I didn't know what he was talking about. He said, I'll get you a free board. I know a guy who'll shape you a really good one.

I thought, *What for? What FOR?* I didn't understand.

I came home and talked to Dad about it, telling him there's this guy with a surf shop down the street who wants to give me a board. And Dad said, Well, what does he want in return? When someone gives you something like this, they're going to want something in return.

I was like, Oh. Really?

Dad said, There's a bargain here, you need to talk to him about what they want.

Charlie explained to me that it was a surf shop board, so

I'd be surfing for the shop, but I still didn't understand it. I just wanted to surf the board. I can't remember it as a big deal other than the fact that someone had recognised me.

And then I got that shop board. I had to swap it for my yellow one, which was okay. It was a beautiful board. I never got one that good again for some years. It changed my surfing, shifted me to another level. I can't remember talking with Rodney Hocker, the shaper. It just turned up. I remember running my hand across the board. It had a sanded finish, a tucked-under edge and a beautiful fin. I wish I had that board today. If I took it out surfing and stood up on it, my blueprint would be in it. I would instantly go back to that original feeling.

When I was young it didn't feel like a natural thing for me to go out into competition with other people in a combative way or try to get the better of someone else.

It wasn't natural for me to run out onto the football field. It was very foreign; I didn't know what I was doing. I couldn't work out what was going on. I understood that I had to play the ball, or run the ball up, or pass the ball out, get the ball in and out of the scrum. I liked the idea of being in the backline and running the ball up and around a couple of guys. I didn't mind tackling. I didn't mind any of these things. But when it came to being against the other team, at a deeper level, it didn't really click with me. I didn't have a strategy in my head for combat, for playing the game. I was completely lost. Where's that guy going? Why is that guy doing that? Why couldn't we score a try then? And I'd walk off the field and go surfing. It was probably really frustrating for my teammates, even though I had Twemlow with me, and he was a good five-eighth. Twemlow knew exactly what he was doing, he knew what was going on and where the game was heading, but he wasn't in there unless he was winning.

But I wouldn't give up. There was something in me that would never give up. I thought, *I'm in here for the long haul. I might not know what I'm doing, but I'm here for the whole game.*

So I knew my competitive response wasn't based in anger or aggression. Even though there were a few times in my career when anger helped, I knew that my best performances didn't lie in that anger.

But I did have an ambitious streak in my head and in my blood. I think recognition, that basic need, was starting to be fulfilled. My ambition came out of this desperate urge to prove myself and get on with what I wanted to do, which was to be a great surfer. It wasn't so much a competitive thing. I was just bursting with a very powerful energy, and all these natural gifts were just sitting there waiting to be utilised.

It wasn't like I was thinking, *I'm going to be world champion one day!* I just knew that I'd like to be a great surfer on the world stage. That was an ambitious notion, and it didn't stop on the Northern Beaches, it didn't stop in Australia.

The surf club was a whole other kettle of fish. Alastair Walker, the oldest Walker brother, was in it, and the membership was really low. He needed to kick it up again, so he recruited a whole bunch of us younger surfers. As long as we did our Bronze Medallion and did our patrols, we could leave our boards in the surf club and use the hot showers.

The surf club interaction was kind of messy and not exactly what I wanted – it was focused on board paddling and swim events that I just hated. I just wanted to go surf. Look, there's waves out there – why am I swimming? It was an uncomfortable feeling being a surfer and in the club at that time, the surfer–clubbie wars were still fresh, but I liked the involvement.

Big Al Walker was from a surfing family and he bridged the gap. He wasn't big, but we had to call him Big Al because he was so stinkin' big, surf club captain, you know? He came by some funds from somewhere and got hold of this diesel bus–van thing. It was falling apart but it still ran, and he stuck some seats in the back so there was room for boards in the front, and we'd head off to these carnivals to surf in the Malibu Board Display.

The first one we went to was at Crescent Head and it was disastrous. There were crazy rains that year and we had to travel through floods, the bus breaking down all over the place. We were the only ones who made it from Newport Surf Club.

Everyone was surfing off the point, the clubbies were doing their thing, and I totally tuned out. I had my beautiful new board and I went off and found this wave by myself and started clicking with this board. I went beyond where I'd ever been. I'll never forget the feeling. It all became one movement. It was no longer me separate from the wave on the board – I felt this one movement, going up and down the wave. There was really a feeling of being complete.

Big Al organised for me to go down to Tasmania for the Australian surf lifesaving titles, to go in the Malibu Display and the board paddle at Clifton Beach. My first memory of that was in a hotel the first night, being woken by this crazy, wild screaming in the street. Big Al goes, Look at this – my God. We looked out the window and there were people running through the streets of Hobart with toilet paper alight and hanging out their arses. I found out later this was called the

Dance of the Flaming Arseholes. I thought, *Wow, that's what goes on at the Australian surf lifesaving carnivals.*

Next morning we went down to Clifton Beach. It was May in Tasmania and freezing cold, so I took a wetsuit. I went out for a warm-up surf and it was ice-cream headache stuff. I'd never surfed anything so cold in my life. I walked down to surf in the event and this official looked down at me – this big guy in a white uniform and white hat – and he said, Hey, Snowy, come here! Take that wetsuit off! That's an advantage over the other competitors!

I went back, took it off and surfed all weekend in my sluggos, freezing, but it was a pretty good feeling, winning Australian gold for Newport Surf Lifesaving Club.

But nobody knew what a boardriders club was until Charlie took me up to join Peninsular Boardriders at Palm Beach. It was a club full of older surfers who were all kind of 70s-era hippies, really, all into long single-fin pintails, Afghan hounds, tie-dye clothes, and Jimi Hendrix and Tim Buckley. This whole other side to surfing was really romantic and created a whole other flavour in my life. Once I got back to Newport after a day at Peninsular it seemed boring.

Twemlow and I met the Ravenscrofts, who were part of the club, and Owen Ravenscroft took me down to Narrabeen. Owen said, Watch this guy Col Smith – he's the most radical guy around by far. Watch him! Col was doing backside re-entries against the morning sun, his whole board silhouetted. The image was imprinted in my mind, and I started trying to put that Rodney Hocker board into a backside re-entry down at the Pipes.

I'll never forget Owen. We were at a Peninsular club

contest and he said, Would you like to go in the Northern Beaches competition, Tom?

I was intrigued and said, What happens if you win it?

He said, Well, then you go to the State competition.

I asked him what happened then. Well, then you go to the Australian championships, and that's a big event. If you win that —

What happens?

Well, then you go to the World Championship.

It lit me up. All of a sudden there was this series of things I could do to get onto the world stage. It was clear as a bell. And I was up at Palm Beach at the time, outside my Newport loop. It was already happening.

Winter, 1975. Southerly gales are ripping up the coast, chased by swells. Our first real swells. Our first real scary thrilling days. Big, bombing six to eight foot mornings out at the Pool as the fronts pass just offshore, black horizons framing grey-blue skies. Surreal graceful Derek Hynd, who never says anything to us, and blunt solid Gordon Walker engaging in mortal combat for the inside position. Cameron Hayward on his long racy Feathers pintail plunging down impossibly late drops. Six foot blown hollow days riding the lefts in front of the surf club, across the May storm sandbars, when every wave feels like a step forward, a step toward the next one and the next and the next.

Waves, waves, waves, there's always more and there's never enough.

You and Twemlow reckon I'm getting above myself in the water and wax my board with soap. Fuck you! I scrape off the soap, deciding I'm going to be Newport's big-wave charger.

I watch you on that little round-tail, the magic board, trying these odd turns, close and under the curl, going up almost square and then turning just under it – *snap!* – so the fin flashes for a moment, then almost falling back down half into the barrel. What are you seeing? This turn you can see in your mind, yet not quite on the wave. You try it any time the wave opens itself to the chance.

The fin flashes briefly in the turn. That's our measure of a good turn – if you can see the fin. We all want white fins in our boards because they're easier to see against the dark blue airbrushed wave faces of that fantastic winter, but we never think to ask for a white fin. We just sorta hope for one. It's part of the magic of a new board, and you can't ask for magic.

Some days the surf just gets too big for Newport or any other open beach, and we get into Gordon's car and drive up the coast to Umina Point inside the mouth of Broken Bay. These crazy thick waves coming past Lion Island and slamming into a rock shelf made invisible by water blackened from the river. Pissing Point, we call it. Nobody else ever surfs it, just us. We hoot and scream and yell at each other, catching waves we can't possibly ride, taking insane wipeouts into the black water that smells like earth.

One wet, blowy Sunday in August that year we hike all the way to Palm Beach for a Peninsular Boardriders club contest. The surf's pretty good, but the older guys in charge of the club decide it's too much trouble to run a contest on this soggy cold day. They don't ask us what we think.

We hitch home, deflated. Then around lunchtime a motorbike roars up the driveway. It's Rod Hynd, Derek's older brother. He comes to the door, helmet under arm, eyes lit up.

'Hey, we're gonna have a contest at Newport,' he says. 'Whoever shows up. What are you doing?'

'Who's in it? Just us guys? Derek?'

We're on our bikes as fast as it takes to yell at Haley next door to get his board and hurry up.

Derek wins the contest, you come second, me third. We can't believe it. We can't believe we're even allowed to have our own contest. It begins to dawn on us that maybe we can just do whatever the hell we want.

I did well at the Northern Beaches cadets. I didn't know how I did it, I just went out and surfed and suddenly it was, You got through, Tom. You got through again, Tom. I didn't have any answers as to how it was working or happening. I had that energy. I'd paddle out, pick the waves and go.

Even though I still didn't quite know what I was doing, and I wasn't ready for my ambition at all. Next minute I'm in the State Titles. I'm down at the car park in Newport and Rod Hynd's down there, saying, The State Titles are on at Narrabeen today and you're in it! Want a ride? I'm freaking out. Cheyne Horan's in it!

I fricken ran for the hills. I kept myself real scarce that day. I didn't want to go down there. I was scared shitless. I was scared of everything. I wasn't ready at any level.

Charlie had pumped me up with the board, and I was feeling pretty good about it, but he was connected in other ways. Around then a big contest came to Sydney's beaches, the 2SM Coca-Cola Surfabout. You would hear that it was going to be held somewhere along the Northern Beaches, and there were surfers coming from all over the world. There was Reno

Abellira and Barry Kanaiaupuni from Hawaii, all the way to Col Smith, the surfer from Narrabeen who'd been pointed out to me. There was Nat Young. All the guys we knew from trawling through the surf magazines, all our heroes, all the men – especially Michael Peterson, because for me at that time, Michael Peterson was the pinnacle of surfing. He was winning all the events and there was no question about his surfing, it was all commitment. There was no pulling back from any wave, he could surf anything, and that was creating this really big story in my head.

One day around that event, I think it was about midday, I had my board in Charlie's shop. I stuck it down on to the seagrass matting floor and waxed her up with a nice fresh block, and Charlie disappeared for a moment. He came back through the back door of the shop and said, Hey, Tom, you wanna take Michael surfing?

I said, What? I was still waxing up. I looked around and there was Michael Peterson looking down at me, with this long hair and this distant look in his eye. Michael Peterson, right next to me, as I was waxing up. I'm going to take my hero surfing.

So we strolled down Coles Parade and over to Ross Street, heading to surf the Pool. It was a solid wave for us. It had an end section that came up over shallow rocks and bits of reef; we thought of it as a bit of a heavy section. I was walking with Michael Peterson toward this spot, across the road, past Seagulls Milk Bar and toward the southern end of the beach, Michael asking me questions about the break. Not many questions though – he was a man of few words, especially around a grom like me – but he seemed happy to be going surfing.

He lived up to everything in that surf, and even if he

hadn't, he did in my mind. Everything he did was blown out of proportion but he was suddenly real to me, Michael Peterson was real and he was staying at Charlie's house.

He came down and stayed every year for the Surfabout. I'll never forget him pulling up with his special board, the Fangtail, hanging out one of the windows of his van in the car park behind Charlie's shop. It had these sharp fangs coming off the back that made it look really fast.

Those connections helped Charlie make us feel really special.

Charlie had a girlfriend, Dale, and she was really smart, really switched-on. Charlie was the showman and had the connections, but the nuts and bolts of the operation was Dale. I remember her telling me sternly, Tom, it'd be really good if you could get to surf places like Narrabeen more often, because that's where all the contests are.

Yeah, I thought, that makes a lot of sense.

In Derek Hynd's eyes we were becoming a little more legitimate. We were surfing the Peak. We'd been admitted. So he began introducing me to Narrabeen. Derek had his little five-speed manual Bellett, and if there was any north swell during the week, he would give you a loose, enigmatic comment about it, like, Maybe Narrabeen on the weekend, it could be on. So early on Saturday morning we'd pile our boards on the Bellett's roof and tie them down with legropes. Twemlow would be with me and we'd pay Derek twenty cents petrol money and jump in the car, a very charged-up bunch of little males. To save petrol, Derek would turn off the engine when we were going downhill, wait until it'd almost slowed too much, then jump-start it at the bottom of the hill. I was always stunned at how good Derek was at driving. He could drive with no-hands, legs on the steering wheel, eating a pie or having a drink at the same time.

Narrabeen was an introduction to a whole other kind of surfing. It had a hierarchy going on. There were these tiers of surfers, the guys who were the best surfers in tight on the takeoff, then a pecking order going right down from the outside break all the way to the end. Being a little guy from Newport, I was at the end of the line. I had to sit down at the end peak and get the dregs. But it was practice.

Dale is smart in other ways. She helps us get judging sheets for our contests. We still don't really have a name for the club, but Dale notices there are other kids wanting to join in from other beaches – Phil Motteroz and Brian Bolar from Avalon, a couple of kids from Bungan. Dale says, 'Well, it's all of you and these other boys now. You want to have surfers from other beaches too, why don't you call it Newport Plus?'

She gets Charlie to give us jobs behind the counter at the shop. Hunter and I work there on Thursdays when the new shopping laws let them open until nine o'clock at night. We take up smoking Marlboros in imitation of Charlie, and do our best to sell the Cream boardshorts with their hand-stitched, flowery logos, the batik Bali shirts, the fibreglass-deck skateboards and the cup-shaped blocks of Honey Wax. The shop is a bit awkward compared with other kinds of shops – no item matches up, every pair of shorts is different, it all feels handmade. But work or not, we're there every minute we're not surfing.

We are incredibly protective of the surfboards. They stand

there in their racks in the western window of Ocean Shores Surf Shop, shiny and unwaxed. We're not blessed with a free surf shop board the way you are, but Charlie gives us discounts. We save and save. Haley gets a pink Morning Star with a swallowtail. Hunter gets a green one with a rounded-off nose. I get one with a yellow spray around the rails, fading to white in the middle.

In the flat upstairs there is another world. When Michael Peterson comes to stay, Hunter and a couple of others go up there one afternoon to peer at the Great One and listen to MP on the phone: 'Hey man, if it's black, fine, bring it down. If it's brown, I don't wanna know.'

What is he talking about?

Next morning they sneak into the flat and nobody's awake. There's dope lying around in piles. They wonder if they should steal some.

Late 1975. We go down to Narrabeen to surf in the Northern Beaches regional competition. You're the only one of us who's ever been in something like this. We don't know what to expect. At Narrabeen there's all these kids cruising around. Long hair and early summer tans, puka shell necklaces. These beautiful boards from Hot Buttered and Morning Star and other labels we haven't heard of. Kids from Manly and Curl Curl, Dee Why and Long Reef.

I feel like a pretend surfer next to these kids – scared of this wider world where everyone looks like they should be in a surf movie.

Then we start going in the heats and, wonder of wonders, we win. Twemlow does. I do.

I watch you, in some heat or another, get a wave that looks useless at first, but then it builds somehow, and you ride left away from the whitewater and toward another mass of whitewater coming from the right. What are you doing? You've seen something. You go up and strike the oncoming surge at an angle, so your board is swung around and back the other way. Then you go directly up and into the whitewater you'd been trying to escape and strike that, very high and on a particular angle. Several different unexpected things at once, yet everything just right, and you so absorbed in the moment you don't seem to notice anything till it's done.

People standing near me just sort of exhale.

Winter comes again, winter 1976, the last winter of big surf in that incredible 1970s. I finally beat Derek in good six-foot surf at the Pool, the first of us to beat him in a Newport Plus contest, and can never remember surfing against him again.

On another wet day at Warriewood Beach, we all surf in the NSW Schoolboys Championships. More kids from other beaches show up, ripping. Livewire George Wales from Bondi. Ant Corrigan and Richard Cram, another one of those Bondi boys. We're not the only kids doing this crazy shit. You win the coveted Under-16 division and the 18s on the same day.

We set up a club contest with the Bondi boys. Their delegation drives out one night to meet with us and plan it. They sit in the Walkers' kitchen and marvel at how far they've had to drive: 'Youse live out in the bush, hey?'

Halfway through the winter, on a big afternoon at Pissing Point, it happens: Tom Carroll Injury Number One. I see you catch the wave but I can't see what occurs. From behind, the wave rips away down the line, flat-backed, then toward the end it explodes into deeper water. You'd pulled into it then tried to second-guess and straighten out. The wave lands across your shoulders and drives you down and across the board, flattening you like a spider. Your right knee buckles sideways. You don't paddle back out. I see you hobbling toward Gordon's car, sitting disconsolately on the bonnet while we surf.

We're young, we laugh it off. It's not your back foot. You get an elastic knee band, hobble around for a little while. In three weeks you're surfing again. But you don't forget. You shouldn't pull back from waves like that. You're safer in the barrel. You're safer if you charge.

At school my achievement was buried. I was State Schoolboys champion, and they didn't even want to look at it. There was no acceptance of what was going on for us. That's how it felt to me. The feeling that I got from some of the teachers was that I was not worth mentioning. And my response to the school's attitude toward me as a surfer was quite strong. What do you mean I'm not worth mentioning?

That set me on a path. I thought, There's something really cool here and they're not awake to it. Something was set off in me. I wanted to make a point, show them that they were wrong. It was as basic as that. I wanted to prove there was more to surfing than that.

There was all this focus on sports like cricket, it was all so boring. I thought here's all these sports being televised, and then I see Michael Peterson – I think it was at the first Surfabout – on the ABC. MP in the living room on TV! I'll never forget it. I thought, *Wow, this is where it should be.* He was being recognised as a surfer, and so it was possible we would be recognised as a sport.

I think that's where a lot of my ambitions were fuelled: the idea that this really cool thing we were doing, something I was getting really good at, could be bigger. That there was a bigger thing going on here. The idea of turning that around was a big motivator.

The flipside was that we had surfing all to ourselves, and it was so special. I didn't even know how special it was at the time. It wasn't like we were thinking, *Oh, this is cool.* It was the water we were swimming in. We were just responding to going surfing. There was something really cool about it later on down the track, I think because we were actually pretty healthy as young kids. You're generally healthy and vibrant as a surfer – that's how things come out of you from being in the ocean – and so there was a certain attraction that some teachers couldn't ignore.

My English teacher thought it was cool that I surfed, and she was open to the whole thing. It was really nice. But I never told any adults any stories about surfing.

I went through a lot of boards. There was a Beacham in there somewhere. All of a sudden I got a really good offer from Henri Surfboards. I stuck it out with Henri, but the boards didn't go as well as that Rodney Hocker.

Then I got to Col Smith. I think Charlie eventually guided me toward Col because Col could drive me to contests and mentor me a bit. He shaped me a 6'3", which was probably equal to that Hocker board. It had the raked fin and rounded tail, and it worked really well for me.

I won that State Schoolboys title and went up to Queensland for the nationals. I'd heard that I was lucky to even be in it because I was a goofy-footer and Stan Couper, who ran the nationals, didn't like goofy-footers. I heard a rumour that Stan was going to stop any goofies from competing. It really ticked me off.

But my journey with Col was full of recognition, full of figuring things out – you get a board and give the other one back each time. Then by the time I was fifteen, I was allowed to have two boards: a 5'10" and a 6'3".

I remember walking down the rocks at a State junior title at Sandon Point with Cheyne Horan. He had this little white round-nose with a green underside, and he just ripped on it. He said, Here, feel this, it's only 5'10".

I was in awe of Cheyne. I thought, *This board's sooo small! This is what I've gotta get.* Even so, I went out right then and kicked his arse. I said, Fuck your little board! No I didn't say that. I thought, *I got him* – now I could go down a size and get better.

I was well on the way by then. Travelling with Col, I'd already done the Southside Open contest at Cronulla with him and got a photo in Surfing World. That was my first photo in a magazine and it was a big deal, more recognition. I got a good result in the Southside Open and kept moving through the event.

I remember driving over there every day, Col in his HR Holden doing 360s on the Cahill Expressway. Fucken hell! I thought it was fantastic. It was crazy. He'd race down that left-hand turn around Circular Quay and just lose it, sliding out, loving it. Luckily there was no cars coming the other way. No seatbelts, nothing, getting thrown around the car. Grommet. Loving it.

January, 1977. The Pepsi-Cola Pro Junior isn't like any contest we've ever been in. It has a logo – its very own logo – a Mickey

Mouse look-alike on a surfboard, which is printed on all the T-shirts and banners. It has prize money, huge money, the unimaginable sum of $500 for first place. It's the Surfabout, but just for us.

Where has it all come from? Vince Tesoriero, one of the organisers, is an older surfer from Dee Why, but Bev Dyke, who runs the promotions company behind it, is from outside the little surfing circle of the Northern Beaches. Bev is fantastically enthusiastic about all the superlative kid talent on the beach at Narrabeen. At lunchtime, suddenly aware that we're starving, she orders buckets of Kentucky Fried Chicken for all the competitors. We compete for the drumsticks the same way we're competing for everything. We scrap and laugh, steal waves in the warm-up surfs, hack through heats, watch these new people who we sense will be part of our lives from now on. Cheyne. The kids from Queensland, Joe and Thornton, who fight worse than brothers. Big tall Jody Perry and sharp-witted long-haired Gary Jardine. Banksy, Ross Marshall and Craig Naylor from Cronulla. Steve Wilson from Maroubra and Alex Basansky, the southside showman. The Narrabeen boys, Greg Black, Shearman and Kenny Oliver. Joey Buran and Bud Llamas, two kids we've never heard of from California who Bev has researched and brought across for international flavour. Mike Newling from Cornwall, England. This is real.

We slash away at heat after heat as the summer nor'-easter pushes at North Narra's long left walls.

On finals day I lose the plot in the third heat of the morning and go right instead of left and end up in 10th.

You put on a sleeveless wetsuit jacket against the nor'-easter, take the little 5'10" round-tail with the fin four inches off the back and get to it.

The three heats – quarterfinal, semifinal, final – feel preordained.

Dougall gives you a run in the semis, but it wears him out. You just stay unwaveringly on message. The mid-sized set wave rolling off the outside take-off zone and resetting itself across the middle section. The bottom turn, top turn, high line out on the face. Then the deep turn laid flat against the water, back around, 180 degrees through blue water to the foam line. Smack, rebound, back onto the face again. What they call your 'nutcracker' cutback.

I walk up the sandy track from Northy to the car park, carrying your board and the little wetsuit jacket. You walking ahead of me, carrying the big $500 cardboard cheque. People are milling around, a fizzy excitement in the air. This is how life will be. I can feel the pieces clicking into place, *click, click, click.*

You're fifteen years old and you're going to be world champion.

We've been surfing for four and a half years.

When I walked down to Narrabeen to surf on the first day of that contest, I saw Joe Engel. I walked to the front of the surf club, looked out and there he was, out there practising. He ripped the bag out of this right-hander at the Alley and I thought, *Holy shit, who's this guy?* It freaked me out. I'd never seen anyone go quite so fast, in his hunched-over style, with this little board. Whoa, I gotta be on my game here. But things kinda fell into place for me. I had a really good board. I'd taken Cheyne Horan's advice from that Sandon Point day and got a 5'10" from Col Smith. Then we had these north swell lefts that were running down the beach at Narrabeen. I thoroughly enjoyed surfing the wave. I'd win a heat, come in, just decide, Okay, keep doing that. It was simple, just so simple. I couldn't get the smile off my face.

Going out there and competing at that point, I got into a rhythm. I tapped into that energy that creates a mass headspace. You're on a roll. You can literally walk into a heat and you've won without even paddling out.

I look at a photo of us all lined up: myself, Dougall, Jody Perry, Thornton, Cheyne, Joe Engel and Gary Jardine, and Joe's having a go at me. I remember having a lot of cramps in my feet. I pushed myself beyond my capacity. We were running around to the paddle-out after each wave, and I was only fifteen, riding long lefts and running around in circles. Coming out the back end, everyone was out there to win. It was all the best juniors coming together for the first time, eyeing each other off beforehand.

I was so toasted when it was over, but Derek wanted to go out. We've gotta go and have a drink with the Narrabeen boys, he said, I'm coming around to pick you up.

I told him, No, Derek, I'm too tired. I can't do it. But he insisted. I went down there and I couldn't talk to anyone. I was looking around; it was the weirdest feeling. It didn't make any sense to go out after doing what I'd done. I wish I'd stayed put and recovered, but I didn't. I went out and found it really silly.

When you have a winning experience like that, you set precedents within yourself. There were two things that went on for me at that point: Am I in this for the long haul? Or am I just here for the glory?

I remember feeling that potential. I was quite young, and I was thinking, I've got a chance here to go further. This is a stepping stone. It wasn't like, All right I'm taking all the glory now, I won and it's over. I felt like it was a real start.

And a lot of things flowed from that. I got the Stubbies

invite from that win and there was a lot of recognition. At the end of the following year, by the time I got to Hawaii, there was already some guts behind what I was doing. It wasn't this fresh kid just turning up in Hawaii. There were eyes on what I was doing.

Part two

The Fluffy Zone

'The only way that I'm going to drive a Porsche is if I keep panelbeating.'

TC, *Surfing World*, 1979

No-one knows what they're getting into when this thirst for fame comes up, when we're young and ambitious. No-one knows what they're getting into. We just don't understand what our ego is doing to us, taking us down this road that seems like it's full of good stuff. The illusion's all about this idea, this fantasy about how good things are going to be, how it's beautiful ... It's this incredible Hollywood state.

But the reality is quite different, and you don't know that until it happens. It's like when you lose somebody – you don't know what it's going to be like until they're gone. Fame arrives and there's this powerful thing happening that's run out of control. And unless you've got a good handle on it and you're being coached into it by a good mentor, it's unlikely you'll fare very well under its influence. Unless you're the one in ten million who can naturally take it on.

MAN ON MAN

1977. The summer rolls on. The summer of the Peak. The big swells of the mid-70s are gone and in their place is this funny little wave, really two waves in one, drawing and breaking left and right off a shallow rock, bouncing its way in toward the sandbar and the inevitable close-out. There's room for two surfers, one on either side of the rock, and every day there's twenty or thirty of us swarming around it, piling in two at a time: Gobbo and Woggo, or Derek and Dougall, or Haley and Newling, or Twemlow with his huge sunburned lower lip, who masters the dummy call so he somehow gets the whole wave to himself, then paddles back out grinning, till we all shove him off the next one in revenge.

Meanwhile Nam, starchy, cheerful, strong-minded at eighty years of age and five-foot-zero inches in height, meets with the Anglican ladies of Newport, then walks along the shops, happily waving at Phil Paso the sports store owner, David Pitt the newsagent, John Kape the barber. They all know Mrs White with her motherless grandchildren and her English accent. She stops at Dependable Butchery to buy chops and sausages for our dinner and discovers the big, young, pale-eyed man behind the counter, John, is a surfer.

She quizzes him: 'My grandchildren are down there all the time! What do you all get up to?'

John the Butcher tells Mrs White all she needs to know and nothing she doesn't, and lets you drive his crazy overpowered racing Mini along the car park, watching with a big grin on his face.

We're a small dirty scraggle-haired muscular tribe. We take over the entire northern half of the freshly laid post-storm car park, kick everyone else out of the water, and catch fifty, eighty, 100 waves a day, 200 cutbacks, 400 top turns, two dozen wipeouts, four near-barrels and half a fight. Nor'-easters blow up little swells on sunny mornings, then southerly busters arrive late in the afternoon, turning the wind offshore at the Path. We sneak down there in groups of two or three and try to ride down the gap where the two waves meet under the headland.

We're surrounded by beautiful girls but we barely see them, these gorgeous girls who'll grow up to be women, who'll become girlfriends and wives and bear children and outgrow us, and we'll still barely see them. But when two – Kay and Julia – dare to come out and trade waves with us, the bad teenage boys of Newport Peak roll over and give them whatever they want. We can't see girls, not the way we should, but in the water they turn into surfers.

The surf movie *Free Ride* comes to Avalon Cinema, and overnight it feels like everything changes. Surf movies have always felt like fantasies – wordless distant dreamscapes we can admire but never inhabit. But this is a movie about surfers only a few years older than us, and they are tearing apart the best surf in the world in close-up slow motion. Surfing like we try to out the Peak, except they are at Sunset, Pipeline, Off-the-Wall. We paddle out next morning two feet taller, our half-lit grommet imaginations inflamed, and instantly nickname the sandbar right just down from the Peak 'Tomson's', after Shaun Tomson, the hero of the film.

We just have a sense. Surfing is too incredible, too magical not to mean something more. It's like a wave. A wave is forming out there somewhere. We don't know how big it is, what shape it is, but we are going to catch it and ride it into the future. A lame metaphor, but it's all we have.

Then the invitation comes in the post. This big envelope with 'Stubbies Classic' stamped in light blue in the top-left corner. Little Tommy Carroll, invited to a big pro contest, the first one of the new International Professional Surfing tour. The first one ever to hold man-on-man heats. Fifteen-year-old Tommy Carroll, man-on-man!

We never think you might be as baffled by this as we are. Instead, we tease the shit out of you: 'Yaaah, Tommy! How are you getting to Queensland? You taking your skateboard?'

You with this distant look in your eye, dreaming. 'Oh,' you say, 'it's all been fixed up.'

'What?' we shriek, 'What the fuck are you talking about? Who's fixed it up?' We're jealous but we are also excited. '*Fixed up?* Bullshit!'

But it has been fixed up. You're gone on the plane, your two boards in towelling socks tied together with legropes, your face lit up with hope.

I saw some classic footage from that event recently, of me getting in a tussle with Buzzy Kerbox. You can see Buzzy trying to punch me in the water, because I was taking him out. It was just this little flash, guys surfing Burleigh, MP ripping, and this altercation with me and Buzzy down the end section.

I remember thinking, *What's wrong with this guy?* He was weird and aggressive, like I'd done something wrong because I was doing well. Really strange. I had no understanding of it. Otherwise, I was just watching all the guys ripping, surfing so well, so cleanly. And Burleigh and Kirra on my first day.

Terry Fitzgerald was on the plane to Coolangatta, and he knew who I was. He introduced me to Clyde and Eddie Aikau, right there on the steps getting off the plane. And just seeing these massive guys – they took up the whole aisle but were really nice, soft-spoken guys. My hand disappeared into their hands. I was just a weedy little *haole* kid.

I had $110 to last two weeks and I didn't know where to go, so Fitzy said, Well, you can get into this motel – it's $10 a night. I thought, I have $110 and two weeks, I've gotta find somewhere else to stay. I didn't know where Col Smith and Ron Ford were staying, but I knew they were somewhere at Burleigh, so I started walking. It was raining. I didn't know where to go. It was stormy and waves were breaking way outside Burleigh – doubling and tripling up on the sandbar and grinding around the point, unrideable.

I was walking along in the rain and looked around and saw Col inside one of the units just before you get to the Burleigh caravan park. A little red block of units. He was living there with his wife, Denise, and their youngest daughter. They were like, No worries, you can stay here, and they put me up on the couch.

Then Ron Ford turned up. He said, We're going down to Kirra – it's booming, six to eight feet.

I gulped. What board was I going to ride? Ride the longest board you've got, he said.

So there it was, this session out at Kirra, with Reno Abellira, Barry Kanaiaupuni, Shaun Tomson, Rabbit Bartholomew, Michael Peterson, Rory Russell, Gerry Lopez – everyone! It was the mega line-up. For a kid to paddle out there ...

I couldn't really surf up close with those guys, but I sat down toward the end of the wave and watched. It was amazing Kirra. I remember looking into the barrel and freaking out. I tried it switchfoot, standing the opposite way, because I saw this kook getting such a good barrel, and thought, I can switchfoot better than that guy. I took off and did a bottom turn switchfoot and stood in the barrel for what felt like ages and came out. I've never done that again in my life.

It was scary going in to compete. It was all so special. You had your outfit they gave you, your name stamped on it, and two different colours of boardshorts – red or yellow, depending on what colour you or your opponent drew. Michael Peterson was the guy, had been from the beginning of our surfing lives, and I watched his every move with eagle eyes, and seeing him up close, making all these slight adjustments and using the rail in a turn all the time, it was incredible. And watching Col Smith surfing out there at Burleigh on the backside. Incredible. He was at his peak and there was no-one doing the stuff he was doing. Maybe a couple of the Queensland guys. I liked watching Tony Eltherington and Guy Ormerod, those guys' backside styles really inspired me, watching the way they used their body and surfed tight and were really stylish and flowed in with the wave. That really defined the Queensland goofy-footer.

But Col Smith brought a whole other approach to the lip, vertical and straight up, there was nothing slow. One hundred and fifty per cent full tilt. I loved that. Staying with Col and watching him surf was a really golden moment for me. His whole body was opened up to the wave, stretched out and just ripping it around super quick.

There was another heat, before Buzzy. It didn't mean much to me, obviously – it's a grey blur. That heat with Buzzy was the big one. I remember the judges calling out scores, or writing them down on a big board that we could see, something. I had him up against the ropes. The waves were perfect and I was overwhelmed by the situation. I wasn't looking at catching a specific wave and getting a specific score – I was just doing the best turn I could on a wave and keeping it together. I came in and Col said, I think you got that one. I had the yellow shorts on. Skinny little kid. Absurd.

I stayed the whole two weeks and watched the final, Mark Richards and Michael Peterson. It was sooo crowded, I was distracted by the crowd, but I was focussed on MP. I was so drawn to him that I didn't really watch MR and wouldn't be able to appreciate him for some years to come – what he had to offer, style-wise – even though I loved the yellow-and-red boards he used to ride, the Renos.

Competitively, the event launched me. Another precedent was set in my perception of who I was and how I was to compete. Here I was, for the long haul.

That year I had a real swagger going on. I definitely had an idea about myself. I'd won the Pro Junior, I'd been in a big pro contest, and I thought I was killing it. I had recognition, social status, money. It wasn't a huge thing, but it was certainly something. My ego had been inflated, and a fresh male ego at that point just wasn't acceptable in the group. People were calling me out on my behaviour. Boj and Squeak, those guys in particular, Haley and Hunter too, though a lot less directly. Twemlow. All those guys.

It was a real struggle. I didn't like to be called out, but in some way I really understood it. They wanted to know I was still with them, and not above them in some way. They were looking at me differently, but they still wanted to put me back in my spot.

I think they had to begin to trust me – trust me to go away and succeed. Before they put their hopes and dreams in me, they had to know that I was fair dinkum. It's almost like they needed to test me.

The tall poppy treatment did a real job in keeping my ego in check, even though it wasn't pleasant. But at the same time it was essential to move past it. I had to look at it clearly. If I was going to become a world champion, I had to be able to see myself as a world champion. I had to clearly define myself and do the work and feel worthy.

I would end up getting smacked in the competition anyway. Eventually that would happen, and I would have to be ready for that too.

field and the hopeful world of the future. I was on the competitive surfing roller-coaster and I'd already had enough winning sensations to want it again. But I couldn't see myself making a living that way and paying rent. I remember saying to Dad that I'd like to get an apprenticeship of some sort, so that I had something to fall back on if my surfing didn't work out.

I finished school in Year Ten and Dad got me three days' work on a job site to see how I'd go. I'd never worked like that in my life. I'd worked with David Pitt and Gordon Walker at the newsagency on the weekends, but this? I was picked up in the morning and taken to the job site, somewhere in Fairlight. I was thinking it might be like the woodwork we'd done at school, but it was all about how many bricks I could stack in a barrow and get across planks of wood through this job site without falling down through them. Sometimes it was six feet up in the air, along scaffolding planks. Then I had to unload the bricks on the other side.

I worked three days full on. I was probably fifty kilos, doing nine hours a day for three days. I got to the end of it and thought, *I can't do this.* The builder agreed. He told Dad, I don't think Tommy's cut out for labouring.

So there was Wayne Smith from Narrabeen, one of Col Smith's surfing buddies (no relation). Wayne and his brother Les had a panelbeating shop down in Narrabeen. They said, Why don't you come down? We'll put you on a first-year apprenticeship. It was four days a week, $50, eight and a half hours a day, and a day at tech learning how to be a panelbeater.

I was allowed to go to competitions, it was understood that I could surf at lunchtime at Narrabeen – but how would I get down there? I had to ride a bike or get a lift with Wayne if he wanted to go surfing. Wayne was pretty cool. Fatty Al Hunt

NO MONEY

It was so raw back then, eh. Everything was so raw. Well, what did we have to pay for? We had to pay for food, a bit of petrol, rent. Then we needed money for going out and clothing. It wasn't as though the surf companies made everything back then. Rip Curl was just a wetsuit. Quiksilver was just boardshorts – maybe a jacket or a T-shirt. You had to buy what you wore, but there was very little to pay for.

And there were no consequences. No plans. I didn't have a big strategy.

I remember one time going to apply for the dole, which was a really strange feeling. I think you got $60 or $80 a week. I was only on it for about a month. But I knew that I had to work. I think as a bloke you really want to do something for yourself – that's a strong natural urge for me.

It was funny because I'd already done okay with surf competition, had made quite a name for myself in the junior was running his own little business next door, rebuilding VWs and selling them, in his way.

I watched some of the things that were going on. It was just the way business was, I thought. You'd charge people for one thing – what you put on the quote – then you'd do another thing. That was business. You were meant to cut out some rust and weld up a whole section for someone, but that wasn't what you'd do. It was sometimes up to me to grind out this rust, bog it up and make it really smooth and clean, like there was metal in it. It was kinda like surfboard shaping and I got right into it, getting the surfaces perfect so they didn't have to replace the door skin. I did about a year and a half.

That job showed me what I really wanted to do. I was making $50 a week, paying $10 board to Dad and doing whatever I could with the $40 – buying clothes mainly. I wanted to look good going out on the weekend. I'd put a little bit away each week. It was a pretty lean existence.

Then this other job came up with another panelbeater in the area, paying $87 a week. The guy said, You don't have to go to Tech, but we'll teach you panelbeating. He knew I'd need time to go to contests. But man, when I went to work there, it was a whole other level beyond what I'd seen at Narrabeen. Far more shonky. There was always two ways of doing things: the right way and the other way. You'd see the customers standing there with these puzzled looks on their faces, trying to work out what they were paying for. It was an environment that made me realise I wanted to be somewhere else, but I was doing it as a means to an end.

I got my driver's licence second go. There was this car across the road from the panelbeater's, an HD Holden, and the guy sold it to me for $250. It had an eight-track player and cartridges in it – David Bowie, the Rolling Stones, bands like that.

Some incredible memories of that car: sex in the back seat and being really, really drunk. Me and Haley, after late nights at the Avalon RSL – if we didn't score a girl, we'd drive to Palm Beach and back as fast as we could. That car was pretty cool – a two-speed automatic, just high and low. I remember once flying along, leaning out the door and looking at the ground. The white line was on the other side of the car – we were on the wrong side of the road. Next morning we were thinking, Holy fuck, I can't believe we did that. But it seemed like the normal thing to do. Girls were pretty rare, so there were a few drives up to Palm Beach and back.

Then Colby came up – Colby Engineering. I got that job through Bluey Norton, middle one of the Norton brothers. That's where we learned about 'Colby Legs'. Colby employed a lot of the guys, Haley and Mike were there, and we were making a hundred and something dollars a week. We punched out various components made from sheet metal. The factory was producing something, I don't know what, though. I was just doing what I was told. The first two days I was there I did too much work. I was too efficient. Bluey had to take me aside and say, 'Slow down, you're doing too much.'

But we couldn't surf after work. We'd stand there all day, come home, try to surf the Peak and discover we had what we called Colby Legs. Some weekends when we'd go to the Avalon RSL, Colby Legs would last all weekend.

Then there was Peter Overy, the gardener. When Overy had landscaping work on the estate homes, we'd get up really early in the morning, jump in the back of his ute and drive all the way up to Castle Hill in the freezing cold. We'd pump it out, get paid okay money, and Overy would pocket the rest. I got to learn how to turf – relentless, fricken turfing – and would come home really dirty, just filthy.

While the labouring sustained me, it definitely taught me about where I wanted to be. More and more I knew that I wanted to get out there and surf. If there was a career coming up, surfing would be it.

The household begins to fracture. Josephine has moved into Sydney, needing to find her own way, and settles her calm caring precision on a chef's apprenticeship. She loves it – the language of the kitchen, the crazy cooks, the intelligent cultured young friends she makes; above all the chance each day to make something perfect.

Dad's life changes in a way we don't quite understand. He doesn't come home every evening. Sometimes he's gone for whole weekends. Eventually he brings her home and introduces her: fellow journalist Valerie Lawson, smart, blonde and careful around these two wild-haired freckly boys and their tiny, starchy British guardian. Around Valerie, Dad is a different man – warm, smiling and a little bit shy. We don't know what to feel about this; we can feel he is torn, unsure of where to place his commitment. But Josephine guides us. It's good, she says. Dad's been alone for a long time, it's his chance to be happy. Be happy for him.

Well, if Jo thinks this is good, then it must be good. It *is* good. We go to the wedding, freckles, hair and all.

Dad sells the house in Newport and moves into the city. Nam, perhaps a bit put off by this whole turn of events, decides it's time to retire to the Surrey countryside with her sister Gigi. You and I move into 23 Hillside Road, Newport, sharing the top-floor apartment with Andrew Hunter: nineteen, eighteen and sixteen years of age.

We're not bad kids. We just do stupid shit. Our whole lives are a rejection of the early 70s Northern Beaches teen junkie scene, of the things we'd seen of the too-cool Av cats and Cookie and the Grots, of smack's downbeat on-the-nod culture. The junkies opted out, we're opting back in; we want to ride this wave into the future, this wave we've caught without even thinking, but we don't know how to do it, not yet.

Let us correct that: you have a dream of how. You think of becoming a commercial artist and draw little sketches on bits of paper: funny goblin faces, waves, cats, things you see. And pages and pages of surfboards with a deck design – this broad, curved sash tapering down to nothing toward the tail.

The same sash that is still on your board models thirty years later.

Meanwhile. The stupid shit we do. Letterbox-stomping episodes that peak one night when we spend hours roaring around in the Norton brothers' station wagon, not just kicking in letterboxes but actually *collecting* them, like trophies, and decorating the beach so people going for an early-morning swim are treated to this very post-modern vision of seventy-three of the Northern Beaches' finest letterboxes neatly arranged in rows along the sand. A Newport Plus presentation night that begins with a group march down the main street of Newport in full daylight with a dead pig's head on a spear. A winter flat spell that lasts too long, so we take to the bush valleys behind Hillside Road at night and engage in crazy, violent battles, hurling huge chunks of fallen tree at each other, screaming '*Bismarck!*', hoping nobody gets hit, but sorta hoping somebody does.

The letterboxes are the only thing we're ever busted for. Probably the least dangerous stupid thing we ever do, but it involves Private Property. And even then, you, Sir Thomas Tom, avoid the rap. When the cops call around, you're tucked up in bed under doctor's orders, suffering from an infected fin chop to the leg. They decide one Carroll is enough to satisfy the outraged burghers of Bilgola Plateau. You stay in bed while the rest of us are hauled off to see the magistrate at Yasmar Youth Detention Centre and be lectured about our foolishness.

And so it goes. You're there but you're not there. We're heaving Bismarcks into the darkness during the flat spell, and you're in Japan with Col on a surfboard sponsorship trip, learning to eat seaweed and dried fish for breakfast. We work at our dumb jobs and hang out at the Newlings' house between surfs, listening to the Clash, smoking joints, sunbaking. Derek christens us The Happy Squad.

Then: Tom Carroll Injury Number Two. Out the Peak one cloudy late arvo. Solid waves. You drop in on Haley on a left. Haley goes up high, past you, drives into a longish turn down the face and around, just as you bottom turn around his spray. Haley is still on his board carrying the turn when the nose of his board strikes you mid-body, just a little off centre. The weight of the collision knocks you off your board. You go in, saying you're winded, but when we come back up to the car later you are sitting in the front seat, folded over, face white.

We take you down to Mona Vale Hospital and leave you with a nurse we recognise, a friend of Charlie's, Helen Porter. Haley and I go back to Hillside Road, where the phone rings. It's Helen: 'We need you here,' she says. 'He has to go into surgery right away and we need an adult to sign off on it.'

Robert Hale has his dad's big V8 Falcon. He drives us the five kilometres to the hospital in just under three minutes. I sign the papers, and the knighted endocrinological surgeon, who just happens to be in the hospital when you're admitted, performs an operation and finds the stomach fully ruptured. The surgery is simple, but it saves your life.

It's a while before I flash on what has happened. I'm the ADULT. I'm the one they called. I feel a whisper of when Mum died, that cold thought: *That's it. Look after each other now.* And of carrying your board up past the Narrabeen surf club, you with the cheque, the future falling into place.

Joe Engel won the Pro Junior after my win, then he won a second one. Two-in-a-row Joe. I was really pissed off. I was angry and I was the underdog and I had to get a second one too and I did.

So me and Joe ruled those four years. Just through being mates and not mates. Two sides of the coin.

I struggled in that 1978 event – I was really nervous – then in 1979 I had a shocker with a bluebottle. It was a really good swell. We used to have these singlets that were tied on the side, really tight, almost like sailcloth. I was paddling out for the final, going out through the Narrabeen Alley, and the bluebottle got under the singlet. I had to take that and I was just thrown.

But I was also thrown by Joe. He was such a good surfer, I was psyched out by him. And he was staying with us, at our house. I was done business in that final. Maybe the bluebottle was there to wake me up but it didn't work.

Still, I was really happy with my board. It felt really close to the wave. The tail was quite thin and pulled in, a little semi-rounded pin with the fin right back, a green fin. God, if I saw that board again it'd be cool.

I surfed that same board in the next year's event and won the 1978 Australian Junior Titles at South Point in WA, surfed it into the ground. It was a big year. The Australian Titles was a hell of an event. I'll never forget my first heat, at Margaret River – massive, offshore and dark and big. Getting out there on this six-foot pintail with a fin-box, I shoved the fin as far back as it could go to try to deal with the swell size. I was out there going, Whoa, what's this? What's going on here?

All the guys wanted to stay on the inside, but the left looked too good not to go out further. I wanted to get one of those. Joe followed me out and it was fucken big, for us. Scary. But I remember getting a wave and thinking, *Yesss! This is it! I'm into this!* The board felt huge.

South Point was a marathon wave, with a long paddle, and it was a strenuous event. But I wanted to win and I'd got into my winning formula, getting results and picking up momentum with each result. I'd get an overall sense of how things were moving in a heat. Not a detailed layout. Not a strategy. But I'd get this sense of what to do in the twenty or thirty minutes of a heat, and that would become my default surf. I'd go and do that, come in, win. Go out again, second. Go out again, win.

Coming out a winner was awesome. I was on the return flight home with Colin Smith – the other Colin Smith from Newcastle, who'd won the open division – and we were talking about my plans to go to Hawaii, wondering how to prepare. And he said, When one of those waves comes down and you've got to straighten out, Tom, it's like a fucken V8 engine up the arse!

FULL-BODY RESPONSE

That first trip to Hawaii. All the things I went through there. Feeling like I was the little guy, this little *haole* in this big world, this dream world. We were thinking about preparation, which was kinda cool, because we were all scared shitless. Derek had gone a year earlier and I remember saying, You might wanna do some preparation for it, maybe some swimming or something? Then later I saw him swimming along the beach: Derek! Swimming. Before Hawaii.

Derek wasn't that impressed when he came back, but I wasn't ready to believe that. I thought, *You've missed the point.*

Col Smith didn't like Hawaii because it wasn't like Narrabeen – he couldn't just drop in on anyone. His take on Hawaii was, Oh, you'd better go and get your boards shaped by Simon. I can't shape you boards for Hawaii. It's not my spot. But … it's dangerous. It's dangerous over there, Tom.

For him to say that it was like – whoa. It pulled me up.

I held on to every word Col said. He'd say about Pipeline, You could drive a truck through that wave! You be careful when you go over there, Tommy – it's dangerous. Col would usually laugh about things, but he wouldn't laugh about Hawaii.

A lot of the stories out of Hawaii were visual for me, from the movies and magazines and books. Not from reading, because I never really read anything. It was all visual. There was a lot of fantasy in there for me, fantasising about what the ride might be, what it might feel like, and then I'd go out and try to duplicate it at my home break.

I remember that Feathers board, the one I drew the lightning bolt on. I used to put it on my bedroom floor and stare at it, and look at photos of Gerry Lopez and think, *That's the Pipeline board! That's the Pipeline board!* I'd match the colour and the light and the visual with what I knew of waves already, trying to re-imagine it. This photo would look like the Pool, or this other one might look like the inside sandbar at the Peak. I'd look at Pipeline photos and think it resembled the Cove in the morning, with the light shining through it.

The light was like a dream. The dreamy idea of it. The dream space. The rehearsal. And there was a lot of rehearsal, because you can't just stop everything in the middle of a wave, rewind it and do it again. There is no same wave. When you're riding it, that's it.

I stood under the garage door at home trying to figure out how big it was, looking at photos and trying to imagine it and the wave size, doing a bottom turn under the open garage door. That door played a big role in me sizing things up. It gave me a gauge for height and what might happen in a wave. It played out a lot of fantasies.

So I'd already seen the waves and the light and the shapes of the waves in a mini-version at my home break. But some of them were so heavy, the images, the weightiness and the size of the board and person compared to the volume of water, I thought it didn't make sense. I looked at photos of guys like Jackie Dunn, taking late drops on deep-dark Pipeline walls, and was just thrilled by looking at them. Thrilled and shaken by the enormity of it. And another photo, a little ad for a large wall poster in *Surfer* magazine. Billy Hamilton. I couldn't fathom being on a wave that size. He was at the base of the wave near the lip, with that Billy Hamilton wide stance, and there was this huge top-to-bottom backlit barrel. I thought, How do you ever ride that?

It was those stories, those images, that made me shit myself when I got smashed at inside Sunset for the first time. The stories were so rich that I actually shit myself. I went over the falls, got pitched. I was fifty kilos, sixteen years old, and I actually shit myself. I remember my arse opening up and it being a really involuntary response to the stories that'd built up in my mind. It all came out in a full-body response.

It was a brutal winter, that year – howling trades, north swells, messy conditions. I didn't know it at the time and I didn't care. I was there for three months, living in these conditions and loving surfing shitful Rocky Point and inside Sunset.

I stayed at the Kuilima condo complex with the Narrabeen guys: Simon, Al Hunt, Brian Witty. One morning Fatty Al shook me awake. It was still dark, around 5 am. Come on, you little cunt, he said. We're going to Kauai and you're going to drive the car back from the airport.

I didn't know how to drive a car at the time, and this was one of those giant American station wagons, like a boat, but I shut up, got in the car and went with them to the airport, where they got out and left me. I don't know how I drove back. It was still dark. I could hardly even see over the dashboard. By the time I got to Wahiawa, halfway back to the North Shore, I was starting to get the hang of it. Then I took the wrong turn and went down the snake road. There's two ways down to the North Shore from Wahiawa; one is the straight road to Haleiwa and the other goes around behind the pineapple fields down to Waialua through all these big S-curves. The snake road. I was roaring through these curves and I half-lost control of this big, sloppy car and began sliding from curve to curve. I was shit scared that a car would come up the other way, but even more scared of trying to correct the wagon in case I flipped and crashed off the side of the road. But no car came up the other way, and I got back to the Kuilima unharmed. It was still only dawn.

Then Pipeline. That first surf at Pipeline is always big. Same thing for kids now who want to do well, the first surf at Pipeline's huge. You have to use all your wits and be completely humble. All that stuff at once.

I'll never forget this day. A big west swell, pristine, clean, the first really good day of the winter. The vibe was that Pipeline was going off. I was hanging out with Critta Byrne and Joe Engel at the time. Those two guys were pretty full-on to hang out with. Simon and the Narrabeen guys were back. All in all, a pretty hardcore environment.

Joe says, I'm going to surf Pipe today. He had his chest out.

I was thinking the same thing: *Right, I'm going to surf Pipeline today!* I'd seen it earlier and it wasn't what I'd thought. It was no good and there was a lot of sand on the reef, but Simon told me that's what happens, and of course I was listening to Simon.

Critta said, Grab your biggest board, we're going to surf Pipe. I was thinking the 7'2" that Simon had made me, but it was a big issue. I'd surfed it once at Sunset and could hardly turn it. I was a pretty small guy, weedy, there was nothing much to me. Could do a bottom turn, but off the top? No. I was full of butterflies.

We got down there and Joe was already out there and there was no question I had to go out. We were such heavy rivals. Critta, on the other hand, was really straightforward about everything. He was mad, you know, Critta's mad, so it sort of fit the situation. He threw me a bar of wax and said, Just wax up, willya, and get out there and shut up.

If it wasn't for that I might have just been mesmerised staring at the barrels.

I took the legrope off – you didn't wear a legrope out there back then. It was serious Pipeline, ten feet. Shaun Tomson, Lopez, everyone in the line-up. I was going, Wooooow. I had boardies and a wetsuit vest on because the wind was a bit chilly.

Critta had said, You don't have to go out and get a big one. Just hang and get a couple on the inside first. So he coached me into it, told me how to get out there, start in front of the break and get sucked out, paddle your guts out, you'll get knocked back but just get out there. So I got out there, fighting with this big thick board, but not losing it.

As I pushed through the closeout bit, I looked over and got my first view of Pipeline from the side. Sixteen years old and looking straight into it. It was awesome, the biggest barrels you've ever seen in your life. So much room inside the barrel. I'd heard the stories, imagined it, but nothing compares with the reality, not in anything. The stories are great but when it's there staring you in the face, gaping holes, your heroes sitting out the back …

But my nature is to get involved. It just wells into me. Only moments after getting out there, I was thinking, *I gotta get one of these.* It was reminding me so much of North Narrabeen. The way the inside section was coming in, with a corner on it, kind of bending in a peak. And guys are ignoring this inside section, and I'm thinking, *Wow, maybe I've got a whole little section to myself here, 'cause there's no-one picking these up.*

I paddled into what looked like a little one, and then the whole bottom emptied out and I dropped down it. Shaun Tomson was paddling out. It lurched and grew, and I felt those backwashy bits coming up the face, and the whole wall opened up and I was in this big thing, feeling so insignificant, and there was Shaun Tomson paddling over the edge of it, looking at me. I was just going, Wow this is phenomenal!

I got out, kicked out, didn't lose my board, and had an instant surge of confidence. Connection, confidence, adrenalised. That got me further into it. I kept edging my way further out, picking off the wedges at the end, the whole time looking across through huge tunnels of water and freaking out, watching guys take the big ones. Like that's where you gotta take off, that's the spot. But how do you do that?

I went over and tried it, and had one of the worst poundings of my life. A second reef set hit and I was so far inside that I could paddle across further toward Backdoor, inside the foam trail. I hopped off as the foam came and pushed my board further over and felt this huge wave surge past, came up and saw my board just flutter off the back of the wave as it closed out. There was another wave coming and I thought, *Fuck* –

and tried to get my board. I swam my guts out and when I reached it I realised the next wave had sucked out and was coming down right on top of me. I'd swum myself right into the impact zone.

I looked at my board and thought I might die here, because it felt like that, that I was going to die.

It broke just on me, but I was a little bit toward the beach from it, so it blew me up into the sky. I came up near the shore and started swimming, but I couldn't get there. Just couldn't. It took me ages. I was way down the beach when I made it. I walked all the way back, got my board and lay down on the sand. A person came down and said, I saw you flying in the air! Are you okay? Are you all right?

I wasn't all right, I was pretty shaken up, but it put me in my spot. The first day at Pipeline, and it woke me up. Go in, you little *haole*.

And I think that's when I started to notice myself separating. I was part of the gang and I wasn't. When I came back home to Newport it was summer again, and it was really hot, and there were two-foot waves and there was nothing to it, and I knew that nothing in Australia could ever really compare to what I just went through.

1979. We've always looked to the North Narra guys – Col Smith, Simon Anderson, Terry Fitzgerald and the rest – for guidance. They're not just great surfers, they don't just make our boards and drive us to contests; they're as close to adults as anyone we know in our surfing lives. They've given us templates to which we're separately drawn: you to Col's flaring extroverted skills, Mike

Newling to Simon's power surfing and beautiful boards, Derek and Haley and Dougall and me to Fitzy's sharp wit and breadth of intellect.

But now this odd shift occurs: we begin to draw energy toward us. This odd shift. George Wales and Richard Cram join Newport Plus and drive over from Bondi every weekend in George's gigantic, overpowered Valiant. We have these insane, reckless contests against Maroubra, where if you lose the contest, you have to win the party. Maroubra always wins the party because they have perfected the terrible art of Spit the Winkle, the garden hose enema followed by explosive public release. We can beat the Bra crew in heats, but we can't beat Spit the Winkle.

We make new friends among people who come to town: the Newlings' English mate Richard Gibbs; Mark Tydeman, whose nickname is Spyder and who never in a million years will cop to what the nickname actually means; Spyder's uni mate Leroy Moulds; Keith Redman, the gnomish cheeky New Zealander, who always knows where the best buddha sticks are to be found.

Tracks, the crazy surf magazine, publishes a mad four-page article on the club, lining us all up next to the surf club toilets and running a series of mug shots with hilarious and possibly defamatory personal descriptions. We love it and use it as an excuse to behave even more disgustingly in public.

Surfing World, the serious surf magazine, publishes issue number 170, volume 28, number 2. On the cover: a photo of you, Gobbo, the archetypal Australian grommet, hair curling down to the shoulders, white zinc cream across the bridge of the nose, looking out of the cover with mouth half-open and slightly quizzical eyes, as if you're only half believing your good fortune. 'Magic School', the magazine is cover-lined. 'Tom Carroll and the Cream of Australia's Young Surfers'. Inside there are photos of all the hot kids. Twemlow trying a 360. Steve Wilson doing a layback cutback. Jim Banks bottom-turning at Pipe. Derek, Crammy, George, Joe Engel, lots of Joe.

There's a twelve-page feature on you, full of beautiful surfing photos and Gobbo quotes. 'I'd much rather surf than work,' you tell *SW*, 'so I wouldn't mind chasing it full-on, but I know that if I keep on surfing there's not going to be too much for me when I get older.'

There's a paragraph each for everyone else. In my paragraph, it says, 'Later on he might get into something seriously, like journalism.'

Is that what I am, I wonder, *a journalist?*

Charlie Ryan sells Ocean Shores Surf Shop; he and Dale move out of our lives as swiftly as they arrived. The shop goes downhill, but despite the never-ending recession of the post-Whitlam years, little surfing businesses are springing up around us. Roger Casey starts KC Surfboards in Ron Wade's old factory unit in Mona Vale and ignites a minor twin-fin revolution. A guy named Norman starts a little wetsuit business called Peak Wetsuits, running it out of an office upstairs over one of the Newport shops; John the Butcher, sick of being a butcher, takes a leap of faith and quits the sausage business and joins him.

In the same way, new events are beginning to pop up on the world tour. That Straight Talk Tyres Open down at Cronulla to which Smithy drives you so, err, rapidly, for instance. It's organised by the guys who started the Coke contest, Graham Cassidy and Geoff Luton. Cassidy plugs it in the newspaper he works for, the afternoon Sydney *Sun*. Dad knows Cassidy, calls him 'Sid', laughs when we tell him about the contest.

Then four contests in Japan, where the department stores have fallen for surf culture in a big way. Hawaii's the premier

Japanese tourist destination, and surfing's Hawaiian. It's new, it's fresh. Why not? You surf in the last one, the JSO Chiba Pro at Isumi Rivermouth, and make it through a heat, then another, then another. You beat Shaun Tomson's cousin Michael. Michael calls you a 'little kucker', some Afrikaans insult, but you still beat him. You make the quarterfinals of a pro contest for the first time.

People keep calling me Tom Carroll's brother. I don't like it one bit. I grit my teeth and win the Australian open men's title, pretty much the only contest in which I don't have to beat you to do it. It's good, but it's not a pro contest.

That December, wishing I was in Hawaii, I go with the Australian amateur team to California. You go to Hawaii and make the Pipeline finals and come sixth. You're only just 18.

You put your foot on the real ladder. The ladder holds steady.

I was venturing out in the world in surfing, but it was nice being able to come home and be in the group. We were all involved with each other, it was this mad Newport Plus sort of gang mentality, and it was understood that we were all on even ground here, and you'd better stay there, otherwise you can fuck off. That was real Australian blokey stuff. They'd take the piss out of you no matter what.

Those relationships were very grounding, but when I'd go away it was new and fresh. Guys like Louie Ferreira, who I met on my first trips to Hawaii, and the local guys there – they were a whole other experience of friendship. I was interested naturally in how other people were, and it was an enquiring open space to see what it was like to be from another place. There was the idea that there's a world beyond this. The dream of having opportunities. And groping around, trying to understand myself in relation to others. I was open to new relationships with people and I was kind of naïve. I was open.

Louie came to stay at our house a couple of times in Newport, in among the relationships I had here, and saw what it was all about. It was a bit like a high school exchange student thing. Louie Ferreira, the Black Piston, unleashed on the girls of the Northern Beaches – that was funny.

There were other guys from Australia too, like Joe, and Thornton Fallander, and Critta. But again I often found myself stuck in between two aggressive characters. My first two trips to Japan were with Joey Buran and Joe Engel. I got on well with both of them, but they didn't get on well with each other.

My relationship with Joe was intense – a jousting. Cheyne Horan was highly competitive, so we had a jousting relationship too, always trying to get one up on each other. How can I get a game of pinball with him so I can beat him? How can I get a game of ping-pong so I can get an edge on him? These were relationships that teetered between friendship and animosity. At any moment it could turn to war. There was always that cutthroat feeling in it, and an edginess that wasn't always nice.

When I watch the young kids relate to each other now, they all seem nice; they all seem to be functional toward each other. I always had to be on guard. You'd never know when you might be taken advantage of, when someone might try to get the upper hand. There was nothing concealed about it, it wasn't covert, it was right out there in front.

I was a late developer on that score and I was really sensitive to it. My idea was to keep it covert, not to show anything, then at the last minute try to whack 'em, or just whack 'em when it needs to be done. Get out in the water and do the talking there.

At the same time, I sensed a real turnaround among my friends. That feeling of being a tall poppy in need of a trimming had almost completely waned. It was a big deal for us to win contests back then, a real big deal to win on that stage, in among our heroes. I'd already made the Pipe Masters final, and coming back from that event in 1980 and winning that second Pro Junior, there was a lot of support from my friends. A feeling of, *Wow we're part of something really cool here.*

There's a black-and-white photo of me winning that 1980 Pro Junior, and they're all crowded in with me – Boj and Scott Lindley and Baley – everyone joining in, happy to see the win.

And I think I was accessible to them. I didn't carry on so much the way I had when I was sixteen. I'd gone through that period where I was thinking I was something really special. I was two years older now, it was a sketchy time, but I was getting a lot of success and I wasn't swaggering with it. I think that helped me avoid becoming unreachable or an enigma to everyone.

That enigmatic image for a surfer, or for anyone who gains some fame, can be powerful because you come to represent a fantasy for people. They would rather trust a fantasy. Maybe because of the way the culture is: media-driven, brand-driven, commercial.

But it's always been difficult for me to sell myself. I think it is for everyone. I don't think it's natural for anyone to be out there constantly selling themselves and being totally comfortable with it. And when you get the tall poppy thing on top of that, it can become quite unnerving. You've gotta be able to laugh at yourself and screw up, that's important.

By the time I won my last Pro Junior, I was starting to be paid fairly good money. I can't remember how the income from Rip Curl and Quiksilver started to pan out, but it was there. Any work I picked up through Colby or panelbeating was to supplement it. I soon had a bit of money and thought, *I'll have to get rid of this Holden, it's gonna clap out.* The Holden disappeared into the ether and I got this little Ford Escort we nicknamed the 'Chookwagen'.

By then I was involved with Byrne Surfboards. At the time I was looking for fresh approaches, and Phil Byrne came out of nowhere and said he'd really like to sponsor me. Byrne was a solid brand and Phil had a good connection to Hawaii through his shaping, and that was where I was aiming – Hawaii. I'd already surfed Pipe with Critta and had seen Phil in Hawaii, and I had some trust in those meetings.

It was really difficult to part ways with Col Smith. He'd given me so much – but I sensed that Col had lost a bit of interest in what he was doing, and he had a family going. Moving on felt like the right thing to do.

Someone, either Mark Warren or PT, came up to me and said, That's a really positive move for you, Tom. Whoever it was, I had respect for them and it was really strong feedback. Plus Byrne had a strong connection to Quiksilver; Phil had been offered a partnership with Bob McKnight in the US when Quiksilver started there, but he decided to stick with his own brand instead. The Byrne brothers had some ambitions. But they were Quiksilver crew through and through, and that helped me a lot as the years went on.

So my surfing really started looking like a career then, and I wouldn't have to go back to Overy Landscaping or Colby Engineering or to that Brookvale panelbeater, getting stuck underneath cars with the toxic fumes and the bog and the craziness of the employees and the puzzled looks on the customers' faces.

THE RUN-UP

You win that last Pro Junior and then you're off and running.

1980. Six of the ten events on the International Professional Surfing tour, two semifinal placings at Pipe and Haleiwa. $2,335 in prize money. You finish the year in eighteenth, two places out of the sacred top sixteen, the elite surfers who get automatic entry into all the events.

In late 1980, Simon Anderson invents the three-fin thruster surfboard. It's perfectly suited to your style of surfing, squared-off, fast and powerful. Phil Byrne immediately makes you one, complete with channels cut through the bottom. 1981 dawns as the year of the three-fin. It's the year of the Aggronauts, as the surf mags dub you and Critta Byrne, Australia's curly-haired hell grommets. They run photos of you both, snarling cheekily at the cameras and winning your heats.

Critta hurts his back and falls off the Aggronaut pace. You just roll on. Third at Bells. Ninth in the Coke. Fifth at the new OM-Bali

Pro at Uluwatu. Ten years since they'd filmed *Morning of the Earth* at Ulus, and it's hosting a contest. Surfing is changing ever quicker, bending itself around the ideal of showing itself to the world in this new guise of professional sport, this wave we've caught almost without knowing it.

Then South Africa, the two events in Durban, where an unknown fifteen-year-old kid named Martin Potter rips his way past almost everyone, beating Shaun Tomson, twice. Two second places in a row. Pottz is four years younger than you, but he's on your mission. Take the reins from the *Free Ride* heroes, if you can. Take over.

South Africa was a real eye-opener for me. Back then, being white meant you were pretty sheltered. I was connected to the guys who I'd met here when they'd come to visit, Dave Hansen in particular. He'd come and stayed at our house, like Louie had, and he was really cool. I stayed with him at his family home in return, which was a unit overlooking north Durban. I was welcome there and they took me in.

At first it didn't seem that much different to Australia, except there were servants and there was that classic smell of South Africa in the air, of the plants and the people. But it just became more and more revealed to me that there was a whole other side of life there, the heaviness of the place started to appear.

The heaviness was in the family homes, in the attitudes toward the servants, in everyday life. Driving out of the units to go surfing in the morning, Dave would remark about the Africans walking up to go into the units, to go to work. And because he was a policeman at the time – six months on, six months off – and had to deal with Durban at its worst, he took it to an extreme. He'd swerve around off the road, onto the footpath, playing with them. It was off-putting to me. I'd never seen anyone behave quite like that toward other human beings.

And he had a gun, his police weapon. Guns were something I had never been exposed to at that age, before that trip. I went out one night in Durban, and someone pulled a gun on the dance floor, and I just hit the deck. I don't know why I did that; I must have seen it many times in the movies. Somehow a gun was out – I remember the shadow of the gun, though I wasn't sure who was holding it. It's a vague memory but still a very frightening moment.

And girls carried guns in their handbags. I'd never seen anything like it. I went back there next year and Steve Wilson from Maroubra wasn't allowed in the pub at Jeffreys Bay because he looked a little dark. So we ended up calling him Steve Biko. The week before, the great Hawaiian surfer Dane Kealoha had been kicked out of the same pub. So we barred it completely: no-one was going to that pub.

Once, coming out of a Barclays bank in Durban, I'd cashed a traveller's cheque and there was a boy begging outside. I gave him a little bit of money, and this lady looked at me in absolute disgust. She was fully decked out – gold jewellery, everything – and she looked down at the kid on the ground and said, Shame little kaffir boy, shame.

I had a sinking feeling in my stomach. I never knew people carried on like that. It didn't make any sense. It never occurred to me that you could behave like that toward anyone.

You get your worst results of the year in South Africa, but you vault into the top ten regardless. Then in late August 1981, some Friday night or other, you're on the way to the pub with some of the crew, jump the metre-high wall between the bottle shop and the beer garden, fall over and can't get up again.

Tom Carroll Injury Number One (b).

What we don't know is that the Pissing Point wipeout six years ago changed your right knee in fundamental ways. Both the anterior and posterior cruciate ligaments snapped and never reset. Now they have completely disappeared, dissolved into the knee cavity. Result: knee dislocation.

Some doctor takes a look at it, bandages it up and tells you, That's it, you'll never surf again, tough luck. Or words to that effect.

At home you just sit there, leg up, shrunk down into yourself. When I'm not around, you cry on and off. I can hear it at night sometimes.

The doctor is wrong. You go to see Stuart Watson, the sports orthopaedist, who diagnoses the knee properly and arranges for you to see the surgeon Merv Cross, renowned for getting footballers back in the game.

In early November, you check into a private hospital on the hill above South Curl Curl. Dr Cross cuts the knee open and grafts a piece of tendon he has taken from your shin into the joint to replace the missing ligaments, drills a couple of holes through the bone and staples it into place. None of us have ever heard of such a thing. I go to see you next day, but you're not there; instead, there's this little morphine-riddled zombie with his eyes rolled back in his head.

For two weeks you lie there in a cast. When the painkillers wear off and you're awake late at night, you begin to cry again, in a sort of existential fear – what if it's over now? Before it's even begun?

I should worry more about this, but I don't, because thanks to my new job, associate editor at *Tracks*, I'm finally going to HAWAII for the first time, so I do not give a fuck about anything else. Some adult.

Fitzy makes me some boards and off I go with fellow team member Steve 'Biko' Wilson for that epic winter, when Simon wins Pipe on his newfangled thruster gun, and I realise, really realise for the first time, what we have got ourselves into. I understand what you'd tried to tell me after your first trip. Sunset Beach, Pipeline, Haleiwa – holy shit. These are the waves that will make us the surfers we know we can be. I write and write. Biko and I run out of money and live on rice and instant coffee for a week.

I come back seven weeks later and you are out of the cast, still using a crutch, the wound a ragged bumpy pink scar that heats up at odd times. You hobble around down at the beach, dragging the leg through the sand, trying to strengthen it. The leg looks alien next to the rest of you; it's wasted, skinny, like a plucked chicken leg. A Chook Leg!

That's what it becomes, your Chook Leg, and that's how your little Ford Escort shit-box becomes the Chookwagen.

But now you're determined. You've got a sniff. You go inward to your little place of concentration. You swim laps with a fin on. You go to a gym, learn to use the weights, build the Chook Leg so it begins to resemble the rest of you. The rest of you also begins to respond to the work.

Me, I'm still pretending I'm in Hawaii. It's January in Sydney, it's two feet, and I'm paddling out every day on my 7'2" gun, trying to hang on to the intoxicating feel of a big surfboard. One morning

I come in; you've just been bodysurfing. There's the board, there you are. I hand it over.

You catch a grovelly little left not far off the beach, trim a line, pull a little cutback, let the wave catch up, go down low and get a short, half-foamy little barrel.

Everything falls back into place. *Click, click, click.*

I stayed with Dad for a while to recuperate after the operation, in the house in Paddington. I had the weirdest experiences there, alone in the house during the day. Long periods of time by myself. I was on a painkiller cycle, taking pills every four hours. For the first two hours it'd be okay, then for two hours the pain would come. I'd have to bite down on things, anything to distract from the pain. I'd have these out-of-body experiences, sitting up in bed, half-awake on painkillers, feeling aware of myself but unable to move any part of my body. It would take every ounce of my will to move the smallest part of myself. I read books – anything to pass the time.

Once I got back to Newport I really wanted a change. It's grey, that moment when I moved out of Hillside Road. I can't recall it well. It was the first time I'd decided to live by myself, outside any of the family, away from my brother. But I looked around and there was a room for rent in a house in Avalon. I felt like I was moving forward and up. I was supported by sponsorship and I felt that I could take care of myself. Maybe it was in sync with recovering from the knee.

And I had the Chookwagen, and I felt like that had been a step up in the world, in a funny way. I was mobile. I would drive down to see the Byrnes in Wollongong and try to break the speed record every time. Newport to Wollongong. I got it down to an hour and a quarter. I don't know how I did it. I had an Alfa later, and I couldn't even break it in that.

THE ARRIVAL OF MONTY

It was a pretty interesting time. I went down to Bells to compete and reached the final and came second to MR. The best I'd ever done. All the boys were on the rocks at Rincon, cheering.

And then Quiksilver dropped me, just like that. It was a big shock. They called me into the office and said, Oh, we can't support you anymore. They said that they needed to support Rabbit and that he was more value to them at that point.

Just like that. I walked out in shock because I was on the way up. I felt really strong. I was on a bit of a mission. I had good support through Byrne and Rip Curl, money was coming in from different areas, but it kind of put a dent in my finances.

Going home to Sydney, I was a bit devastated, didn't know what to do. Then I got a phone call out of the blue from this guy, Peter Mansted. He said, I can see some opportunities for you, I think this is a really good time. He was a fast, enthusiastic guy, and he had a contract for me to look at.

We went to the Black Stump restaurant in North Sydney. I drove there in the Chookwagen. And there I met Monty. We talked about things; he was planning to become a sports manager of other athletes. I've got big ideas, he told me. How much are you making? How much do you want to make?

I was on a mission and Mansted could see that; he'd been following me, saw that I was on the up and up. He told me there were other opportunities outside the surf companies, that we didn't need to be dependent on them. I was suspicious. I didn't really trust him straightaway. I didn't know business very well, other than that I was living really simply on what my sponsors provided. I didn't know my value, really. I was just out there surfing and competing, doing the best I could, looking at ways of improving.

The very next day, Shaun Tomson approached me from Instinct Clothing, based in South Africa. I didn't want to deal directly with Shaun like that because I was competing against him, so I thought, Perfect, I'll put Mansted in touch with him.

He actually calls me first. At *Tracks* magazine. 'Hi, my name's Peter Mansted. I think Tom's got a lot of opportunities. By the way, do *you* have a manager?'

What the hell, I think. *Who is this person?* But he wants me to like him – it's important that I like him – and I do. There's nothing foggy about Mansted. He's a red-headed, freckly ball of energy in a suit. I like that he can see a path ahead, a way into the future, and he's willing to plan for it, commit to it, to say: I will do this and get this result. He wants to catch the wave we're on and make it bigger.

The Newport boys, on the other hand, don't know what to make of him. They've never met anyone so flat-out uncool. Hunter is dumbfounded. He takes pretty much one look at Mansted's jutting jaw and near-military bearing, and dubs him 'Monty', after the famous British general. Monty! It fits so well – you can see him in a uniform, piercing gaze fixed on the troops, revolver in hand. Over the top! Charge!

I sense he will be able to do what I don't want to do: drive you. Light a fire under you. Be the doer to your dreamer.

I'd never met anyone like him before. I'd never met anyone quite so needy, but also quite so forceful, with bigger-than-Ben Hur kind of thinking. Maybe his level of ambition would be normal now, but back then it was different. He couldn't wait to get to America and be American: I'm gonna get you on Letterman! He had all these dreams, these massive delusions of grandeur, like overtaking IMG, which I found out about later, but he was shooting higher than anyone I'd heard of before. But that's the sort of thinking you need in management, to get results out of people at the bargaining table.

He would say, I don't care, I'll bang on the door and walk in and tell 'em how it's gonna be.

I'd hear about it and be like, What do you MEAN you did that?

But he got me moving on the Instinct contract, made it better than I could have and made sure everyone's responsibilities were clearly laid out. Getting in there, boldly saying, This is what we're worth, we're not backing down. This is what we can deliver. Making a commitment. It was really cool. I learned a lot about that back then. And we shared the idea of a surfer being a professional sportsperson, turning it into a job, into something we could make better and improve on from its current status. We shared that vision.

But I remember being overwhelmed by the amount of energy he was putting forth – a lot of opportunity, a lot of fast talking, a lot of action that I wasn't used to. My energy was different; it was ocean-focused, and on the land I was a lot more subdued. I had to learn how to get out there and make myself valuable to people. Monty was really aggressive in that way, and at first he was getting good results. I was his main guy and received a lot of media, newspapers, loads of little stories, columns in the *Sun* with Graham Cassidy, all these things that I wasn't really interested in but did anyway.

And I started getting exposed to his dream, which was to make me a big star, a big personality. It was his thing, eventually it was more his thing and less in line with what I wanted to be. But at first it was good and we were getting results. I was open to him and to his influence.

Mike Newling was competing too, and Monty thought it would be great if we travelled the tour together. I liked the idea but Mike would have found it frustrating at some level. He was a really good influence, and the antithesis of Monty. It was like I had two things either side of me again. It was amazing, like polar opposites floating around my head, and the gravity between the two things was quite intense at times.

1982. $20,850 prize money. Ninth Straight Talk Tyres contest, ninth Stubbies Classic, second Bells Beach, ninth Coke, third OM-Bali Pro, third Gunston, third Mainstay Magnum, seventeenth OP Pro, second Hebara Japan, ninth Pipeline.

Sunkist World Cup, Sunset Beach, Hawaii. First. A win.

Ranked third in the world.

The second place at Bells paves the way for the win at Sunset. MR beats you at Bells, but at Sunset you're riding these beautiful narrow pintails shaped by the incredibly accurate designer Bill Barnfield. The final day the surf is eight feet and excellent, and you make one of those pintails hum and sing all over that complex bumpy wave. Young Aussie Glen Rawlings is second, MR third, Shaun Tomson fourth.

It's so easy. It's easy to watch. The natural ascent of the young champion.

MR comes back to Australia and tells the media, I think Tom Carroll is first in line for the world championship. He's a power surfer and that's what the sport needs.

Out there, your true opposition is taking shape.

Tom Curren from Santa Barbara, California, the quiet 19-year-old with the perfect surfing style, who makes the Straight Talk quarterfinals on his first outing, and marries his childhood sweetheart the next day.

Gary 'Kong' Elkerton, the frothing outsized Queenslander who comes down to compete in the Sydney junior contest sponsored by the radio station 2JJJ. Kong knows Gary Green, the Cronulla superkid who has been drawn to the Newport talent hub and has moved into Hillside Road. Each night during the JJJ event, Kong rolls up at Hillside with his new mate Ross Clarke-Jones from Avoca, and the four of us engage in massive bong wars till we can't talk. Kong wins the event and Ross comes second.

Martin Potter, who went on tour straight after his double finals placings in 1981 and who is now sixteen years old and travelling the world full-time.

Barton Lynch from Manly and Damien Hardman from Narrabeen, still kids but on the fast track.

Then this other kid from Cronulla, Mark Occhilupo, who gets a sponsorship from John the Butcher's wetsuit company. The kid comes out the Peak with his Peak wetsuit in its insanely bright 80s colours: hot pink, electric blue, lemon yellow. John wants to expose him to some heavy Newport energy, but the kid seems on another wavelength; it's hard to pin him down. He's kind of clumsy still, but his movements in the water seem measured to some other rhythm.

He's a freak. Everyone is. It's the 80s, when nobody can do any wrong, and it's just beginning to roll.

I moved house again, out of the place in Avalon and into a house in Foamcrest Avenue, Newport, where Keith Redman and his girlfriend, Jill, were staying. It was a two-bedroom place; I took the front sunroom and made it into a room for myself. It felt good, stepping back into Newport again, being able to run down to the Peak for a surf, being a bit of a larrikin with Twemlow and Keith. I'd stretched the Newport umbilical cord but it hadn't snapped.

That was the first year I really felt like I wanted to do the best I could on tour. It was also the first year I had a girlfriend.

Elizabeth was my first real love. Well, I thought it was love, anyway. She was a really good friend of Mike's girlfriend at the time, Nicole, and I really connected with her, I really felt like I was gone here. She was everything for me, in many ways.

Elizabeth was a strong character, a strong woman, and she had a strong influence on me. She decided to become a policewoman and went through the police academy. One night she came home with a revolver – unbelievable, a 19-year-old girl with a revolver! I remember pointing it at Twemlow once. Twemlow shit himself. He knew it was unloaded, but he still shit himself.

We ended up living together at that place with Keith and Jill.

Monty didn't trust the relationship at all. He was always in the thick of it, trying to challenge me on it. He would say, Argh, she's a woman. She's in the way and she's distracting you. You gotta concentrate on the events. He kept me focused on my travel and questioned what the relationship was all about, why I was in it, saying, You've got a lot of time left, you don't have to do this now.

It was a real conflict having Monty around my friends. It hurt because he really wanted to be involved in it all but struggled to fit in. We were a close-knit group of guys – if you didn't fit in you were just cast aside, and it'd been that way for years, it wasn't going to change just for Monty. But he really wanted to be a part of it, and I think that became difficult when he wasn't accepted that well into that group. It was hard. It was an intrusion, and it created a bit of conflict for me, because I wasn't mature enough to deal with it and be honest with him. I didn't know how to explain to him, Not now, Monty.

Instead, I'd avoid him where possible. I'd do underhanded stuff and try to run away from the situation. It was uncomfortable being direct with him anyway; it'd usually go volatile. And he struggled with it too. Monty knew there were some dangerous people close to me. He knew there were people in the group who didn't have my best interests at heart.

Keith had a grip on me because we were living together. He acted like a really good friend at the time, while I was flitting around, in and out of the country, doing my thing. It was a good escape being in this relationship with a person who was ingratiating, who seemed to have his own thing going, and who supported whatever looked cool. I wasn't savvy to that. I just thought he was being a good bloke. That's the way I was, quite vulnerable.

And it was very convenient. He was a friend, he'd help out, he'd go surfing, we shared the rent. He and Jill were a stable partnership for me to be around. It was almost like a family to come home to. Eventually that all came undone.

I'd decided to spend a lot of time in Hawaii that year, and I spent a lot of time just thinking about Elizabeth and how much she meant to me. It was really strong, and she'd made it clear that that was where she wanted to be too. She came over to Hawaii with Nicole for a weekend; it was my twenty-first. The Pipe Masters was on and I had a shocker. I was totally distracted and didn't want to be in the event. I wanted to hang out with Elizabeth. When she went home, we all focused and I won the World Cup. Really charged up, freshly twenty-one, beat MR.

After that win I came home and Monty told me, Right, you've gotta really concentrate this year coming up, we've got big plans, and so forth. But with me, whatever Elizabeth said went. I didn't really know how to draw a boundary between us very well. Then she moved in, started talking about kids and wanting to go look at houses! I had some money coming in and I could look at property, but I hadn't even thought about it. I was trying to open my mind to it, but I was in shock.

I was just a kid really and was scared by what she was putting on the table. But I was very much in love with her. Monty was questioning it, saying, What are you doing, buddy? She'd get her goat up about him: He's not gonna come around again, is he? So I was stuck between them a bit. I didn't know how to manage a love relationship, let alone manage a relationship like I had with Monty.

Then I won the Coke Classic and started travelling, and that's when Elizabeth couldn't deal with me being away. Plus it was becoming more and more focused on me, I think. Me and who I was and everything in my little world.

Early 1983. A power shift in professional surfing. A new organisation, the ASP, wins a short fight with Fred Hemmings's IPS for control of the tour. It throws pro surfing into brief disarray. To cover the confusion, Sid Cassidy invents something called the Australian Grand Slam: the first four Aussie events are sequestered off by themselves, outside any world championship calculations – a little tour unto itself.

The break in rhythm throws off the old guard. Tom Curren wins the Straight Talk event, Pottz wins the Stubbies. Joe fights his way through the trials rounds at Bells Beach and gets his one great victory the only way he ever knew: the hard way.

That leaves the Surfabout, and that one's yours.

Watching you plough through the final day, I get odd flashes of that first Pro Junior win. The North Narrabeen lefts running down the beach, the cutback laid flat and around, the spray line matching the sash on the board. You versus Crammy instead of you versus Dougall.

But today there are thousands of people on the sand, and Dad and Valerie among them with our weeks-old baby sister, Lucy. First and only time they see you win. A little familial moment in the middle of the ruck. The TV cameras follow them briefly, then cut to you, triumphant, holding the trophy, on the stage.

Winning the Coke means winning a 'surf van' from Bill Buckle Motors in Brookvale. But you don't want a surf van. Some quick-talking from Monty and some stardust from you and a few days later there's the picture in the paper. You with the sales manager of Bill Buckle, being handed the keys to a Toyota T-18, the closest thing they have to a sports car. 'Surf Winner Collects Prize'.

Goodbye, Chookwagen. Haley ends up driving it for a while till it dies some ignominious death. Meanwhile you rip about the place in this flashy bronze hatchback, people seeing you coming a mile away. Tom's got a new car. Look out.

A few months down the track, early one Sunday morning, the phone rings in Hillside Road. I answer blearily, and you tell me the following:

You've been fanging around Mona Vale in the rain and lost it around one of the curves along the main road, slid out and hit something. A telephone pole. Maybe a parked car. Anyway, the police were called and you're worried about being busted. Surf star on the way up and all that.

'So I said I didn't have my licence on me,' you say. 'And I told them I was you.'

'You told them you were *me*?'

I don't know what to say.

'So what do you reckon?' you ask. I still don't know exactly how to say what I'm thinking. Luckily, you save me the trouble. 'I've got to tell them, haven't I.'

Yep, you do.

You don't wait for me to call them and you don't ask Monty to call them. You just immediately call the duty sergeant who'd attended the scene and make the incredibly embarrassing admission, and go through uncomplainingly with the whole thing, local newspaper reporting and all. You're a dreamer, but you've got Dad's sense of right and wrong.

There's a postscript: twenty-seven years later, while researching a documentary on cars, I cross paths with Bill Buckle, the grand car dealer himself. Bill, getting on in years but still a very sharp customer, pulls up to the side of the road in his Audi R8 supercar, hops out, looks at me, and without even blinking, says: 'How's your brother's Toyota?'

When I went away to compete in 1983, it was my year to step right up. I was getting wins, starting to feel the energy. I had people like Tom Curren to keep at bay, and Pottz. I could feel a world title but I didn't know how to win it.

I did okay in South Africa that year and beat Curren, which was good. Went on to California and didn't do so well there, got beaten. Came home a bit dejected. Went to England and won Fistral.

And I think that was the time when Elizabeth could no longer deal with us being apart. She was too feisty. She needed a man around. She was always looking for that connection and she jumped on opportunities when she could, I think. By the time I got back from the UK I was dying to see her. I knew straightaway something was wrong. That's when I found out she was having an affair. I was devastated: Fucken hell! What's going on here?

I had no idea how to run a relationship.

Keith and I found a place just over the back behind Newport. It was a pretty nice little spot, hidden away. I was asked to not go to Hawaii because the ASP and IPS were having a big falling out, and Fred Hemmings had refused to support the ASP. Monty said, You've got to support the ASP, so I thought, *Fair enough, I won't go to Hawaii*. It was really hard to forfeit Hawaii that year.

And at the same time I was trying to cope with all the pain around the breakup, Redman and I started getting into cocaine. It couldn't have been any better, to run off into the abyss. The cocaine was there and Christmas was coming and fuck … I was in Australia, not in Hawaii.

Spyder had opened a café, it was Newport's first at the time. I remember being in the café one evening and something went on between him and Redman. Spyder was saying, Right, let's go up there and let's do it!

I was like, What's going on?

Redman said, Spyder's gone in and we've got a whole lot of coke, like an ounce!

What? You got a what? Wow! Let's go!

The timing was perfect: the pain, having the addict there inside me, ready to go. It was fuel to the fire, and it blew up in my face.

I made it to the New Year and then kind of woke up, thinking, *Fuck!* I'd been going for one surf every couple of days, feeling like half a human, completely dislocated. I said to myself, Right, fuck this. I'm pulling my shit together. This is ridiculous.

Monty saw me and said, What's been going on? I haven't seen you for a couple of weeks – you look fucked!

I said, Oh, it's just been Christmas, whatever.

He said, Well, you better get to work – this is the big one. You've gotta get training. We need to turn this into work.

We'd talked about it before, but it was time for action. Monty said, Right, you're gonna come over and live in Cremorne; we're gonna start five days a week, six hours surfing a day. You're going to do aerobic training every morning, we've found this gym in town. Mike's coming over, he's training with us.

Boom! It was on. The discipline started from the first week of that new year and went for two months, and by the end I was so highly tuned. The program was an early surf, then aerobics class, breakfast, then five hours surfing: two hours, then lunch, then two more hours, then a rest, then an hour before dark, then home to sleep. Mike had already started looking at our diet and he was coming up with a cool nutrition plan. It all started making a lot of sense and fit in with the results we were beginning to feel from the training.

We were surfing in the worst waves we could find because I was so bad at surfing shit waves compared to Curren and a lot of the top guys. My style just didn't fit, so I had to bring all my concentration to bear. One of the worst waves in the world was South Bungan, the close-out before Rock Pools there in a nor'-easter. We'd usually surf it on a Friday afternoon. That was a good day. The weekend was for fun, just going surfing wherever and whenever we wanted. But it'd be back to Cremorne on Sunday night, then the days would start again. Surfing those crap waves, it felt like time was going backwards.

And living with Monty really focused us. We went through the shit we needed to go through, and you always get closer that way; you get to know each other. I remember pulling out of Mike's place at Bungan on a Friday afternoon, that cool calm sense of a job done, the work put in for the week. Self-esteem. Pulling out from the Bungan house and on to the main road and feeling good.

Then I focused on that first event, the Straight Talk Tyres, when Occy beat me in the final. Then I won the Stubbies. Then I went to Florida for that little B-grade event, the one that would close out the world championship. That was insane, a very surreal experience. I remember thinking, *Why do I have to do that?* I looked at all the points on paper and realised: I've gotta go to fricken Florida! I was with Mansted and he was looking at me with that insane look, saying, Right!

And then I looked again and thought, *Well, it's only a couple of days, I won't even be out of the time zone.*

It was the last little piece of discipline I needed, and it was an easy win. I remember coming back home to Australia with that world title locked up, flying over Sydney. I was feeling really good about myself. I'd nailed it. I was so stoked. I didn't care how I'd done it – I'd done it. I could relax and enjoy myself. It'd been a lot of work; I'd done shit I didn't really want to do and learned from it. And I looked out the plane's window and started noticing how many swimming pools were in Sydney, in people's backyards. Incredible. I don't know why I picked up on it at that time. I guess I'd always had the beach in my backyard, and I'd never thought of pools before.

Anyway, won that one, and came back to Bells and was beaten by Cheyne in the final. But I already had the title by then.

1983–84. $47,825 prize money. Fifth Gunston, third Renault Pro Durban, ninth OP Atlantic City, second Lacanau, France, a win at Fistral, a win at Hebara, a win at the Stubbies, second at Beaurepaires, a win at a B-grade event at Deerfield Beach, Florida, second at Bells.

Ranked first in the world.

THE FLUFFY ZONE

I'd reached the goal of the world championship. I was in that fluffy zone of being a new champion, of realising the goal that I'd thought I could do but hadn't seemed real until now.

I went down to Bells Beach on a high. There was a lot of media going on around my win, various funny bits and pieces that Monty was organising. One in particular was the *Bert Newton Show* in Melbourne. I'll never forget going in to see Bert, they called him Moonface and it was amazing seeing his head: huge, round and happy, and very professional.

We got hold of some gear and it all started happening. I went into party mode, but I also wanted to do well in the contest. I was in rhythm with my equipment. I could go out in a heat and take command of it pretty quickly. I didn't fall apart. It was all there. The momentum you gain from that world champion aura, everyone's thinking, *This guy's done the hard yards and he really deserves it. We have to take a step back here and hand the power over to him.* People build up a story about it, and once that's happened you can really hammer the story home.

It becomes really hard to lose at that point, because you've got the judges onside, and you've got the momentum; people are talking around the event, maybe they're even dreaming about you.

So you get this grace period, this space.

And back then, 1984 Bells, it was a lot simpler than now. Less stuff going on, easier to get around. The surfing was still of a similar energy to today.

The surf got pretty good as the event went on, and I really disliked losing to Cheyne in that final. I really felt like nailing that event. I beat him in the first of the three twenty-minute heats. We spent a lot of time in the water back then – you got scored on three waves, there was a priority buoy and paddle races, no jetski assist. Paddling was big. I can't remember the lead-up to the final, to be honest. That trip was about letting loose after three or four months of knuckling down.

And I guess I was still dealing with the break-up. Or not dealing with it, more like it. I was sucked into myself and shut off that part of myself. Elizabeth had laid a blueprint of what a female should be physically, and I must admit, it wasn't necessarily good. I felt like I was being ruled by her. I didn't know how to express that at the time, but I'd handed over so much of my power. I looked upon her as It, the magic person, thinking, *Without her I'm fucked!* Which wasn't true and didn't feel right.

A lot of the energy that came out of me and my surfing at the time came through this pent-up energy and frustration.

I'm going to nail this world title just to show her I mean business. I'm moving up, I'm a champion, and you missed out.

I look back and think it was a blessing she broke my heart. It worked out well.

~~~

Back from the Bells bender, it dawns on me that you really are the world professional surfing champion.

Seven years from the first Pro Junior. Eleven and a half years since we started.

People think world titles are just labels, trophies perhaps. They are not. They're the air you breathe, the blood in your veins, your sense of self enlarged to regal dimensions. The title wears you and you wear it. Weedy little Gobbo, the panelbeater's apprentice, suddenly seems six feet tall, golden, smiling, smooth. Gobbo is glamorous. Gobbo is a god.

With it comes fame. Actual fame. You've been well known for some time; I've long since grown used to it, the guys who say, How's your brother? How's Tom? I have pat replies to that. Yeah, he's good. He got a third in Europe last week. He's going to Hawaii tomorrow. Yeah, I'll tell him you said hello. It's mostly cool – surfers interested in surfers.

But now, jeez. People know you whether they've surfed or not. You're part of this new post-recession Australia, Bob Hawke's Australia, America's Cup-winning, INXS-saturated 1980s Australia. The TV shows, the newspaper covers, the social pages, the *Vogue* fashion spreads. The 16-page Coke contest colour lift-outs from the *Sun*, orchestrated by Sid Cassidy.

The fame begins to distort our little universe. It forms the world into concentric circles, lines of orbit around the increasing gravitational mass of Tom Carroll. There is the outer circle, the world at large, then in ever-tightening circles they grow closer – the surf community, the fan base, the acquaintances and allies, then the inner circle – the bubble now forming around you, opaque, shutting out the world, reflecting back the Tom the world wants to see.

The Newport boys drift through space, unaffected by this distortion. They don't give much of a fuck about the bubble; it's irrelevant, even kind of funny. They come and go as they please. In the surf, David Jones drops in on you, you on him. Haley and Hunter make jokes about Mattel producing a line of Tom Carroll Dolls, and laugh at the people queuing up, hoping for Bubble entry.

Monty's in the bubble because it's his invention. He works it: the SKI Yoghurt deal, the Qantas deal. Mike's in the bubble, a bit uncomfortable about it, but keen to train and travel and surf. Keith's in the bubble because he understands it at some level; he understands what he needs to be and do in order to maintain a place on the inside. There's a transaction here somewhere, and he's a natural salesman. He takes a job selling *Tracks* advertising and turns those casual Tom-and-me stories into gold.

I am in the bubble because I've got to be. That's my job, after all – protect you. *That's it. Look after each other now.* Remember? How could I forget. I write about the heats you win; I write about your training, about your opposition. I never write about the drugs.

You? You are in the centre of it all, the apparent *raison d'être*, yet you're oddly passive. Monty's there to look after things, Keith's there with the good fellowship or its simulation, I'm there, Mike's uncomfortably there – and you're there. But all you're thinking about is the surf.

I was in a bit of a blur. Monty was around; he was trying to get in between Redman and me, and joining in the partying to some degree, which was uncomfortable, but nevertheless we were getting things going. Monty was trying to do new deals, and I was just hamming it up as world champion. I'd walk into places and start prancing around, thinking I was The Shit. And I was The Shit. The proof was all around me.

It all started to change at that point. They gave me more space at first. And then they didn't. The space changed. There was more intrusion in that space. I felt more responsibility to the world. It was scary. All of a sudden more people knew who I was, more people were giving me attention – and sometimes very strange attention. Being naturally curious, I was enquiring as to why. Why was that person doing that?

I recall it being scary and overwhelming at times. It was cool when I was partying, because I could get a break, run from it to some degree.

I'd had a lot of attention before, actually, just from having had a brother and sister ahead of me at school. I'd get it through Jo's friends in the hallway. When I was in Year Seven at Pittwater, I'd be walking down a hallway and some of them would see me and say: Look! That's Jo's little brother, Tom! Look how cute he is! Look at that smile!

I'd be thinking, *Shit! What am I supposed to say?*

I'd just smile my way out of it. The Smile Technique. That's a big one, and you can see it on my face today. It's a default mechanism. I'll walk into a situation with a smile and it tends to keep people at bay; it tends to keep people at a positive distance. I have a good smile, I have a charming smile. So the charming smile was something I was able to use, a small way of moving through things without having to reveal myself.

I used it to deal with situations where I was exposed to a lot of people I didn't want to be around or didn't feel comfortable with.

But I naturally sensed that as world champion I had a responsibility to the sport, and I think people felt that. It wasn't like I was belligerent or weird or distant. But my escape route was not necessarily healthy.

Something else changed, though. Some part of me relaxed. My posture changed. You can see it in people's body language, the weight of the world lifts really quickly when you achieve at that level. Then it settles back on, heavier than ever. It moves on: okay, next goal.

1984–85. $32,300 prize money. Fifth Spur Steakranch, Cape Town; fifth Country Feeling Classic, J-Bay; fifth Renault, Durban; a win at the Gunston; second Lacanau; fifth Fistral; seventeenth Op Pro; second Stubbies, USA; a win at Hebara; seventeenth World Cup; ninth Stubbies; second Beaurepaires; third Bells.

Ranked first in the world.

I got smashed straightaway. I got over to South Africa and went down to surf a B-grade event at Cape Town, at Outer Kom. The waves were really good, beautiful lefts, but freezing cold.

And Occy was out there ripping. Surfing in that cool style of his. He was so low and heavy in the ankle, and so nice in the twist of the upper body that the technique was hidden. It was like, *How does that fit?* He'd do these incredible turns. The board would be so on edge, and he'd just pull it in tight in that beautiful, classic Occ style – super young and super vibrant.

And I was thinking, *Shit! How do I get to that point?*

It was a real challenge. I was world champion, but I was put on my knees straightaway. Then I went to surf J-Bay and there was Occy going fricken bananas. He was the best surfer in the world at that point, and everyone was going, Oh, my God. Backside at J-Bay on that little Rusty Preisendorfer, and the board doing whatever he wanted it to do. He was dictating it, reading it perfectly. It was groundbreaking surfing.

On top of that, he was leading the world ratings and the ASP was calling him the ratings leader – it made him sound like he was the world champ.

I was really unnerved by the whole situation. I'd kinda let myself go a bit. I'd tried to prepare for the tour, but I was still in party mode. I wasn't fully committed the way I'd been before the world title. I knew that that was real commitment, and I knew I needed to be at that level to get back on top.

My response to Occy was that I had to accept he was in a really good spot. I was with Mike at the time and talked to him about it. I tried to absorb it and turn it into a plus somehow, because I could feel the negative response within me. Fuck him, fuck all of 'em! I could feel it growing in me. How dare they call him the world champion? How dare they do that?

I had to learn a new approach. I was at Durban at the Gunston 500 after this humbling run through Cape Town and J-Bay, and I had this board I didn't like. It was a Phil Byrne 5'9", belly channels, and it had a little too much curve up front. I needed it to be a little straighter; I couldn't run it on the rail the way I wanted and I fought the board all the time.

And I thought, *Okay*. This is an exercise in getting myself together, disciplining myself to come back and make a mark, to win on a board that I didn't like. To set myself a challenge and wash everything off.

I wasn't going to get rid of Occy, I knew that. I wasn't going to get rid of Pottz and Curren and these young guys coming up. But I had the ability to shift my perspective. I could do that pretty quickly. I had to concentrate on shifting my dislike for the board and making it work. And I did. I won the Gunston 500.

Winning the Gunston was a big step for me, but being in South Africa that year was really uncomfortable on a number of different levels. I was world champion and it was made into a big deal in the press that I was going to South Africa. Yet on a personal level, each trip there was more intense than the next, as I became increasingly sensitive to how people behaved and treated one another under apartheid. Each trip I found myself conflicted internally about what was going on. It had a real big effect on me.

I got that leg of the tour out of the way and went over to France for the first time, and on to the UK, where I didn't do very well at Fistral. Then Occy beat me in the Lacanau Pro final. But I was on a bit of a roll. I was starting to feel physically strong again, and really studying Occy's surfing, looking at his boards. They were still saying he was on top of the world and my response to that was getting more intense, more focused, knowing what I could do and breaking down what it would take to win. I was also doing a lot of rehab on my right knee, trying to get my leg stronger, working out, stretching, working my physical abilities. It was good hanging out with Mike, and Haley came over too, and hung out with us in France. It was funny and loose, and a real asset to have those guys around, because of the intensity and the idea that Occy was the inevitable world champion. It wasn't a good idea, that one, not in my head, other than the fact that it refocused me.

Everything else was good, but I needed to gain some confidence in my equipment. I went to California and hooked up with Rusty Preisendorfer and worked with him. I knew there was a secret in Occ's board that was working really well for him. Rusty shaped me some nice boards and I got a second to Brad Gerlach at the Stubbies event.

It was all about pulling myself back together and regaining my balance. I liked the idea of retaining the world championship, just to put the nail in the coffin. Mark Richards had got four; it'd be hard to get just one.

We were all very young still. I was only twenty-two.

One thing punctures the bubble world – surf. Another thing – friendship. November 1984, we rent a house at Log Cabins on Oahu: you, me, Mike, Haley, Spyder.

We're already a part of it, part of the deathless young brigade assembled on each of those incredible 1980s North Shore winters. The Hawaiian kids. Louis, of course. Carvin' Marvin Foster. Ronnie Burns. Mickey Nielsen. Marty Hoffman. The Kinimakas from Kauai. Tim Fretz, who they call 'Taz' because he is like a Tasmanian devil. Max Medeiros from Kauai, smooth smiling barrel-riding Max. James 'Bird' Mahelona, who switches feet to get backside barrels at Sunset. Johnny Gomes, fourteen years old and big as a man. The Sunset crew: Richard Schmidt and Allen Sarlo from California, Don Johnson, Jeff Johnston, Bradshaw, Kong, Butch Perreira and Michael Ho at the top of that tree. The Pipeline Underground crew: Bruce Hansel, Chris Lundy, Bulkley, Adam-12, Tony Roy. Jeff Hornbaker and Aaron Chang the artist photographers. The one-offs: Joey Buran, the California Kid who's known on tour for pulling his backside turns short, but who at Pipeline becomes a different surfer altogether, wild and willing. Derek Ho, Michael's brother, smaller than you, clinging to Pipeline's face like a fly on a wall.

Later, many years later, I think, maybe this is our version of a war zone. Our generation is spared the nightmare of war, yet we still go looking for it, some simulation of it, the adrenalin, our young blood risen to the risk of that amazing surf, waxing our guns, dodging the fifteen-foot bomb sets detonating on Sunset's west peak and Pipe's second reef, the fear and exhaustion and strange peace at the end of a hectic day.

Then the emptiness of the flat spells, the stillness between the madness. The fidgety stillness.

There's a little basement apartment under the Log Cabins house. About a month into it, Taz rents the apartment for North Shore recreational purposes. Taz calls it 'The Lab'. He shows up on Fridays from Honolulu and goes in there with a skinny blonde girl and a buddy, a big local kid called Manson.

Every now and then we get hold of an eight-ball of cocaine, snort it up in the evenings (Newling the clean-living one sensibly abstains) and talk shit half the night, then end up on the beach at Logs or Ke Iki, smoking joints in a vain attempt to come down, staring up at the brilliant tropical stars, trying to pick out the northern hemisphere constellations and counting the swell interval as the shorebreak hisses and booms invisibly in the dark.

We count the seconds between booms. Like kids trying to count between a lightning flash and the sound of thunder. Ten- or twelve-second gaps, the swell is dropping or dropped. Seventeen seconds, it's here and you'd better be ready, coke hangover or not.

One stoned Friday night, the interval stretches way out past seventeen seconds. We get a fitful three hours' sleep, listening to some sort of crazy shit going on downstairs in Taz's Lab, and wake to a grey, hazy light and a deep thick swell from the west, glassy and breaking with a flat booming crack along the Log Cabins reef. How big? The bulk of the swell is moving off up the coast to our right, but even then it's eight feet plus out front.

Taz, already down on the sand with a tiny little twin-fin board, waves to us and sprints through the shorebreak in a lull, then picks up a solid one and tries his signature Taz move, a sliding 360 in the pit, and gets obliterated, just blasted. Shakes it straight off and races out to try it again.

You point down the beach where half a mile away, huge clouds of foam are rolling off the back Pipeline reef. This'll be Pipe Masters final day.

Newling and I drop you down there with your new Rusty widowmaker guns and head to Sunset Beach. It looks deceptively small, the only sign of anything more dramatic being the cluster of small dots way out on the west swell peak. A lonely little pack on a big day. Hawaiian surfer Keone Downing has just come in. He says, 'It's one of those days when you don't see the one that gets you.'

We surf for hours. I don't think Newling even wears a legrope. I do, and eventually snap it under an immense series of waves. It's like being run over by several apartment blocks. I swim and swim, dazed by the adrenalin, and hitch a ride with Sarlo for the last 100 metres against the rip.

At Pipeline in the afternoon I sit with young Australian pro Graham 'Ces' Wilson and watch you surf into the final. You're quite calm, not adrenalised, and the eyes of the small crowd are elsewhere, on Joey Buran, who is claiming the day, wave by huge gaping spitting wave.

Joey is in the lead when you pick a wave off, a big wave, slightly wide of the reef. The wave stands up square on the sandbar – a wall, not a barrel. Someone else is hunting the next one. Eyes swing away.

Then you come off the base of this wave and drive straight up against the backlit water, the board suddenly like a sword, and at the last possible moment shift all your weight to the other rail. The board tears around in an impossible arc. It's the turn from ten years ago, from the left in front of Newport Surf Club, but this is a twelve-foot wave at the Pipeline. It is not possible.

You make it halfway out of the turn then catch a rail and fall. Ces and I look at each other. Did we *see* that? Did anyone else?

The irony: Pipeline, the greatest wave in the world, this wave that defines you and that you redefine, and it's off the tour. It never helps you win a world title. Later, it will help to take one away.

I write about it all, but not about the drugs.

We made a lot of money that year. I won something like seven cars.

I wasn't paying a great deal of attention to it, but I remember having a fair amount of money in my bank account, looking at it and thinking, *Wow!* Monty was high on the whole thing and we were driving around, looking at all these different cars. We went out to the BMW dealership in town and the cars felt really nice. I took a BMW 323i for a drive, a car I'd really liked from years before. It reminded me of driving around in the

Chookwagen for years and thinking, *How bad is this car? Look at that person's car – why don't I have that?* Keith Redman was all keen about cars, so I was influenced there.

But the prices didn't make sense to me. We looked across the road from the dealership and saw a Mercedes convertible, gleaming in the sun. Monty said, You can get that! You can!

I was like, I'm not going to get that! That's ridiculous.

I was changing tack; I was already beginning to think about buying a house, getting into property, see what I could get. We went back to Newport and saw the little house at 66 Foamcrest, just down the road from where I was living. I'd seen it before and thought it was a really nice little house, so I put down as much money as I could. It was a $120,000 house and I put $30,000 down and went into a twenty-five-year loan. I thought, Whoa, twenty-five fricken years. I'm never gonna get there! It was an obscure, surreal concept. Interest rates were around fourteen per cent and ended up around eighteen per cent. I thought, I don't wanna see that, just let me surf and I'll bring the money in.

It was a big move in everyone else's eyes. Owning a house! I didn't feel any more separation from my friends, other than I was well on my way.

Monty kept doing the deals. He was pushing the Instinct crew to the edge. Shaun was always trying to deal with me and get away from Monty. But then I ended up bringing it all to a head, in a way.

Again, Bells Beach is your victory lap. You come to this event in a very different state to last year. There's no DHL cocaine deliveries, no world championship overwhelm. The mid-year paranoia about Occy and Pottz is past. You carry a certain weight with you now which has replaced the sense of power and expansion and grandeur of the first time. Nobody seriously doubts that you will be world champion again.

Nobody, that is, except Shaun. The hero of *Free Ride* has done the unthinkable – in pursuit of his last shot at the title, he has given up his seed in the event, thinking to qualify through the trial rounds and draw you straight-up, turn it into a face-to-face duel.

Shaun easily makes it through his first heat – of course he does. He is then drawn against Gary Elkerton and a young Brazilian surfer, and me.

The heat is at midday, a beautiful four- to six-foot Bells day, a strengthening offshore wind, blue water. I feel no nerves whatsoever. I know Kong doesn't. We are both riding Allan Byrne six-channel boards, the most advanced surfboards in the contest, in the world. The Brazilian kid tries but he is like a marker buoy. Kong and I lap him over and over, set wave after set wave. Shaun gets the leftovers and does what he can, but the wave and weight of history breaks on his head and rolls over him and passes him by.

Later, in one of those sensitive surf-writer moments, I try to interview him. Like the gentleman he is, he gives me an address and a number, but by the time I get there he's gone.

So the script follows its natural path, and a day or so later we are in the Torquay pub for lunch – you, me, Monty and a journalist from the *National Times*, who has come down from Melbourne to research an in-depth profile of this small yet beautifully formed young two-time world champion, who also happens to be the son of V. J. Carroll, whom no journalist cannot know.

The Torquay pub is almost empty except for the four of us, which seems to free Monty up more than ever. He regales the journalist with stories of triumph and magnificence. Tells of how the entire pro surfing world is at our mercy. 'They call us the Holy Trinity,' he says, 'Tom, Nick and I. They are cowed because they know that together we are unbeatable, together we cannot be touched.'

The journalist is polite. I watch him, thinking, *He is watching more closely than we think.*

I am not watching you very closely.

The journalist asks you about next season, and out of nowhere you drop the bomb.

You tell him, 'Well, I have decided not to compete in South Africa this year. I feel it's important for me as world champion to take a stand on apartheid. I feel strongly about the issue, and if I can do something to help bring change, I think this is it.'

The Holy Trinity is thrown into some disarray. I'm secretly thrilled and fighting not to show it. Monty is almost apoplectic. He dissembles superbly: 'Tom's not absolutely certain about how he'll do this. We were going to announce it in a week or so.' It's a statesmanlike move on his part.

It's all off the top of Monty's head; neither of us had a clue.

Later, when it's all settled somewhat – after Instinct has ditched you and Monty's gone in and salvaged an entirely new, fresh and bigger deal with Quiksilver from the carnage, when some surfers have slagged you off and others jumped on board, when the nasty letters have stopped coming and the letter of support from the Prime Minister has been framed and hung – I think to myself, *Well, Thomas, you did kind of chuck Monty into the fire there, didn't you.*

But you chucked yourself in first. Like a wave at Pipe. Sit, wait, feel for the wave, the moment. When it comes, trust your sense of things. Turn, paddle, freefall in.

Like a wave, but it's not a wave. It's your sense of right and wrong. Somewhere in that dreamy cloud of a head of yours, among the waves, is this other thing, this small hard core of a thing. The waves break on it without effect.

It's harder than anything in my head, for all my energy and half-craziness. Would I have done that, in front of the reporter at the Torquay pub? Throw my career half out the window because it's ... right?

I found when I made the boycott decision that a lot of sensitivity came up around the fact that the same stuff goes on here, the same stuff goes on in our backyard, the same stuff goes on in my head. So I make this stand, but then I get reflected back onto me this incredible responsibility to stick by the decision.

But I wasn't going to buy into all the activism around it. I know that only fuels it, another layer of crap. I had all this stuff coming at me about joining this or doing that, and I wondered, What's wrong with me? Why don't I want to be an activist for the cause? But there was something in me saying this is not right. I was travelling with a guy at the time who was thinking of going into US politics. I caught up with him a year or so later in California. We had a chat about it, and I'd gone through a lot of confusion in my head about how I was supposed to work with this decision beyond just the making of it.

But he made it really clear: if I'd made just one person question that system, I'd done my work.

And those words really clicked. That's where I'd been trying to get to with my conscience the whole time.

South Africa, where I stood in my power as a world champion and as someone at the peak of their game and could have the most impact – that was big. When it comes to the other stuff, the human shit, I haven't always been able to be so big. At times I've acted outside myself, or not been true to what I felt – probably because I didn't know any other way to act. I didn't know how to stick by my convictions, I didn't have the tools. I didn't want to listen to that voice going, *Okay, you're going to have to act this way here, Tom.* The voice of conscience wasn't listened to.

Making the moral choice to come clean, that was something of a healing measure, but it was a very, very painful choice. To strip back the masks and step back into myself, knowing it would affect everyone around me. An awakening.

MONKEY IN THE LAB

1985–86. $32,925 prize money. A win at Nii-jima; a win in
Allentown; fifth Atlantic City; seventeenth Lacanau; ninth Fistral;
ninth Hebara; third BHP Steel Newcastle; second Op Oz Bondi;
a win at Margaret River; third Beaurepaires; a win at Bells;
seventeenth Coke.

Ranked third in the world.

Tom Carroll Injury Number Three (the ankle version 1).

I exited the fluffy zone with an injury. I remember the moment
quite clearly.

I won the first two events of the year. I was kicking arse,
straight onto the tour. I kicked Curren's arse in Japan, then
won the Allentown wave-pool event. They had this stupid
interference rule in Atlantic City where if you were caught

just paddling on the same line of swell as the guy with wave priority, you were done, even if you were miles away. Even if you made a move for it. So I got done on an interference shortly afterward against Bainy in the quarterfinal. I dunno where they got the line of swell from. I was smashing him. I was on fire. I felt really strong.

I ended up coming home, needing to get back to training, focused and on top of the ratings, aiming up. I was training at Whale Beach, surfing the south end and working on critical moves, sharp turns into the lip. I landed a big floater just as a backwash came toward me, and it shoved the board back at me. I heard this *crack!*, and I was rolling around on the sandbar, feeling like I'd broken my leg. I'd separated the two bones at the base of the ankle, a syndesmosis tear, though I didn't know anything about that at the time. The injury rearranged a couple of ligaments that flopped over each other and made the ankle feel really weird; the whole leg was really weak.

And that was it. My year was completely fucked. It put me out. I couldn't come back. I lost all my confidence in the surf. I look back on that injury as the most devastating one of my career. You're in your prime, on top of the game – and bang. No-one knew about ankles the way they do now. Today they'd have operated, pinned it, held the joint in place till it healed, two and a half months and I'd be back. But then they didn't know what to do with it. They said, Ah, it's just a ligament thing, you'll be right.

I got this special brace that tied up around the ankle, and that made it feel okay, but trying to turn back to the foam, and then brace yourself against the foam? Everything was clunky. I went to France and tried to compete and it was just like, pain. I had acupuncture on it. I iced the daylights out of it all the time and got the swelling down, but it'd rearranged the way the muscles were behaving. I was struggling and I couldn't get rid of the pain. It put me into a negative hole I couldn't climb out of.

I got to California and there was a guy in Encinitas who Kong knew, called Garth Murphy. Garth said there's this lady in Encinitas who does a heat energy treatment. I'd try anything, because I was completely distraught.

So I went to see this lady in her garden flat. She had a room set up; it was all orange and she had candles going, but she seemed really switched on. There was no messing around. She got me on the table, lying there in my underpants, and she started moving her hands just off the skin, building this heat up. She gathered it from around the body and brought it all down to my ankle. My ankle was on fire. I looked at it and it was bright red, sweating.

She grabbed my ankle and said, This might be uncomfortable, and holding the base of the heel with her fingers, she pulled the whole joint apart. She had her fingers actually inside the joint, fiddling around with something. I was going into shock. I didn't know whether to scream or vomit. Then she let it go and it just went twang and flopped back into its spot.

I thought, *She's completely toasted my joint.* She said it would be uncomfortable for about a week and told me: I want you to come back then, but I think I got what you needed. There were some ligaments out of place, one was overlapping the other, and they needed to be put back in place.

I paid her and walked out of there, thinking, *She's stuffed this, she's screwed it up more.* But a week later I went back and saw her and it was feeling okay, and she was happy. She said,

It's doing exactly what I want it to do. And I was surfing within a week. It got stronger and stronger. I was back.

But it was too late. Tom Curren had taken full control of the tour. I was so over that but I was stoked to be back surfing. I had a really good Pat Rawson 6'8" that got all my confidence back, and I remember coming back to Margaret River and getting really intense on that event. I had to beat Tom in that final. It was ugly Margarets, big and north-west – ugly but perfect for the 6'8". It was all starting to click again.

It was an extraordinary experience of healing. That ankle joint's been good ever since. There's extra movement in it, for sure. But it works.

It was about a month before I could start surfing really well on my ankle, the way I wanted to, and settled in on it. And I wasn't treating it easily. I was desperate to give everything that I had to my surfing. I'd already gone through months of frustration and not letting go. Curren, Occy and Pottz were pretty much my focus, as far as rivals went. I was older than them, so I was trying to stay on top of it all the time, trying to learn how to surf better, finding new ways of doing it. Curren was on a roll. I had a chance to beat him at Margaret River and I did. Then I beat him at Bells Beach, when he first won his world title. It was overshadowed by his great semi with Occ, but it still felt good to win.

I started experimenting with different kinds of training – more core work, some really bizarre stuff, with a guy named Nigel Websdale. Nigel had very strong ideas about how athletes should holistically go about their day and approach their sport. He was big on nutrition, lots of miso, grain-oriented stuff. He'd get you to use the bar to work on the core, so you'd be hanging and doing straight-leg raises, and plyometric work with the ball, jumping and bouncing. Pretty cool and very much ahead of its time.

He was a pretty mad, intense sort of guy, but I tended to attract that sort of person. I think I gave off a feeling that I was a really intense competitor, I'd attract all these intense people who had unconventional ideas and pursued them in a very intense way. There was a lot of madness around. And it was never unconditional, so at some point I'd find that my reputation was being used at some level to help them along their path. This was usually unspoken and sometimes underhanded.

It's like chalk and cheese compared to who I am now. It's like a completely different me. I just feel so different. Looking back, I can see I was not a naturally competitive surfer. I don't know how I even made it as far as I did. I still get it from guys like Bruce Raymond, who will say to me, I mean this as a compliment, Tom, but you were possibly the worst world champ competitor ever ... Had you been better strategically, you could have had many titles. When I competed I brought along this idea of who I was viewed from the outside, Tom Carroll Surf Star, which conflicted with the person inside me at a deeper level, who was not hyper-competitive. It all felt like such a forced issue. I look back and think, *No wonder there was a lot of conflict going on in me at the time.*

Part of me, at some level, was probably wanting to run away. Like, Well, I've lost my world title, now I don't want to engage at all. I'm extreme by nature – it's all or nothing – and there was a part of me who wanted to jump off the train. I still didn't have an idea of how to separate the business of surfing from everything else. In my head, I was still a pro surfer

24/7. That's a lot of doing and there wasn't enough room for anything else.

If I could have had a rest from it all, that would have been the ideal time – a chance to come up for air, go off and recalibrate. My injury was forced upon me to try to make me take a break, probably. But my nature would never allow it. And no-one ever had a rest.

1986–87. $31,940 prize money. Seventeenth Marui, Japan; seventeenth Gotcha Pro; seventeenth Lacanau; third Fistral; fifth Op Pro; seventeenth Brazil; second Stubbies, USA; a win at Margaret River; third Op Oz; second Pipe, seventeenth Bells; a win at the Coke.

Ranked second in the world.

The older Carroll kids are both married: me to my dark-haired blue-eyed *Tracks* art director Wendy Harvey, Jo to her chef-in-arms, Damien Pignolet, and their restaurant, Claude's, is the talk of the town.

Me spending time with Wendy and you being on the road so much, we drift just a little apart. We surf together less. I watch less and less of your heats. You go away for months at a time and return subtly different each time. Always returning with unexpected bits and pieces – things you've been given, books on odd subjects like numerology or astrology, stories of odd people you've met on the road.

And photos. You take roll after roll of photos. Pics of your tour mates on trains in Japan. Weird miniatures of plant and animal life. Broad views down favela streets and French laneways. Your artistic traveller's eye occupied by the worlds through which you

Above: Uncool 70s, Newport car park (l/r): Scott Beggs, Robert Hale, Peter Phelps, Greg Fearnside, Rod Hynd, Andrew Hunter (bike), Nick, Sam Seiler and Derek Hynd. (Photo: TC)

Left: Haley and Hunter, backyard pushbike wars, 1982. (Photo: TC)

Below: Bedroom at Keith and Jill's, late 1982.

Fools on tour (l/r): Kong, Ross, Rod Kerr, Dooma Hardman, Jeff Booth, Bryce Ellis, Glen Winton and Simon Law in Hebara, Japan. (Photo: TC)

On the beach at Logs, 1984. Back row (l/r): Mike Newling, Peter Crawford, Haley and Spyder. Front row: Tom and Nick.

Clockwise from above:
Haley on the '85 French mission with Mitch Thorson and Kingsley Looker. (Photo: TC)

MR, PM Bob Hawke and Tom, Federal Parliament, 1985.

Tom Curren, quiet moment at the Op Pro, 1984. (Photo: TC)

Jeff Hornbaker, in front of the lens for once, Mexico. (Photo: TC)

Opposite: Tiny Jenna, happy in a swing in France, 1992. (All photos: TC)

Top: Kong and Pottz, stranded in Allentown, 1985.

Above left: Monty with friendly beast, US stopover, 1986.

Above: Self-portrait in Tokyo, 1986.

Left: Bryce Ellis, Kong, Rabbit and Gary Green, France, 1985.

Opposite: Jenna on Silly Dad's shoulders, Newport, 2001.

Rogue's gallery: Martin and Ross, bliss attack on *Indies Trader*'s roof deck. (Photo: TC)

Below: Naughty girls: Mimi and Jenna acting up in the Volvo, 2003. (Photo: TC)

Ross and Tom, eternal grommets, off the transom during the Crossing, early 2000s.

Below: Mother Lisa with her two older girls. (Photo: TC)

Below right: Young Grace storming into view, 2004. (Photo: TC)

move. Like another small fascinating life you're living beneath the big life, the Tom Carroll International Sports Star banner that Monty's continually stitching and re-stitching together. There are almost no photos of any surf.

You and Newling are like monks. Everything is cleaning out of your life, even the body fat. Newling reckons you might get down to three per cent. You're impossibly fit and clear-eyed, yet you're also becoming oddly distant. You switch off at times.

We'll be talking on the phone and mid-sentence, I'll suddenly be aware you're not there. You're holding the phone at the other end, but your attention has wavered for a moment, shifted from the conversation, and gone – off, light as a feather. Dreaming.

'Hello?' I say, into the space. 'Hello?'

'Oh! Oh, yeah,' you say. 'I'm with ya.'

But are you?

I stuck to that training program for quite a while, off and on. The idea of eating a lot of miso was pretty good. I was working on diet the way Mike had opened my eyes to it. I was eating buckwheat, vegetables, vegetable juices – a lot of juicing – as much natural, raw food as possible.

But on the other hand, I was doing the opposite. There was this clean life, but every now and then, when there was a chance, there'd be this cocaine explosion, this binge. I would give myself permission: if I did well in competition, or if there was a gap in the schedule or some pressure valve opening, it was on.

I came into contact with people in Hawaii who dealt large amounts of cocaine. They were surfers too, and kinda heavy, and I was vulnerable to people with that kind of intensity. You wanna have as much as you can, and I could get access to amounts that I'd only fantasised about. The cocaine, when it came out, went with my pathology so well that whenever I'd get a chance to do it, I would. And there was never, ever gonna be enough when it came round. It really went with who I was inside. I just bit in and loved it. I figured that was how it was for everybody. I couldn't imagine anything else. There were plenty of others hoeing in too; there was a lot going on.

I never thought of it as being illegal. When I think back, I was following the path of all the people I'd admired – Michael Peterson and Jimi Hendrix and all the rest, the people who were just great in my eyes. And it was fresh. There's been a lot of time and human experience since, but back then we were squeezed up against it. They were there in the 70s, those guys; I actually watched MP perform and fall apart, and I thought, Well, that's normal. At some level, that's what you just did.

It was cool to live hard and party hard in those days. It just seemed normal. Being illegal – whatever. Intensive drug use in a lot of the circles I moved in was quite acceptable. And if you could back up next day, get on with whatever you were doing … you could handle it. You were on top of the world. You were The Man.

I felt like a rock star. I felt like I could do it because I was special.

And this illusion carried out on the broader level, not wanting to look at the implications … even if at the back end of using there was this slash-your-wrists kind of feeling. Oh shit, there's no more, I'm gonna have to come down out of this. The high disappears, and you get drained of everything you are, and it feels like there's nothing left of you.

Surfing, food, everything you love – it all goes away. Just for that moment.

Then you start to come good, your body starts doing what it's always been doing, always wanting to be alive. It all returns and – *bang!* – I'm back!

I was like the monkey in the laboratory who keeps pressing the bar for treats. I'd just keep pressing till there was nothing left. Those were wild years in Hawaii. I dunno what else was going on out there, but where I was it was heavy.

IN THE MEMORY OF MY SISTER

I'd really dislocated myself in Hawaii that year, spent more time there than I should have, I was partying, surfing some big waves, hanging with Mickey Nielsen. Mansted was trying to get hold of me, get me out of there. It got to New Year's Day and I thought I'd better ring up and tell everyone I'm coming home, give 'em a little faith. I got back to Sydney and into my training regime, and that's when I got together with Lisa Merryman.

Lisa was working with Mansted in his office. She helped him out at the front desk. Pottz sort of took her out. She was a friend of Boj's and she became a surf buddy with Stuart Bedford Brown, who'd come over from Western Australia to hang out and train. I was training with SBB, trying to clean myself up from all the partying, following the template – party then train, get myself back on track.

I was really attracted to Lisa, but I never thought I'd be able to reach her for some reason. And I was still in a lot of pain from Elizabeth, so I still didn't know how to process that. There was no processing it! I was twenty-two years old, the world champion, what the hell? I'm the King! I could do what I wanted.

But my female relationships were dead in the water. I'd always look for what I'd seen in Elizabeth, whatever I was looking for in her. After my second world title I went out with Sandee Jonsen for about a year, and I just couldn't connect because I was too in my head, on another planet, not really ready to open myself up to another girl. And she was beautiful! These beautiful girls. Fuck! I had no idea what was going on with me other than that I was still hurting from three years before.

And then with Lisa, it just happened, we got together one night and something clicked. It was just a lot of fun with her. It wasn't like my relationship with Elizabeth, like whoa, boom! It didn't have that intensity about it. At the time it was really nice to have a female friend, and I thought we could be more than friends eventually. I wasn't ready to open my heart to anybody, I was a closed shop really, and I was still very self-centred with my surfing and life on tour, and I had permission to be like that. Being in a relationship with someone the way I was at the time means being subservient. I know it sounds bad, but anyone was going to be second to the surfing, to the sport, and my commitment to that.

I was still doing my world champion thing, my public Tom, and this other part was boiling away, getting bigger.

1987–88. $34,000 prize money. Fifth Stubbies, USA; seventeenth Op Pro; ninth Lacanau; second Hossegor; fifth Fistral; third Anglet;

a win in Florianopolis; ninth Hebara; a win at Margs; a win in Newcastle; seventeenth World Cup; thirteenth Billabong Pro; a win at Pipeline; seventeenth Santa Cruz; second Bells; third IMB; fifth Coke.

A win at Pipe.

Ranked fourth in the world.

Tom Carroll Injury Number Four: The Fin-Up-the-Arse Incident.

In Japan, you're having a pre-event practice surf and your board flips underneath you during a top turn, the nose wedges itself in the sand, and you land on the tail bum-first. Result: large, disgusting laceration right next to the anus. They can't stitch it properly because it's more of a hole than a cut. The doc secures the wound and packs it with gauze and gives you a bottle of heavy-duty antiseptic solution to ward off the glaringly obvious chance of infection.

Dutifully, you use the solution night and day, not knowing it's supposed to be applied as a one-to-ten dilution with water.

You end up running out into the Tokyo streets at 4 am, screaming in agony because the stuff has burned half the skin off your balls.

Monty's reaction is the best part. He *plays* it. He organises an ambulance to pick you up from Sydney Airport and alerts the media. Surf Champ Injury – Rushed To Hospital From Airport! Surfboard Up The Arse! The price of fame, or one price, anyway. The Newport boys are crying with laughter. They love it. Another story they can gently torment you with.

A nurse has to come around to your house for regular visits to clean your bum.

A couple of days before I leave for Hawaii that year, Jo and Damien ask Wendy and me to come to dinner at Taylor's, their friends' Italian restaurant in Darlinghurst. Damien is late; he's driving back up from Melbourne where he's gone to buy the car of his dreams – a late 1960s Citroën DV6.

It's a great dinner. Jo almost never has a night off from Claude's and she's in excellent form. We're joined by more and more people, the Taylors and their close customers, and the conversation flows, lifted by some deep undercurrent of optimism and happiness. We're in our late twenties and early thirties and in control of our lives. The future spreads out before us, like the meal on the restaurant table, and we all together feel ready to relish it, live it all, leave no crumb untasted, leave what remains of the past behind.

In Hawaii, it does something you and I have never seen before. It begins to rain. The rain comes in one afternoon, grows heavier overnight and never stops. Insane, drenching tropical rain for a week, a morning of half-sun and small surf, then more rain. The Pipe Masters is on hold, but there's no running contests in this weather. Everyone's stuck indoors, except when we crack and go out to play touch footy in the mud.

Late one afternoon it eases and the surf begins to build, and we surf Sunset in water that is now almost black with run-off, a lividly setting sun staining the surface red.

Next morning the sky is clear, the roads are steaming dry, and Hornbaker's house, where I'm staying, is shaking from the impact of swell on the reefs 400 metres away.

I race down to see Pipeline and watch, awestruck, as dead glassy fifteen-foot waves roll off second reef. Tom Curren is out there and Kong, maybe one or two others. Curren gets a big, big wave and eases off the bottom, the dirty brown water looming overhead, like a cliff pushed into surrealistic motion by some giant hand.

Wondering what to do, which board to ride, I head back to Horny's house, where he tells me, 'Wendy's been calling you. It sounds urgent, man.'

International calls don't happen every day, not when you're in Hawaii and it's the 1980s. I dial my home number with some apprehension. Wendy answers. She's crying.

'Damien's had a car accident,' she tells me. 'They'd gone to Canberra for the day and crashed on the way home. He's alive, but Josephine was killed.'

There's no fending this off. It just goes straight in, all the way, cold.

I comb the North Shore for hours, on the edge of panic, till I find you, thinking the whole time, *I've got to be the one to deliver this news*. I've got to be. We're brothers, for fuck's sake. He can't just *hear* this.

When I look back now, my first response was anger. I didn't cry or anything, I just was angry, really angry. Classic grieving response, really. After trying to get some reasoning around it, I talked with Dad on the phone and was figuring on coming home. He said, No, don't do that, stay there, I know Jo would really want you to win that event.

Then the next day the Pipeline Masters was on, and whatever else went on that day, I've never experienced anything like it since. The trivial things completely dropped away. I was completely raw and in the moment. There was very little between me and what I love doing in the surf. It was amazing having Fate say, Okay, we'll give you a day out surfing Pipeline now, here you go. Here's an opportunity to win in the memory of your sister.

It was incredible to have the opportunity to express that. I had no idea what was going on, but nothing got in the way, I couldn't make a wrong move, and every wave was just there.

I had an incident with Johnny Boy Gomes in the water that morning. I'd paddled in with Doug Silva from Rockpile, around the back of Pipeline. It was a windless morning but the water was brown. A fresh west swell. I didn't know how big it was. It was a dark morning, but it was really serene. The sun was still well down behind the escarpment and there were already a few guys out there. I saw the back of Pipeline exploding, and I realised it was pretty big. It was scary Pipeline. I had my helmet on. I paddled into it and got a couple of waves. It was really heavy, with a backwash coming into it. Doug got slammed. I paddled into a second reefer and Johnny Boy Gomes paddled around and on top of me and grabbed my legrope and pulled it as I was taking off on this wave. I couldn't get to my feet and got pitched with the lip. It was mindless behaviour, dangerous and stupid, and my automatic response was to paddle straight up and tell him it was a really stupid thing to do.

He was fuming. But he could see my eyes were different – he could see I was different – and he wasn't quite sure, I could see him backing away. I had my helmet on and I didn't care if he hit me. Normally there'd be no way I'd have confronted him like that. And instantly I felt different, I felt the difference for what was going on for me that day.

And then it just played out.

At the end of the day I honoured Jo in the ceremony, and then all I wanted to do was party. I wanted to escape from all of this craziness. I didn't get what was going on, all these journalists talking about our sister.

And I remember Nick saying, Look, these people are going to come at us, and they don't have any business in this. This is between us.

I thought, Yeah, this is a very private thing. I've never really known where to go with something like that. I can't remember the interviews, but I remember some feelings of distrust, which I'd never really felt before, so I wanted to sink back into myself. I was with Lisa, it was our first full trip to Hawaii together, and I still wasn't sure where we stood. I was still kinda caught up in myself. The first opportunity I could, I got on the gear, trying to drown the feelings that I was so confused about.

And that's how I dealt with it for the following week and probably for a long time after. I disappeared into myself. I blacked it out, shut it down. It was a deep family message for me: *you'll be right*. It was sad, but that was how we dealt with things. It was clear and very devastating. It really shook me up.

It's all over the papers: Surf Champ Tragedy. Tom Carroll competes at Pipeline, not knowing of his sister's death. Another price of fame: Josephine is turned into headline fodder for the afternoon tabloids.

You stay in Hawaii with Lisa. I get on the next flight home.

Two days after Christmas, Dad and I drive down to the Goulburn Police impounded vehicles yard, to check the car she'd died in for any personal effects. Dad never speaks directly during that drive about how he is being affected by the sudden death of his first child. Instead, with a slight smile or frown of recollection, he begins to tell me all he knows of our extended family background. Stories I've never heard, about goldminers in Ballarat and publicans in Kalgoorlie, about the Great War and boarding school in Charters Towers, and the oxcart track from there down to the coastal plains beneath the Atherton Tablelands, where his half of my family eventually settled, helping found the vast sugar cane farmlands of that broad coastal plain.

I listen, fascinated, to this history I've only half-guessed at, thinking at the same time how thin these strands are that connect us – how those goldminers and farmers can't ever have seen where their seed would be cast, into these two boys released into travelling the world, obsessed with riding waves.

In the Goulburn Police car yard we come upon the Citroën in which Jo has died. The car is heavily buckled from the front bumper, testament to the combined speed of the vehicles involved; they'd collided head-on at 100 kilometres an hour. Damien is still unconscious in a Sydney hospital. In the ruins of his car we find Jo's purse, one or two small items, and her small polka-dot umbrella – white on a deep-blue background, her favourite.

We sign for her possessions and drive out of there, passing the odd, almost surreal curve in the road where she'd died.

I am given the task of calling Nam with the news. She responds to it with her usual cheery stoicism, but I don't believe she ever quite takes it in. Sometime later her sister Gigi grows ill, and I travel to Surrey to organise better accommodation in a comfortable care home. Nam is in her nineties yet is still fairly sharp; at several points she asks me about Jo, then corrects herself: 'Oh, of course.'

Not long after this, she dies, at the ripe age of ninety-seven. The last connection we have.

I knew there were a lot of gifts that came with Jo. In many ways I kept looking at my last memory of her. It was at the house in Foamcrest Avenue. She drove up, parked outside and came in. She was quite sad, quite concerned. She was in a soul-searching kind of space. She said she'd really like to have children. I can't remember if it was an organised visit or if she'd just come out from town. But she came to see me, and she thought it was coming to the point where she'd like to have children. She was thirty-one. I was really happy to hear that; I thought, *Wow, I'm going to be an uncle.* I felt a lot of joy for her.

And so I kept going back to that memory, and over time I started to look at the gifts she'd been given. I'd drive past Claude's and want to go in and have dinner every night. I wasn't too good at dealing with the memories or with the emotions around the memories. I'm more adept at denial: closing off my emotions and denying those memories.

And I never held anything against Damien, but I still wasn't quite sure why that was. Why I didn't question him. Why I didn't want to question him. I knew there was no way in hell she was coming back. And I'm probably better at escaping things like that. I did a lot of crying down the track. I'd cry privately.

It didn't follow me back out to Pipeline, though. I detached. But at the same time it allowed me to know Pipeline much better. It brought me a lot closer to Pipeline. It was a bonding experience. A surf spot bonding experience. When you're feeling every part of the wave and there's nothing between you and it.

Part three

Adulthood

'Strange as it may sound, Tom Carroll's mission in life has not been to seek eternal glory on a surfboard, but confidence and belief in himself. In Carroll's words: "I need to work on my confidence. It's always been a problem, but it's very hard to get out of that groove. I'm self-critical. I give myself a pretty hard time, which has been pointed out to me by friends many times. But I want to do the best I can ..."'

—*The Sydney Morning Herald*, October 1990

There's no moment when I've feared for my life in the ocean. I don't think there's even been an all-encompassing freak-out, that total frozen sensation of fear. Nothing like that. The ocean is more like home for me, at some level. But you can see how quickly the ocean can take you, it'll take you in a second. It's a part of being in it. It's a possibility.

I was out Sunset once, just me and Mike, it was onshore and crap and big. I got pounded on the takeoff and Mike had paddled over to get me because he saw my board tombstoning, and he'd just got there when I came up. I floated to the surface. I'd lost my limbs. I had no feeling of control over my arms and legs. It was dark, but there was a pinhole. You know how people say, 'I was looking through a tunnel into the light'? Well, my consciousness had shrunk down to a really small hole. I got to the surface and took a breath, and as soon as I took a breath it opened back up, *whoosh*. Luckily there were no other waves coming. I came to pretty quick.

That was the closest moment I can remember. I don't have the delusional idea of being immortal that comes along with being younger and less aware. But rather than being completely frozen with fear, it's more like, *Okay, where do I move here now?* I've got a lot of confidence in the ocean.

I'd have more fear for my life out of the ocean, with other human beings, especially when I see how people can behave towards each other. Whereas a wave? Being held down by a wave? For other people, maybe it would be cause for fear. Not for me.

April, 1988. Monty pulls it off. The deal of the century. Five years solo with Quiksilver. Boiled down, it's an average of $200,000 a year, the first million-dollar surfer contract in history. It sets a precedent that will roll into the future, when surfers will ride a wave we haven't yet imagined, signing exclusives for ten times the sum with surf companies worth billions.

You and Bruce Raymond and Monty pose for the cameras, the pens ready, the contract laid out – a scene rehearsed for its media value and played out clean, yet it feels oddly elegiac. Not a beginning but the faint whiff of an end. You and Monty are walking away from each other, though neither of you are willing to say it.

In the middle of that year somebody, maybe Bruce, decides to send Tom Carroll, Quiksilver's new million-dollar man, on surfari to Grajagan, the epic, still-mysto left reef break on the jungle-bound southeast tip of Java. It's gonna be Adventure Surfing's New Dawn. We fly off to Bali with a film crew – you, me, Spyder and Hornbaker – then you let on that you've brought a bunch of acid with you, hidden in your shoe.

Not for a moment do we think, *Oh God, we'll all be arrested and thrown in jail,* even though back at *Tracks* I'd carried on a correspondence with Jimmy Cook, a kid from Cronulla who'd been chucked in jail in Denpasar for twenty-five years for a lot less than a few squares of acid. Nah, that's never going to happen to us. Invincible.

We come into G-Land by boat across the bay from the village, and forget about the acid for days. Grajagan is too much all on its own: the vast reef bending into the bay, the long improbable stretched-out waves, the languid afternoons waiting for the tide; the big paw prints in the sand and the rumours of panthers in the jungle.

Then comes a night when the tradewind dies, and a morning arrives shrouded in strange mists drifting off the jungle canopy. Surf photos can't be taken. Hornbaker the angler decides it's time we went fishing, and Paul King, who's managing the camp excursion, heads off to set up the Zodiac he's arranged to have available while we're here. Tom Carroll! Gotta have a powerboat.

We decide it's time for the acid.

A half hour later we are in the Zodiac with a few handlines, trolling up and down off the back of the Money Trees reef. Time passes, no bites. Still no wind blows. The day grows steadily warmer and the haze thins under the sun. Everything seems entirely normal. It is very disappointing.

Then – *bang!* – something hits Hornbaker's lure. Hornbaker is a hippie but he is also a Hemingway; no fish takes his lure and survives. He wrestles a giant trevally over the side and into the boat.

We're stunned, but not as stunned as the fish. It thrashes about, a veritable scaly Mike Tyson, but Hornbaker hurls it dismissively into the stern. 'Just knock it out,' he says, waving vaguely at a fish club, but Spyder and I can't think of anything except getting more lures out.

Slowly the excited chatter of the witless rookie fishermen dies away, and only then do we become aware of a thudding sound coming from the stern. The sickening crunch of flesh against something a bit harder.

We turn to find you, eyes narrowed, muscles clenched and fish club in hand, smashing repeatedly at Tyson's head.

Many seconds pass as we all stare, jaws agape at this incredible farcical scene of Gobbo versus Fish. Blood and scales fly, Tyson's long since dead, yet you swing on like some crazed warrior engaged in ancient Celtic battle, giving off an odd grunt now and then – almost a muffled cry of triumph.

What the fuck?

Then you seem to come to your senses, turn to us with a terrible smile, and just as the acid bursts through the surface of our minds, you say: 'Catching that fish kicked me in.'

I write about it all, but not about the drugs. Well, nearly that time.

Back in Sydney, ten years of effort, MR's and yours and Occy's charisma and skills, Cassidy's event promotion and media savvy, and a lot of possibly slightly puzzled sponsors' money have helped turn surfing into the pro sport of the decade. The footy commentator Frank Hyde says he reckons it'll end up bigger than Rugby League.

You're the Australian sporting star *du jour*, and you need a car to match. You shop around and get the red Alfa Romeo GTV6. Hell, it's the 80s! The fizzy boom days of the 80s. Leigh Moulds gets his canary yellow Porsche and after late nights at Metropolis, his North Sydney nightclub, you two conduct races up and down the Roseville Bridge at 220km/h. The sports star and the nightclub owner: what a couple of bouffant-haired success stories you are.

A house comes up for auction, high on the cliffs above the Path. A trophy house. The real estate agent can barely believe Tom Carroll is planning to bid. At the auction, the price climbs, higher, higher. It breaks $700,000 on your bid, an unheard-of sum. Going to Mr Carroll, says the auctioneer eagerly, seeing the headline, going ... and another bidder carries it out of your reach.

You relax, and spend a lot less on an old brick-rendered place on the hill above the Peak, a couple of doors up from Bill Wawn's parents.

They feel like golden days. I begin to relax too, and to concentrate on my own life, try to stop worrying about how you'll do in the next heat, the next contest.

You're twenty-five years of age. Nobody's ever won back a world title after losing it. It's a goal, a good one. You go back to work.

I wanted to get a third world title. I'd just come out of a few frustrating years, toing and froing with Curren, Elko, Barton and Dooma and all those guys. Occy was out of the picture. I was trying to get back to that world champion headspace, regroup and get a third one. I'd had a good year or two training with Mike, mentally approaching things, and I felt really on top of my surfing, everything really clean and crisp.

Lisa was living with me at 66 Foamcrest Avenue. Redman was gone. He'd already shown his colours by then. I'd barred him. I had to pay a lease out on his car because I went guarantor on it which was about $8000 – a lot of money in those days. I kind of just wrote him off in my head.

At the time our area, the Northern Beaches, was definitely the focus of a lot of talent. The scene was really on fire. People were moving here to take the next step in their surfing. Pottz was here, pushing his style; he'd joined Newport Plus and we were training together. It was really peaking, that 80s style of surfing: all power, muscle surfing, very macho and competitive, and very uptight in a way. Tight boardshorts. Tight. Neon. Bright colours.

I was still up there in the top three or five, punching away, and 1988 was seen for me as my year.

It was a bit different this time because my relationship with Monty had become strained. In the previous world titles it was a real team effort; this time I felt separate from him. I was trying to grow up and didn't want to go the way he was pushing. I didn't even know which way he wanted to push. He'd been running his own race without communicating to me, and he'd done a few things that didn't appear to be managing from the background; he was trying to push his own barrow, and not necessarily managing in my best interests. I'd try to find out what Monty was dealing with, and he'd say, No, I've got it sorted, don't you worry about it, go and do your thing.

I wasn't really willing to confront the situation. I decided I didn't have time to be suspicious. I felt like my only way of dealing with it was to get back into a winning phase. I just wanted to surf, compete and do the best job possible. I was travelling a lot, and when I came back home I was focused on training, improving my boards. It was all about improvement, growing my performance – almost an obsessive drive after a few years of getting knocked back or injured. I was getting closer to my best form, closer than I'd been since I'd last won a world title.

And I was dealing with living a more public life, driving around in my Alfa and being a bit of a hoon. I used to do time trials down to Wollongong and back, still not beating the Chookwagen's record, though. I dunno how that happened. I must not have got the timing right because there's just no way. I mean, in the Alfa I was doing 230, 240 down the freeway.

But I was really serious about that year. I put a big focus on performing. And my relationship with Lisa was blossoming. We were making a little home together. It was a really good time for us, even though I was still completely and utterly self-centred and blind to it. Nobody was saying anything to me, like, Maybe you should listen to someone else other than your own self-centred stuff. Everything was entirely about me. I was living in classic 80s style: raw. We were making it up as we went.

In training we were using bikes a lot, and swimming early in the morning, doing sprint work at Bilgola Pool which was really good. We'd do the swim and the bike, then a weights session later. Pottz would come along and join in, along with Justin Rose, who Monty had somehow involved, I think partly as a buddy for Pottz. Monty was doing his marriages and break-ups and divorces, living at Whale Beach one minute then Drummoyne or Bondi the next – it really got hectic. He'd had me on a really good deal with Qantas one year, travelling a whole year first-class, but the deal fell apart. One time I didn't even turn up to one of the meetings; we'd been partying and I went AWOL. I got to the end of the Wakehurst Parkway and I was late in traffic, so I just turned around and went back home.

But by 1988 I was a bit more grounded with Lisa in my life. I wanted to be the professional athlete I was meant to be and regain the world title. Around Newport, it felt like we were at the top of the game. We were just feeling really good about ourselves and our surfing. We'd go out wherever we wanted and push it when it got bigger – Deadmans, Dee Why Point – really going for it and really enjoying it.

1988. $65,750 prize money. Ninth Nii-jima; fifth Gotcha; second New Smyrna, Florida; fifth New Jersey; fifth Stubbies, USA; fifth Op Pro; a win at Lacanau; a win at Hossegor; second at Fistral; third at Anglet; second Zarautz; a win at Florianopolis, Brazil; seventeenth Hebara; seventeenth Bondi; seventeenth Newcastle; a win at Sunset; ninth Pipe; ninth Billabong Pro.

Ranked third in the world.

I can't remember all the results. Europe was a big shift for me. I got a few good results in a row – a win and a third – and it really lifted my ratings. Then in Spain I got a win. Beat Barton Lynch. Barton was spinning! He accused me of taking anabolic steroids and amphetamines, all these performance-enhancing drugs. Barton hated me because I was beating him and he thought I was rigging it. I had momentum – I could feel it – so I started lifting my game.

Hawaii was tricky, though. I got a win at Sunset and was feeling really strong, but then I got sick. Surfed massive Pipeline the day after Sunset on my 8'6" with Stretch and Pottz, and the day after that I came down with this incredible lung infection. I could feel the pressure mounting on my world title chances.

Every time I saw Monty he would be visibly tense, and I would respond to that. He was carrying the pressure more than me, and I felt like I was carrying him. I didn't know how to deal with that stuff.

I had to go down the sports medicine road with Horny's doctor. I was coughing up yellow stuff all night, dizzy and spaced out. The Pipeline Masters was coming up in a couple of days and I had to be tuned for that. It was an important event; I needed to keep my ratings up. I was really stressed and it all came out in that infection.

So I went to the doctor and he's like, Look, Tom, there's medicine, and there's *sports* medicine. We can go the medicine route – antibiotics, rest, taking it slow – or we can go the sports medicine route, which is to take these steroids.

It just knocked the crap out of whatever I had. One day I was whacked, couldn't move, coughing and feeling like crap, then in two days I improved radically. I was still spaced, though. I wasn't there.

I remember trying to get my brain working: *I'm going out to Pipeline. I'm going to surf the Pipe Masters. It's a competition.* And after feeling so sharp and on at Sunset, I felt so disconnected. It was small Pipeline, raining, and Rob Page won the event. I rode my 7'2", which was a small Pipe board then, and couldn't figure out what the wave was really doing when I took off. I was surfing by Braille, in a sense. I was lucky if I got through a heat. The infection was gone, where it went I don't know, and I could walk around and act like I was all right, but I was pretty toasted.

I was still in the title race, of course, with the Billabong event to come. There was a lot of hanging out and waiting for that event, which was brutal. If you think about the Sydney

Northern Beaches at the time, there was Barton, me and Dooma, all in the top five in the world, which was pretty cool. But there was no camaraderie between us at all. There was no friendship like we have now. A lot's happened inside us since then.

By Hawaii it's a big deal. Three surfers in the title race: Barton Lynch, Damien Hardman and you. You're strapped in, committed, confident, but you want the backup. You ask me to travel with you, help walk you through these last three events to what surely seems your destiny.

I want you to win. But I don't know if I want to watch. Watching you in a heat is sometimes a delight. Mostly it's a torment. Over the years, instead of it mattering less, it just gets harder. Me, the natural competitor, and my little brother the brilliant surfer, powerful, intuitive, yet as Bruce will later point out, the worst competitor ever to win a world title.

I sit there, my heart in my mouth, unable to protect you or myself, trying not to second-guess your decisions and watch them pan out – good turns, wipeouts, priority battles, a win or a loss. Having to talk to people afterwards. How'd Tommy go? Yeah, great.

I don't want to watch. But I'm going to worry, whether I'm there or not. I sign up, what the hell.

You, me, Wendy and Lisa take up residence in a big glossy Kuilima condo. Pat Rawson and Jack Reeves, the greatest surfboard builders of modern times, prepare a quiver of surfboards, both eclectic in design and honed to perfection. Incredibly specific craft for the world's most dramatic surf.

And the first contest, the World Cup at Sunset Beach, is a gem.

The final is all time. You and Elko in perfect airbrushed ten- to twelve-foot Sunset, me and Darrick Doerner caddying with spare boards in the channel. We can almost reach out and touch you both. Gary comes fanging out from behind the north-west peak on his 8'0" AB six-channel at a million miles an hour, this huge grin on his face. He's already spending the prize money, and so is DD; he keeps yelling, 'What's one-tenth of $15,000?' Referring to the caddy's time-honoured fee.

But you get the next wave, and instead of driving parallel to the wave line the way Gary's doing, you just go straight down the face, mid-peak. Just slow the whole thing down. Then throw the big new 8'3" Rawson straight back up again – a pure muscle move, but done casually, like it was a lazy day out the Pool ten years ago.

Just superb.

You get sick and we pretty much write off the Pipe Masters, which never gets over six feet anyway. Then it goes flat, and rains. It's like a replay of 1987. It gives you time to recover, yet the tension grows. We go for these desperate surfs, the waves one foot, the wind howling, nobody else in the water.

Then the swell comes for the Billabong Pro final day. The event is mobile; it can be held anywhere on the North Shore. They set up at Pipeline: perfect, dead glassy, big, square, still building. It looks like the old posters of Jackie Dunn.

Derek Hynd, now a coach for the Rip Curl surf team, a job he's more or less invented, is in charge of your number one rival, the rankings leader Damien Hardman. Derek comes up to me, says, 'What do you think is going to happen today?'

I say, almost without thinking, 'Tom's going to win the contest and the world title. I mean, Derek, look at it.'

Oh shit, I think immediately, *what have I said?*

But I've never been so sure of you winning anything as I am that morning, with your new transparent blue helmet and needle-thin Rawson gun. Everyone's eyes are on you as you dance easily through a first heat against Hawaiian Noah Budroe, shaking off the nerves.

Then you're in the water with a young, fired-up Florida kid, Todd Holland. And you forget the dumbest, most unnecessary, most obvious rule in competitive surfing. Priority paddling interference: if the guy with priority paddles for a wave, you can't.

You do.

That incident, it's caused a lot of scarring for me. I was fired up and trying to calm myself down. I don't think I was mature enough at that stage to manage it or to understand the situation. I was so caught up in trying to control the day. I was clearly winning the heat and didn't need to catch that wave, didn't need to catch any wave, but I wasn't connected to the situation. My warped idea was that I needed to look at every single wave, I needed to be on top of everything. I wanted to get the best score I could get.

It was serious Pipeline. It was kind of ugly at that stage; it wasn't great Pipe. The wind wasn't on it yet. It was a good swell. But it was feeling like a good day for me. The heat with Noah that morning had been really clean, really nice.

The heat with Todd Holland was a bit chunkier and less predictable. I'd been noticing all winter that Todd was just going for anything, going mental. He was a bit crazed and I sensed he had no regard for his own safety. I pulled up at Pipe a couple of times that season and watched him get absolutely annihilated. Surfing out there by himself on onshore days. He was a pretty good surfer and I always got on with him, but he was on a mission.

So there I was in a heat, feeling like I had to be on top of my game because he could possibly get a really high score. I was at odds already with that priority paddling interference rule. I'd been called once on it that year, way down the beach from the other guy, totally separated, and that blocked me in a quarterfinal. I just didn't get that rule.

And I was so fucken arrogant I thought I could do without it. I'd brushed it in my head. I was that arrogant – fuck the rules! Arrogant and ignorant.

So I wasn't ready to deal with it correctly.

I was looking at this wave coming through. It looked like it could be something – enough for me, anyway, in my state of mind. I thought, *I'm gonna have a look at this.* I sensed that Todd wasn't in a position to go, because he was further out than me and over, keeping the inside position. He didn't care where he was as long as he had my inside. He had priority. He was twitching on every move I made.

I remember turning round toward Ehukai, looking down the line, realising it wasn't such a good wave and pulling back. Then when I turned around, he was gone! He went for the wave. And because I'd made a move for the wave as well, I knew it could be an interference call.

He went Backdoor and got obliterated in a closeout and they called it an interference.

I went in and punched the steering wheel out of my rental car.

Up on the cold morning Pipeline sand, next to fuming Monty, I realise at that moment just how much I hate watching your heats.

Just hate it. Always have. Hate the worrying, hate the caring, hate the impotence.

Barton rolls on, beats Luke Egan in the final, wins the world title from the back marker in one of the greatest performances in pro surfing history.

We all go out to dinner, Team Tom Carroll around a big table at the Turtle Bay Hilton. Monty talkative, you withdrawn, untouchable, a slight smile – the mask smile – on your face. For an hour we sit there all together, not talking about the only subject on anyone's mind. Nobody knows what to say to you or what to talk about at all. It'd be hilarious if it didn't suck.

Sitting there, I think, unkindly, *I would never have done what he did, give away such a chance.*

Then I have a little brotherly revelation. I think, *Ahh, so what? It's past. It's done.* Tom's never going to commit to the world title like that, not ever again.

I know then I'll never again have to give much of a shit about your heats, because I know you won't. Not the same way. Never again.

I didn't know it at the time, but that day I lost faith in the way the whole judging system worked. I'd been done by that rule a couple of times already, and I felt absolutely powerless and voiceless around it. I would never go up and question the judges. I would always accept the judges' decision no matter what. Just perform. Don't get caught up in that. So I would try and let it go, or I'd internalise it.

A few hours later they made a decision to scrap that rule. So how could I put my fate and future in those hands?

And I decided I was not going to put that kind of effort into a year and suffer that kind of result ever again. No way. I was just gonna go for the events I wanted to go for. I still wanted to reach new levels in my surfing, I knew I had a lot left in me, but I wasn't going to give it to the tour.

I started stepping away from competitive surfing at that point. I started my slow step away, because it couldn't be fast.

1989. $43,525 prize money. Third Cronulla IMB; seventeenth Bells; fifth Coke; seventeenth Nii-jima; third Gotcha; ninth Op Pro; fifth Fistral; fifth Lacanau, seventeenth Hossegor; seventeenth Biarritz; ninth Hebara; second Margaret River; a win at Newcastle; ninth World Cup; fifth Pipe, fifth Billabong Pro.

Ranked fifth in the world.

1989 was a really tough year. Trying to come back after losing that title chance and trying to hold up this idea that I was the same competitor I'd been in '88 ... it was horrible. I couldn't get through a heat.

Earlier on that year I'd decided to call off my relationship with Monty and not have him involved at all in my business. It had been a couple of years coming, trying to drum up the courage to make the break and get out there on my own.

It was a really insecure time. He was starting to put all his energy into Pottz then anyway, and that was cool – I was happy for them. When I look back on it I think Monty may have put all the energy that he wasn't able to give to me, because I wouldn't allow it, into Pottz, who was open to it.

Monty knew what was good for you. He could manage and focus people's wild energy; I think that was one of his best talents. He couldn't manage his own, but he could see what other people needed and he could help them get it.

So he coached Pottz into that extraordinary world title. Pottz completely annihilated everybody. He was on such a roll and I couldn't even get through a heat. It was killing me to watch that go on. I took it all on board. I was fucked, just gone. It was a dreadful year of competing when I didn't want to, trying to make out I was something when I wasn't. I was in all kinds of trouble.

Everything was telling me to step off the train and take a rest at the station. And eventually I did, around the European part of the tour. I came home with my tail between my legs, really worried that the whole thing was going to blow up in my face and I wouldn't be able to take time out. Would Quiksilver support me? I had all that stuff going on. But they supported me.

I wanted to clear everything out of my life. I came back, broke it off with Lisa, got everyone out of my house, severed ties with Monty. I got my home back to myself but it was a really sad time. It all came up one day when everyone had gone and I was alone there, and I just had the horrors, I was really sad. Crying a lot. Emotionally really distraught and not knowing who to turn to or where to go.

I had a red Commodore wagon, the bomb surf car, and one day I had to get something out of the back. I had to have a piece of wood to prop the hatch open, because there wasn't enough pressure in the rear-door shocks to keep it open. I got the piece of wood and propped it open, and just began crying uncontrollably.

I hadn't seen Lisa for a while and she just happened to be driving by and she saw me, and came over and comforted me. It was a big moment between us, and I realised she was someone special to me, and it reignited something. We slowly began seeing each other again, and by 1990 we had really reconnected. It was much fresher, and all that other stuff, the horrors and the sadness, was behind me.

1990. $42,525 prize money. Seventeenth Bundy Rum, Burleigh; seventeenth Bells; third Coke; ninth Oceanside; seventeenth Op Pro; second at Zarautz; seventeenth Hossegor, Biarritz, Sopelana, Hebara and Margarets; twenty-fifth Haleiwa; a win at Pipe; seventeenth Billabong Pro.

Ranked thirteenth in the world.

Pottz's win punctuates an era in surfing, though we can't see it then. The 1980s are passing. Then they're past, those mad tight-boardshorted, buffy-haired days of muscle and neon, the Aussie dominance, the great ascent of the surfing image on the back of Coca-Cola and OP and Foster's and Subaru and various insurance companies and Japanese department stores and sixteen-page *Sun* wraparound sections.

The world changes. *The Sun* has already closed; Graham Cassidy is now chief of staff at *The Sydney Morning Herald* and running the ASP out of a post office box on Broadway. Pottz's and Monty's relationship goes south under fantastic Taxation Office debts. John the Butcher, now a fully-fledged rubber baron, sells

Peak Wetsuits to Rip Curl for a lot of money and begins casting around for other opportunities. Newport Plus wins its last great national teams challenge and blows the entire prize purse on a party in a hotel suite, and the club pretty much implodes.

In the middle of it, you seem lighthearted in a way I haven't seen since you won that first world title. The bubble Monty once formed around you has popped, and you're still there – still the Australian sports star, but not quite as opaque, no longer Gobbo the Glamorous God. You seem to travel less that year. We surf together a bit more. You and Lisa come to dinner, like any other suburban couple.

You're beginning to come back to yourself, I think. My dreamy little brother with the vague phone manner, the freckles and the cheeky grin, the grommet everybody loves.

And you've always been lucky. Lucky with Charlie Ryan, lucky with Col Smith, lucky with sponsors, lucky with friends, lucky with allies. Lucky now with Lisa.

It's all been fixed up. It's always been fixed up.

In December, our worlds collide. Dad, now retired from the newspaper game and keen to see the place we keep going back to, comes to the North Shore of Oahu for a holiday with Valerie, Lucy and our other new little sister, Annie. *Crikey*, I think anxiously, *I wonder if this'll work* – it's not exactly Paddington.

We rent a big house on the point at Backyards. It's a bit uncomfortable at times, but Dad seems to enjoy it, his curious observant mind engaged by the differences in the coastline, the tradewinds and the huge swells that arrive overnight and explode across the reefs. He meets Doerner and Marty Hoffman; they discuss the surf, and part with a sense of mutual regard. He has a soft spot for rogues.

I watch from the lanai as he walks away along the beach toward Sunset, thinning hair whipped by the wind, and wonder if he misses this, in his new city-dwelling life – misses an open beach, the space and solitude he had when we were kids, and maybe long before that, when he was a kid on the Mackay sandflats.

So much of him is in you, and you in him.

We surf our brains out together in that lovely consistent late-winter surf, knowing we'll soon part ways. I have a job offer from *Surfing* magazine and a US work visa. Wendy and I sell our cars, pack everything and go to California with our ten-month-old daughter Madeleine Rose, not knowing what we're getting into, but irrationally sure it'll work out fine.

Fuck it. Time for us to grow up.

TRANSITION

I guess it's funny, looking back. I'd started making decisions in my early twenties about where I was going to go with this surfing career. Back then there was no such thing as a pro tour surfer over the age of about twenty-five. The idea of a thirty-year-old pro surfer just didn't make sense. It wasn't in the scope of things. It was considered that by then you'd have moved on. And that's how I'd placed things, in those sorts of boxes: I've got that ticked, that's when I'll be doing that.

Certain things were now becoming a reality for me. I was world champion, I had a certain command over the role, and at the start I'd set limits on myself in order to control my life as a world champion. By the time I was thirty, I'd figured, I'd be beginning to think about having kids, even though the whole idea had really shocked me at twenty-two, and I'd thought I would probably be ready to retire.

And lo and behold, it started happening right in front of

me. I'd made a decision that I'd better settle down, I'd better get married, dada da da da da ... and time would march on the way it does.

These decisions were a way to assert some sort of control over my existence, compared with competitive surfing; the more I tried to control that, the less control I had, which was immensely frustrating. But I still wasn't ready to let go of competition, the structure of it and the tour, or at least the parts of it I enjoyed.

Curren came back and won that third world title in 1990, my goal from 1988, which really made me cranky – my ego didn't like it, but I could see I wasn't really up for that goal anymore. He really cemented his place with some beautiful surfing. I wasn't in the space to counteract that, but I still didn't want to accept it. All these sort of issues were playing out on all these different emotional levels; we just didn't have the tools and understanding that we have today, the sports psychologists, mentors and counsellors. It was more like, you just had to man up and deal with it. It wasn't even the subject of conversation. It was an unspoken thing. There was no feeling involved. It was a really different way of behaving. All these things were left in the dark.

I focused on the Pipeline Masters and the Margaret River contest – events I really liked to surf in and to lift my performance. I started getting into yoga really hardcore. I met Simon Buttonshaw and started doing extended sessions of yoga that were really intense. It was a whole other kind of intensity.

Then the two-tiered system and the qualifying tour came along, and Kelly Slater arrived.

I remember thinking there'd been other times when the choice was really clear: I could either resist this change or embrace it. It was very clear. It'd happened before when I was dealing with Occy in 1984, when he was dominating, and my ego was saying, Fuck this guy! Fuck this situation! It was either resist it or embrace it, work with it, try to improve yourself and do what you need to do to get the best out of yourself.

And that same thing came up with Kelly: who's this young guy coming in? You start getting chesty about it – well I did, inside myself. There was this challenge to who I was within Quiksilver. I didn't really take the matter on board, but I could see it coming up.

I was in Tavarua, Fiji, in 1990, with Bob McKnight and a few other Quiksilver people, and they asked me about Kelly Slater. What I would do with this young guy. I said, Well, he's really modelled himself off Tom Curren; he almost looks like a new Tom Curren.

This young guy. I'd already seen he'd done well. I remembered Mike coming back from this run of B- and C-grade events along the East Coast – he'd gone there to try to get some points – and he came back saying, This little dickhead! This little boy, he creamed everybody! We knew Sean Slater, and here was his brother, Kelly, creaming everybody. He just rips, Mike said. He dominates.

Kelly had already smashed the US, and he had all this ammunition: a wealth of surfing knowledge that he'd already shown on the North Shore. I remember seeing him surf at Off-the-Wall, then he came and surfed Ke Iki Hale, in front of where we'd stayed near Log Cabins, on the wobbly messed-up left that comes off the edge of the Ke Iki rocks. I thought, What the hell? He's only young, but if he can surf backside off that weird left, he must be an incredible talent.

That came up in conversation at Tavarua, and I said, Well, he's got that Curren thing: he was sponsored by Curren's sponsors – OP and Channel Islands. He had a real strong focus on the Curren style, and we'd have to break him out of that mould to make him work for Quiksilver.

As it was, his surfing was one of the reasons why I started to see there was no real choice in the matter. He was too good. I had to step away. His surfing was inspirational, though, and my decision to embrace it really helped me see that.

Then another thing happened that helped me make the transition. John the Butcher came to me at a San Diego Action Sports trade show in 1990 and said, I've got this really good idea. The trade shows were pretty big events back then. It was full-on party time. We were away from the surf and in among all these people. We'd party at night and go to the show all day. I was walking out of the show about midday – I think I was trying to get out of there – and there was John coming in.

He just stopped me right there and said, How would you like to do Quiksilver wetsuits?

I said, Yeah, what the hell? Let's do it!

I didn't think about it too deeply. I just saw it as a good opportunity to get going down the track, something where I could be further involved with Quiksilver. I knew that licensees with Quiksilver were doing well, making good money. And Quiksilver didn't have a wetsuit at the time. I'd been wearing generic suits with Quik labels for a couple of years, so it made sense.

From there on in it was getting money together and getting someone else involved. Bruce had been policing the licensees for Quiksilver, a really hard job, travelling around the world trying to keep them all in line, and he was right up for it. So the three of us chipped around $30,000 each.

It was the first real move I'd made after Monty and I felt freer in a lot of ways. It was independent of my competing on tour, Lisa and I were thinking of getting married, and I was looking for something to support us. I knew John had been quite successful with wetsuits at Peak, and I had faith in his ability to get the rubber out. I thought maybe we could make a really nice product for Quiksilver.

But I didn't know what it was going to take. When you go into partnership with others in business, it's a real marriage. A lot of faith has to be put in by everyone, a lot of communication. You have to rely on each other and back each other up, even when you don't like the way your business partner is behaving. All this stuff! I didn't know what I was up for.

By the beginning of 1991 I'd got myself another Pipeline Masters. I was starting to feel good about my surfing and where I wanted to take it. I was still engaging with the sport, my name was carrying me in many ways, and I could play that pro athlete role really well by then. I already had a great rapport with people. It was valuable and I knew it. Getting a world title wasn't in my sights anymore, but coming along with that shift in focus was the underlying commitment to moving on in life.

And Lisa and I were married. May 4, 1991.

It seemed to be the natural progression for the relationship: to commit to it, to nail it down. That was the movement of the relationship, and the inertia of it. I was still very selfish and my life was definitely still all about surfing and my complete involvement in it. Lisa, from time to time, would come into the picture. And that's what my relationships have been like.

That's sad, but that's true. I can't say it's anything but the truth. Or maybe it isn't sad, I don't know, but that's how it's been. I didn't know better. I was in the dark about myself.

But we had a good friendship, Lisa and I, and a really good partnership. We enjoyed each other all the time; it was the most comfortable I'd ever been with a woman. I wasn't needy, I wasn't crazy, we didn't have some insane need to be together all the time. I found it easier to concentrate on what I was good at, and she supported me in that. We had fun travelling together, and we got to know each other pretty intimately that way – or as intimately as you can get with someone so self-obsessed. I think that probably suited her at some level, even though it probably left her hoping I might change.

Then I finished third in the world in 1991. I wasn't even trying for it.

1991. $57,375 prize money. Fifth Clearwater Classic, Manly; fifth Bells; seventeenth Coke; ninth Op Pro; second Fistral; a win at Hossegor; seventeenth Biarritz; fifth Hebara; seventeenth Miyazaki; third Haleiwa; a win at Pipe; twenty-fifth World Cup.

The year of the Snap.

It's like a gift, that year. A return on all your work and commitment. A reward for it, all the sweeter because you kind of don't care. I come back home for the wedding in May, then watch from afar as you fly through the year, the last year of the old ASP single event structure, the last year B.K. – Before Kelly.

The year is scheduled to finish in Hawaii. I'm too busy trying to make magazines to come to Pipeline. The night of the final,

I hear you've won. Then, next morning, I begin to hear about how. Everyone is talking about how.

It doesn't make any sense to me until I see the photos. A crazy twelve-foot plus day, windy and dramatic, lots of people charging, Derek Ho in the box seat. Then in the semifinals, an incredible split-second decision changes the day. A very big wave rears in the middle of First Reef, you're paddling up and across the face, Derek in the take-off slot.

Derek takes a quick look at the drop and thinks, *Nup, too late.* Pulls back. You're under him. The wave's already vertical; it's Pipeline, for God's sake.

You turn under him and go. Nothing between the thought and the movement. Alone in the moment of freefall to the base. Straight into a bottom turn, squared off, stall, barrel, spit. Perfect, impossible surfing.

Then I see the sequence from the day before, the thing people can't seem to explain. Another set wave, bigger this time, and you relax further into yourself, come off the bottom … and see something. Go up the face and reset the big smooth Rawson Formula One of a board and just rip it around.

It's that turn from in front of the surf club sixteen years ago. The turn you'd almost pulled on that backlit hungover Pipe afternoon in 1984. Now it's the Snap Heard Round the World, as someone later christens it, the greatest turn ever done on the greatest wave in the world.

Weirdly, I wonder why everyone's so shell-shocked. I've been waiting for you to finish that turn for years.

I've missed the show of the year. Instead, I go over for the ASP awards night. That's what surf mag editors do – they go to social occasions.

The night is a crazy binge: booze, ecstasy, heaps of coke, just ridiculous amounts, and a Honolulu hotel room watching the sun rise, everyone wondering if anybody can handle the drive back to the North Shore ... or even remember the way.

I've always thought of this shit as basically just fun, a way to bond with your mates, a way to blow up an evening. Now it begins to seem a bit weird. For the first time, I begin to think, just a tiny bit, down the lines of, *What the hell are we doing?*

Someone's going to write about this one day. I wonder if I should. I'm supposed to be a journalist, after all. I try to imagine the stories hitting the newspapers: The Truth About Pro Surfing. Surfers Use Drugs! How cheesy it will be, how sensational! How inane. Yet how surely it would fuck up careers.

The danger, the real danger, I haven't even thought of yet.

Lisa and I thought maybe we'd wait a few years before we had children. I'd proposed to her in Portugal the year before and when we got married, of course, Jenna was already there, and we didn't even know. She was born on 31 December that year, and she changed everything. It changed me because all of a sudden there was this new person in our lives, and it took me a while to realise I was a father – I was no longer that person who could give 100 per cent of myself to surfing. I struggled with that, I fought that. It was a big thing, battling the idea of being a parent, then eventually embracing it, after being so self-centred for so long.

But good stuff was happening around the Mentawai Islands and the exotic surf trips – the fantasies that were about to affect the marketplace in surfing. It'd already begun happening in the

80s, with our trip to G-Land, and surf mags had been doing adventure stories for years, but no-one had been up there, to that amazing island chain.

And then we had that crazy trip. I look back on things like that and think, *Wow! How did that happen?* We found the goldmine of Indonesia. It was literally like finding gold.

THE EDGE OF THE WORLD

The timing was insane. I was coming to the end of my competitive career and thinking about my options, when out of nowhere came the idea for this trip.

It was Boj really, and Boj's connection with Paul Graham. Boj had met Paul on a surf trip to Nusa Lembongan in 1984. Paul had a connection with someone who was doing diving work for the Indonesian oil platforms and who knew there was surf on some of the islands off Sumatra. He raised the possibility of getting a charter boat up there. We needed to get six of us to add to a couple of Paul's mates from New Zealand. No photographers, no media, no nothing. Just a boys' trip.

There was Pottz, Ross Clarke-Jones, Stuart Cadden, Michael Wyatt, Boj, Leigh and me, and we were all really excited. It felt like a reversion from the whole pro surfing scene. Wyatty's a stonemason, Boj is an electrician – I might just as well have been a panelbeater, after all. It was a really good feeling, going travelling with mates. I'd done some trips away to surf, but most of them had been to promote the brand or get shots for magazines. They always had a promotional edge to them. This one was purely about exploring with your mates.

And I'd never been on a boat. Maybe I'd gone fishing with Mike, or rode on the surf club's rubber ducky, but they were brief trips. This was an adventure. We had to hand our passports over to be held and we had to apply for permits. And we were going to these places that no-one we knew had been to, let alone surfed. We were like, Yeah! Let's go and rage in Bali, then we'll just head up into the jungle!

It was all about escaping and being blokes, and I really need that to connect in a raw sort of way.

So away we went, in late May/early June 1992. I couldn't go to Bali. Jenna was fresh on the scene. Lisa said, Well, it's cool, but I'm back here with Jenna on my own – you'd better be careful. Leigh had his son, Lucas, who was only two, so we skipped the Bali raging and met the guys in Jakarta.

Martin Daly was the bloke who had the boat. That's all I knew of him then. He met us in Jakarta where we hopped in a Mercedes, a guy with the boards in a van behind us, and went on a long drive through Jakarta. I was still a bit soggy from the plane. We got to Merak Harbour and found the other guys – they'd discovered this nightclub in the backstreets and were carrying on. We got on the boat, motored out and squared up straight into a very short sea, maybe a metre and a half, maybe a bit bigger. *Boom, boom, boom.* Martin was all gruff: This is a staunch boat, the MV *Volcanic*, she'll handle it. I said, I think I'm going to be seasick. He just said, Keep your eyes on the lights on the horizon, you'll be right. I went downstairs into a bunkroom and went straight to sleep.

I woke up at first light and we were still going through this chop. But I was all right. I'd somehow slept my way into my sea legs. Martin was still there at the wheel, banging away, and we connected on a blokey level straightaway. He liked that I was feeling good. I was just happy to be on a boat in the middle of nowhere. I went down the back and found Wyatty and Boj all green in the face, not looking good at all. But then we turned the corner around Panaitan Island and it was okay.

Martin was this really raw Australian. He told me he'd been thinking of a dive charter business, but he'd had friends who'd been surfing up here on and off for a few years. I didn't see it developing into a big operation. He was just working with the Indonesian Government on oil rigs and wanted to come out and have a bit of fun.

The first surf I saw him in was at Lances Left. It was well into the trip and about six feet. I hadn't gone out yet. I just heard this screaming, and thought, *What's going on?* I looked through the doorway of the boat and there's this guy in diving overalls and a pair of Dunlop Volleys, riding this wave and screaming. He would scream on every wave, start to finish: Yeaaahhh! Look at this! Yeaaahhh! He was like a kid in a candy store.

He told me then that he'd been a Newport boy. He grew up in a house on Wallumatta Road, three streets away from where we'd lived in Nullaburra Road, and went to Newport Public School. To me, it seemed like something must have troubled him back there, something from his past. I don't know what. But he needed to be the boss of his world, he needed to be the captain – having the boat as his own island and having full command of it, full responsibility. He liked feeling every inch of the boat; he liked the idea of having a boat he could do anything he wanted with.

I liked that idea too. I found I loved boats, and I loved the stories he would tell. I would wake up on some later trips at three or four in the morning and go up to the wheelhouse, and we'd have a cup of coffee and get to know each other.

We surfed a little right down the inside of Panaitan. We were so stoked to be in the middle of nowhere. We saw a little left further down, paddled down and surfed that. It was only small. We really felt like we were adventuring. I took off on a wave on the left and rode it down the reef, seeing how far I could go, then I got a waft of something, a scent arising from the jungle. It was like incense, and my whole body took it in – this exotic scent. I rode along, feeling inebriated, euphoric. I let go of all the other stuff that I'd been involved in, in my other world.

Martin packed it up after that surf and said, Ah, we'll just crank it on up to Enggano. It was a long passage over a day and a couple of nights. We were getting used to the boat, getting up to all that male-bonding stuff: giving each other haircuts, fishing, hanging off the transom. I'd get up, hot, in the middle of the night and go down to the back of the boat, have a piss, and wallow in the water kicking back up over the transom. The boat was going ten to twelve knots, forming a wake, and I would just slide off and bodysurf the wave behind the boat. Anything could have happened. I could have missed grabbing the transom to climb back up. Insanity, really – I could have just disappeared. Not even the captain knew I was there. But it was so warm and beautiful.

Martin didn't want to show us where we were going on the maps. He knew we were keen to know, but the word was going around that he was putting other maps out on the map table to fool us about where we were. That's not the real map! He put a smokescreen up between the real world and the one he wanted us to see. I don't know if that really happened or not. But it felt like we were on the edge of the world.

We got to Enggano and surfed this right, and it felt like a wave anyone could surf. There were guys on board who were average surfers, and it was fine for them. But the rest of us were thinking, *We wanna surf something heavier.* We were pretty hectic, running around, doing whatever we wanted, the poor Indonesian crew looking on. We were a bit nuts, feisty and basically just having a good time. Martin was stand-offish. He'd never met any well-known surfers before, and he would sit back and just watch us, watching and thinking, *Whoa, look at these guys!*

We headed around to the west and north. It was early afternoon after lunch, everyone was passed out. Martin, Pottz and I went up to the flybridge, where you could see a long way out over the water. We were going up and down these huge swells. Pottz said, Look at that, what's that in there? We saw a right, then a left. There were bombies going off everywhere, a real groundswell hitting.

Martin said, Yeah there's a sort of wave in there, and Pottz said, Let's go have a look at it! What are ya doing?

Right, Martin said, swinging the boat to the right. I'll never forget that turn he made. It was so exciting. We were going to check another new wave.

We went down inside the left and watched as it lined up and came around the corner. Like another G-Land. We were freaking out: What's this? Wake up, everyone! Have a look at this left! Everyone was clambering around, getting boards together and trying to figure out how big it was. I got out a 6'9", an average-sized board back then, and we paddled out, everyone trying to beat each other to the line-up. And … holy shit.

That was my first lesson in how a wave looks way smaller from a boat.

I went back and grabbed a 7'4" and my helmet. Pottz and Ross took that precaution too. Then we all decided to drop a tab of acid. We thought it was an opportune time.

Every set was getting bigger. There'd be six waves: *bam, bam, bam, bam, bam, bam*. Then there'd be a decent lull, so you'd paddle back in toward the reef a little bit. Then a bigger set would come and you'd get caught way inside. A lot of the guys said, This is far too big and went in; me and Ross and Pottz and Daff stayed out.

My 7'4" got too small, so I went and got a 7'10" Rawson, a beautiful board with a double concave, Bonzer-style down through the tail. A yellow swallowtail. And we ended up having the session of our lives. We'll never forget it. Ross got caught inside by this massive set! He paddled for a wave and missed it and then there was this set. It was getting *big*. Me and Pottz paddled over the set, just making it. I looked back and saw Ross in there and thought, *Oh, he's fucked*. Pottz, we're gonna have to go in there and rescue him. Ross was held down for two waves and ended up ripping his helmet off; he thought it was gonna drown him.

They all went in then, the light was fading, and I sat out there by myself. It just got too big. I think I might have caught a small one in, I can't remember. We ended up parking the boat inside the reef and having a crazy night on board.

Martin couldn't believe we were out there surfing. You could see he was blown away, thinking, *These guys will surf anything.* And we would. We were catching waves together and doing go-behinds, laughing at each other, everything.

I met the real Martin Daly at our next stop at Sanding Island. On the backside of the island there's a string of left reefs. They probably don't break often, but when there's a lot of swell it'll wrap around the island and come into this string of reefs. And each one has a little bombie outside it. A little pattern of reefs repeating themselves.

Martin pulled in behind the left and spun the boat around to check it out. We were inside both waves now. I liked that, but I was watching it, thinking, *This is kinda suss.* I was on the flybridge and saw the bombie was going to break. Martin said, No worries, and punched it straight toward the bombie. I went, Oh no, we're going to get creamed! What are we going to do? The wave started to feather, and there wasn't just one – there were a few. He hit the throttle and we came over it with a big splash. He punched it again toward the second wave and the propeller caught at just the right moment and we teetered on top and – *splash* – again we made it over. The third wave was the biggest and we actually teetered this time before *just* making it. I was barely hanging on. There was shit everywhere.

By then we were calling it the Wherethefuckarewees. The Wherethefuckarewee Islands.

We found a harbour where there were actually communications; we could find a way to call home. I wanted to check in with Lisa and let her know everything was okay, and Leigh wanted to do the same with his family. Leigh was losing it at the lack of communication off the boat. Martin was puzzled by this: What are you talking about? You want to call your *wife?* It didn't make any sense to him.

We somehow got into this harbour and slept on the deck. I woke up in the morning and there were mosquitoes everywhere. I thought for sure I would come down with malaria.

We surfed all these incredible waves. It was so clean and crisp, a beautiful swell. By the end we were all surfed out and began to get itchy feet. Ross is super restless and doesn't like to be hemmed in, so that was on display. Daff was a bit cranky. I had a sore back the first surf we had at Macaronis and had to watch everyone else. We really couldn't imagine anyone else ever being out there. We pulled up stakes a bit early and went into Bengkulu and caught early flights home. We made a pact between us that we wouldn't show anyone else our photos or anything. It was too amazing.

That was one of the classic trips. It'll never be like that again. They were some of the best times of my life. Martin used to call it a Bliss Attack: in the evening, after a long day of surfing, dropping anchor, the wind calm, those beautiful anchorages in the Mentawais. It was absurdly perfect, and I remember thinking, *We are in this tiny percentage of humanity who knows this exists*. I liked to think about that.

I didn't know what was going to happen. I was pretty naïve. I didn't know the whole world would set their eyes on it that quickly.

In California, I begin to wonder what the hell I have done. I've moved my family across the ocean at what appears to be just the wrong moment. The surf industry, hit by its first big recession, is in a flat spin; surfing is suddenly dorky next to skate, and the big advertisers are dropping up to thirty per cent of their revenue.

My bosses at the magazine don't have any more idea of what to do than anyone else, but they put on a good show, for a while. 1991 is weird, 1992 weirder. By early 1993, half the staff has been fired, including Dave Gilovich, the guy who'd hired me.

But then things start to bounce back. Kelly and his crew somehow make Surfing USA look cool again. Showcasing their talent gives the magazine an urgency, a reason to be. I forget about the possibility of being sacked, and get a corner office with an ocean view.

You tell me a little about the boys' trip, but you're so sworn to secrecy that you won't even show me the pictures. All I get to see is a short video clip of Ross's hold-down from the mega left. The counter on the videotape shows he's down for forty-eight seconds.

The secret doesn't last a whole lot longer.

Hornbaker, on the other side of the world, asks us to send him another 100 rolls of film. He says he's going on a boat trip with the captain from your sworn-to-secrecy trip. A month later the film comes back in a big bag for processing. Three days later the slides are on a light table in the mag office. That's how it works in 1993.

I look at the photos, and realise – it's another world.

Six months later, the surf company boat charters begin in earnest. The Mentawai gold rush is on. And still nobody's even published the islands' name.

DREAM RUN

The trips came hard on each other's heels then, going up and shooting stuff and coming back with a wealth of imagery. It was so valuable for the surfing market and the brands. My relationship with Hornbaker was really strong from creating images in the 80s, so we knew each other really well and could work efficiently together. Ross too.

Horny could be hot-headed at times, but I was on his good side because I was easy to work with. I wasn't getting in the way. I'd always really liked photography and making images, and it was fun. I never seemed to pose any kind of challenge to him on an ego basis. His job was to create campaigns and images, which meant a fair amount of responsibility and control. I could see the image and I could understand what he was shooting. He was at the forefront of the surfing market; he knew what to shoot and how to get people into situations to shoot them, and knew how to present it all. Quiksilver brought him on as a staff photographer, and Kelly came on too.

Our early trips were to Tahiti. It was a central place, in a weird way. Hornbaker thought he could bring in all the crews from round the world – from the US, Australia, Europe – sit 'em there for six weeks and shoot the whole range out off Moorea. That was particularly challenging. Tahiti's not always nice; it gets a lot of weather. It rained for about three weeks straight, and you can imagine the morale.

Plus the place we were staying gets these weird gnats that chew your legs up – tiny ones you can hardly see that live in the chicken poo, of which there's plenty. We ended up with these big fricken craters in our legs. It was horrendous.

We did a couple of those shoots, one at Teahupo'o, which was pretty amazing because there was nobody there. Like – why would anyone go there? It's at the end of the road from Papeete, two hours' drive away. You can't even *see* it, let alone realise the kind of wave it can turn into.

I remember Mickey Neilsen freaking out about how we had to surf this End of the Road wave: We're gonna take you there, you've gotta come along. It was 1992, the same year as the MV *Volcanic* trip. I was with Titus Kinimaka, Ross, Doug Silva and Horny, and Mickey came to pick us up from Faa'a Airport with this tinnie on the back of his car.

Mickey said, Right, we're going to the End of the Road, and Horny, you're not coming. He didn't want to have to deal with a photographer out there. He was like, This is the End of the Road and nobody's gonna find it, so you can piss off. It was really touchy for Horny because he hadn't been allowed to go on that first Indo trip either. He had that pursed face; his mouth just winces right up and everything pulls together.

That introduction to Teahupo'o was dramatic. It took us ages to get down there. Mickey decided not to take the tinnie out, so we had to paddle out from off the point. The first wave came out of nowhere, this amazing barrel – it didn't even look like a wave. The swell was real south and I stood in this barrel as it got bigger and faster, and I came flying out.

Those trips were all cool; it was a part of the 90s theme of finding new places to shoot and market the brand, get it out there, and Hornbaker did a really good job. He produced vast amounts of material; I don't know what they're going to do with it at Quiksilver or even if they know what they've got. One day someone really creative will come across it, take a look and say, Oh, there we are!

I was compulsive with photography myself. Compulsively looking through the frame. Whenever I had the opportunity, I was shooting photos or stashing film, trying to stockpile it because I knew I was going to run out. I'd buy heaps of film before a trip, and it was never enough. I'd end up hassling Hornbaker or whoever else had come along. I'd take cameras on every trip. I'd even bring a Super 8 camera on board and shoot bits of film. But mostly it was stills.

Ross would say, What the hell are you doing? You're insane! What are you taking all that shit for? I got some good photos of him. He was a good subject along the way, because of his head.

It was a dream life really, a dream run.

I was still competing. Even though I'd just lost my confidence in competition. In 1988 I'd already let go of half of it, and now came the time to come to terms with the fact that I was no longer fully on the job. Again, it was subconscious: the conscious part of me was out there trying to put on a show, but the spark, the desire … I wasn't fully there. It wasn't a pretty time. Probably my last hurrah was winning the 1992 Margaret River event. That was all I had left in me.

Lisa and I tried to do the tour with Jenna, taking her around the world. It was really challenging, but we did it for almost two years.

Then, in early 1993, Lisa fell pregnant with Mimi. It became hard for her to travel while pregnant. And it was hard for me to compete, because I couldn't be so self-centred anymore. It couldn't be just all about me. And that challenged a lot of ideas about who I was. I didn't understand how to channel my energies like that, into separate things; they'd always bleed into each other. I'd always feel like something was in the way.

I was still reliant on my surfing for my confidence. Still relied on that. Still very linked, probably in a very unhealthy way, to my performance in the ocean; how I was surfing was how I was feeling. It was all about maintaining those skills, and so I started training with Rob Rowland Smith, getting stronger, building myself physically to help me feel better and more in control.

We took the girls to Hawaii, but it was much better for Lisa to be at home by then, with two kids. It took me the whole year, till the end of 1993, before I was able to let go of the tour and come back home.

So that structure was out of my life and it left a big hole.

That was the first time I began struggling with my demons. That's what Dad used to call it, later on. He'd say, Have you got a handle on your demons, Tom? And I'd put up the charade and say, Oh yeah, I'm sweet. Whether I was sweet or not.

This is what was happening: the disease, the addiction, was starting to get a grip on me.

I didn't like the way I was feeling a lot of the time. I didn't like the way I responded to the world. I wanted to respond differently, in a really 'up' way, the way I thought my family wanted me to respond, and that need became more acute, because I was less secure − less structure, less money, more responsibility with the kids. It was very confusing, I didn't know quite who I was. I hadn't really planned on being a father so quickly, and I wasn't anywhere near emotionally equipped to deal with it. All of a sudden I was trying to work out how to fit together our new life, and we were still partying. We were still kids, Lisa and I, when I look back on it, just trying to make it up as we went along, and all these responsibilities, the daily routine around children, the hecticness filling our house.

My basic reaction was fear. I'd want to run away, get out and not deal with it, and surfing was great for that. If I could have seen it then, I could have used surfing as a great balance for all of the stress. Instead, I used it as an escape − get the hell out, go training, go surfing, go on a trip, lemme out of here. And that filled me with conflict, because I wanted to be a good dad, a good husband, but at some level I was still trying to run.

So my idea of a good time was to get a gram or two of cocaine and go on a binge, snort it up. Lisa would get the whole of Tuesday to do a ceramic course, the girls would be taken care of by their grandma and I'd have the day to myself. I didn't have any big responsibilities. I didn't have any mission, any direction, other than the wetsuit business, which was moving along. And that was my day.

I was in contact with a guy who had a really good supply at the time, and I'd be jittery over that fact alone. I'd say, Line me up some for next Tuesday, okay?

It was really well defined, the urge, but that day was always a rough ride. I'd think I could get through it all and come back down so I was ready for Lisa to come home and pick up the girls around 3 or 4 pm. But of course that didn't really work. She'd pick up on what was going on and be really angry. It'd turn into a roller-coaster ride.

It soon turned into a fortnightly pattern of behaviour. To me it was completely baffling. Quite often I would think, *Why am I doing this? It just doesn't make any sense.* But the pull, the drag toward it, was so strong. Looking back at it now, it's classic really – the thing that was inside me all the time had been built up over years. And with all the pressures of change taking place, all the stresses, I just wanted to run.

And I'd get relief from it for about an hour. Maybe. *Maybe.* Snort up a couple of lines and feel good and then think, *Oh no, now I've gotta do all the rest of this.*

I was always by myself. No-one else had a Tuesday off. No-one had time to come and do that sort of thing. No-one thought about it. I felt really alone in that space. I really felt that loneliness and isolation, and that shame, that really deep-rooted shame that comes with it, to have to face Lisa, the possibility of having to face others.

But the addict was starting to hone my personality. It started bringing in all the personality traits and behaviours that come along with being a finely tuned cocaine addict – ways of manipulating situations, and being secretive, and lying about things, and covering up, so the addict could survive. I began to find ways to get away with it, fix it all up, whenever the situation occurred. I wasn't that good at it yet, though. I didn't have any control over it.

I did think at some level I was bulletproof. I'd pull right up and wouldn't use anything for a few months. I'd get really fit and strong and focused on what I was doing. I'd be in the zone. I was being a father, to some degree, because I was still a pro surfer and self-centred in many ways, but I was doing the best I could, and I wouldn't use until … something would happen. A number would pop up on my phone. Or a big party or function would come up, and that would trigger the response.

The only way to come off it sometimes was to drink alcohol, just to get that comfort zone back, because it was so uncomfortable. I remember one time Lisa was very worried, she didn't know where I was and realised something was going on. It made her panic, of course. It would get her very angry. And she must have known I was under the house. We had a little storage space down there, where I'd hole myself up, dose myself with alcohol, to get the stuff out of me. I'd get smashed, but normally I'd be somewhat coherent. This time I was more smashed than normal. Rob and Bruce came around and dragged me out. That shook me up a lot.

September, 1994: We're in different worlds. You're on these incredible exotic surf trips and I'm working my arse off. I'm running down to Lower Trestles in the dark, keeping my surfing alive on a drip feed of swells from the same storms that light up Tahiti and the Mentawais. The swells arrive in California perfectly shaped and almost completely exhausted from the trip, and collapse on the Lowers cobblestones with crinkly, watery sighs of relief. I ride as many as I can and get home in time to take Maddie to school.

At the magazine I rip through Hornbaker's submissions, pile them on to covers and poster spreads: you, Kelly, Ross, Hoyo, Pottz, Braden Dias, Kelly again and again. Like postcards from this other world – this new bubble you and Captain Daly inhabit. The surf zone with no name. The photos of you and the Captain, grinning like pirates, you with one eyebrow raised, cheeky quizzical Gobbo on the edge of the world.

Then people start telling me about the shit you're getting yourself into. Bingeing alone on the gack, disappearing for days, crashing into terrible post-binge depressions. Hiding under the house and refusing to come out till Rob Rowland Smith and Bruce Raymond respond to Lisa's terrified calls and spend an hour talking you down. Or up.

I carry this information around with me for a day or so, not liking how it makes me feel. For all the weirdness of California, this prosperous shore has given me an unexpected freedom: I've somehow escaped being your brother. You're still a legend, of course, the echo of the Snap Heard Round the World still shaking its way through the core surf culture. But when I walk into work or paddle out at Lower Trestles or talk to one of the San Clemente boys on summer morning surf checks, your name doesn't precede mine in the conversation.

It's a strange little liberation, this non-brother-hood, a subconscious lightening of the days, and while your news causes me an instant jolt of concern and fear and love – *he's in the shit and I'm not there* – another smaller part of me feels itself slide half-resentfully back into the old groove.

And along with that an even smaller, darker thought: *Get yourself out of this one.*

On the phone, I can hear your shame and remorse. You tell me how you're seeing that Hampshire guy, Dr Robert Hampshire, psychiatrist to the stars. The special guy. Surely he can help. We agree to check in every week, and hang up, me feeling a vanishing ripple of guilt.

Months pass. You're due to visit California for a trade show. I look forward to seeing you, find out how things are with Dr Wizard Hampshire, but you're evasive and uncertain about when you'll be available. The odd tone of voice, distant, always slightly hurried, as if you want to end the conversation before it begins. There's not a thing about that voice I like.

Then I hear the name of the person squiring you around SoCal – a good-time guy on the Quiksilver payroll, renowned for seeing to the illicit needs of surf stars and their entourages. Not someone who deserves a pseudonym, but here's one for him anyway: Jamie.

I get the guy's phone number from one of the ad sales crew at the mag, and sit in my office for five minutes looking at it, feeling quite calm. Then I dial. It rings three times and is answered.

'Is this Jamie? This is Nick Carroll – you know, Tom's brother.'

'Yeah!'

'So Jamie, tell me, are you right-handed or left-handed?'

'Right ...'

'Okay, look. If I hear you've supplied my brother with any cocaine, I'm gonna come up there and break your right arm.'

'What?' says the voice at the other end.

'And after that, I'm gonna call Bob McKnight, and I'm gonna tell him why your arm's broken.'

Nothing. Silence.

'Is that clear?'

'Yeah.'

'Good.'

I hang up, still feeling entirely calm, even slightly amused: I wonder how that'll go.

That weekend, you come by San Clemente and spend an afternoon playing with your super-excited niece and nephew. You're completely normal, not jittery or distant at all. A normal adult.

Relieved, I don't tell you about the phone call. It's not for at least a decade that I discover I don't have to, because Jamie wasn't the one who picked up the phone that day. I'd delivered that threat with all its hard certainty, its lifetime's weight of care, to my own brother.

In my mind I make up reasons, excuses. It's understandable, after all. No world champion steps off that stage without some sort of pain or confusion. The binges, every few weeks, seem curiously in line with the rhythms of the world tour. The way it used to work: There'd be a contest, a win or a good placing, or maybe just the relief of the pressure coming off, then a party – a select few and a little pile of marching powder, whatever. Then back to training, boom.

He's just hanging onto it, I think. Like a recording stuck in a groove. Cocaine, the hero drug, the one you take because you're The Shit and you deserve it. This is just a short struggle. He's not on tour anymore. He'll pop out of the groove and he'll be fine.

I really wanted to address the addiction, so I started to see James Pitt; he's a counsellor who used to run Odyssey House.

I'd go and visit once a week, and he would try to give me some feedback. It wasn't a waste of time because I think any work is beneficial on some level. But it didn't stop me using, not completely. I was also using the sessions as a smokescreen, making it look like I was doing something about it, while I was still using. It's the cunning nature of the disease, the baffling nature of our trickery. One minute I'm in counselling, then the next day I'm using ... something, anything.

I needed a group to work with, a group who was fully in on recovery and understood the nature of what I was going through. But because I was special, I was Tom Carroll, the world around me told me I needed someone special to look after me. That's why I went to Dr Hampshire. But only for three visits. I remember breaking down with him, saying, I've got to really get on top of this. I've gotta come back to myself. I really don't want to do this stuff anymore, I really truly don't.

At that point, had I been introduced to an abstinence program, I may have bit down on it. Because there are windows of opportunity for recovery, and a window was open. But he only gave me the perfect excuse to go back and use – he was as buggered as anyone, on pethidine. Poor guy! He must have been toasted. Opiates look horrible to come off, waking your nervous system back up.

It never came close to being made public. No journalist ever rang up. There was never a sense that I was about to be revealed as Tom Carroll, Secret Drug Addict. Somehow I was able to hold up this facade. There was probably some confusion at home for the girls, to some degree, but I really kept as much of the stuff away from them as I could.

But I did a lot of damage to my relationship with Lisa;

I confused the hell out of her at a time when it would have seemed to others like the relationship was pretty good. A lot of damage was done, and a lot of repairing, or trying to repair things. We did get married under those circumstances, we did have children under those circumstances, and we tried to do the best we could with my addictive behaviour going on – and it was an absolute nightmare for Lisa a lot of the time.

And the whole time I was trying to hold up another picture to the world. The person who was hiding under the house, who had to be dragged out, was also the upstanding sporting hero Tom Carroll – the professional surfer, business guy and father, whom a lot of people were looking up to.

But that was part of the thrill of using. Secrecy. Taking the risk. It was a big part of the ritual, that feeling that I could get away with something others didn't know about. It's a little private world that's another level of the disease; it wants to isolate you. It feels good at first – it really does – until it turns back in on you. My experience was that the whole excitement of getting the stuff and simply *having* it was better than actually putting it in me.

I just couldn't hold it up, really. But I did hold it up. It's amazing what we do to ourselves to try and keep up that front, but there's no emotional growth in it. The whole time you become stunted. Emotionally I couldn't get anywhere. I still find it really hard today to tell where I'm growing, and whether I'm really supposed to turn into an emotional mess in order to grow, or just hang on to being stable.

But back then there was no such thing as falling apart – didn't even enter the picture. The result is that eventually you do. You have to.

THE RUBBER WARS

I took a reduction in salary when I stepped off tour, right at the time when we were having our daughters and renovating the house on the hill – it was a real challenge trying to figure out how to do it all.

The wetsuit business looked like it might fill some gaps. I was a non-executive director, so I didn't take any day-to-day part in the operations. It was still pretty exciting, getting involved with John the Butcher. It was back in the 90s, and we were all on the way up. He grabbed the bull by the horns and was very aggressive about the business, charging forward and seeing opportunities, and he doesn't like to back away from opportunities.

John, the way he is, you can see his heart on his sleeve, so you can get past his full-on behaviour – you know he's got a big heart. He got busy lining everything up so the margins would be right and money would be injected back into the business as soon as we started selling. We had to guarantee personal lines of credit with the bank, which felt like a pretty heavy commitment until the business got rolling.

At first we were making wetsuits in Fiji, and they were falling apart. We had quality issues and I wasn't all that happy with the first designs. I was concerned, but I didn't know quite how to voice those concerns.

Then John found another source of manufacturing, a company called Riot Wetsuits in Wollongong. They were a pricepoint wetsuit and did okay in their local area. John went down and saw the owner, Michael Bates, and started doing a deal around Australian production for the next year. We had an order to fill pretty quickly and Bates did a good job at first; the quality was better. But then things got weird.

What then happened taught me a lot about transactions and expectations. I think Bates saw the Quiksilver gold. He thought he was going to be a millionaire. And that was through an expectation that wasn't communicated, that wasn't understood on both sides.

It was a handshake deal at first, and we thought we could work the backside of that initial agreement to get the details in place. When we went in for the next load of production, Michael Bates had changed his tack. He wanted to add all these things to the price of production, things we hadn't agreed to. John's response wasn't conciliatory. Bates was withholding a bunch of stuff from us that we'd paid for – neoprene, suits that'd been made – so John decided to set up our own factory. He went down, opened up the Riot factory, got the rubber, got the suits and set up a factory down the road with a number of Bates's employees.

It sent Bates into a full spin. He didn't know he was messing with Butcher, but Butcher didn't know he was messing with Bates.

One afternoon I was cleaning my Alfa in the driveway when this guy pulled up and walked over the hill, with a bigger guy behind him. I thought, *Hang on, who's that in the background, is that Michael Bates?* The guy in front was a bailiff and he served this claim on me. It was the size of a telephone book. I just said, okay, whatever; I didn't know what it was. What the hell? I rang up John, who was going off his head.

The original claim was for around six million dollars. At that point I knew we were in a bit of trouble. It put some very strange thoughts through my head. I really felt that I could lose everything.

It took five years to work through the courts. The company just survived. It was able to tick over through the whole thing; John just kept running things. He put accessories into the line – backpacks and other stuff Quiksilver was yet to make. We also produced wetsuits and accessories in Europe with Pierre Agnes, and manufacturing was going well out of Wollongong. Eventually we ended up with a factory in Chiang Mai, Thailand, and the wetsuits were getting better. But wetsuits are very hard to make, and we had quality problems.

There was really quite astounding behaviour in the marketplace by various companies. They didn't like the idea of Quiksilver making wetsuits, so they tried a lot of stuff out there to slow us down. Derek Hynd was even in there, working on behalf of Rip Curl. Some of the tricks going on by people trying to score market share got me more tuned in to surf shops and how the good ones work. We travelled around the country selling the suits. I was never much of a salesman – I never felt qualified – but I would go along as part of the product. Even that got challenging. We were putting the Quiksilver branding on this product that kept having quality issues, and I felt like I was part of the problem; I didn't like that. It was frustrating and disheartening, and I felt really powerless at times.

By 1997 the lawsuit was coming to a head and it was a very intense time. We got the best lawyers involved. We tried mediation with Bates through Sir Laurence Street. He said, No, I want my day in court. Sir Laurence raised his eyebrows at that and said, You've got a real beauty on your hands here.

I kept wondering how this guy got us into this situation. How was he going to hold up in court?

Eventually it went to trial for eight weeks. I attended the court, but I didn't have to give evidence. John and Bruce Raymond were trying to make sure I didn't, because they didn't know what I might say on the stand. I definitely didn't feel confident enough. Being involved with legal teams, preparing for the court case, watching the company spending thousands a day on a QC – I was in shock, but also fascinated by how orderly and sophisticated it was. Things are so subtle in a court; it was so strange sitting in the courtroom after being in the real world, where things are aggressive and abrupt and the language is raw. In court it's all these subtle gestures. The judges and lawyers move in their own world, and they speak to each other in their own language. I was taken by that.

Michael Bates represented himself in the first half of the trial. He received assistance from the judge on how to conduct cross-examinations and so forth. Then halfway through, when it came time for him to be cross-examined, he showed up in court with a QC, saying, I have representation now. His QC tried to have the case shifted sideways and tried under another law. The judge didn't give him the same amount of latitude after that.

He lost all his millions of dollars in claims except one. The court held that we shouldn't have terminated our contract without notice and ordered us to cover his loss of profit to the tune of $6200. In turn, all our costs were awarded against him – over a million dollars. Bates immediately declared bankruptcy and was gone, *pfft*.

I was shell-shocked after that. It was my example of how the court system worked: we were guilty until we proved ourselves innocent by defending these massive claims against us. I thought I was going to lose my house, everything. All of a sudden everything I'd done in my career was going to be gone.

Not much of this makes it across the Pacific. But it kinda doesn't matter. Madeleine's turned seven, Jack three, and we've come to a turning point. It's either stay in California for twenty years, or come home. I can't stand hearing about the boat trips, and there are grandparents involved, so we choose the latter.

You pick us up at the airport and chauffeur us home, blinking in the flat hot light of a Sydney summer.

Over the next three weeks I hear more and more of the story, how the rubber wars are panning out.

And all I can think of, all I still think of today, are the ironies – how you'd got yourself wrapped up in business with John, pale-eyed John who'd been selling our grandmother sausages when you were twelve years old and telling Mrs White white lies about our surfing. And there's Derek, enigmatic leader of our youthful surfing gang, the person who once could have shown us how to live a surfing life, out there trying to white-ant your business.

But you're past all that, it seems. Past those dark mid-90s days. You're running training sessions with Rob Rowland Smith for some of the young up-and-comers on the Quiksilver surf team. 'Want to come up to Muscle Beach?' you say.

Muscle Beach turns out to be RRS's backyard, where he's set up a sandpit full of weights, chin-up bars and who knows what other terrifying fitness machinery. I sweat along with the supergrommets, watch and listen as you hound them: hearty, blokey Tom and Rob, kings of the kids, with your one-hand pull-ups and your Friday afternoon award ceremonies – the Hero Award for tough guy of the week, the Cyril Award for the softest.

The kids sneak looks at you in awe, and I feel my old fears evaporate.

One Sunday morning I leave Maddie with the Newport Nipper under-eights and head down the sand for a swim, and something odd catches my eye. A dad and a couple of kids, playing with what looks like some sort of tiny toy surfboard with a tiny man on top.

They laugh and toss the little man into a shorebreak wave, and I suddenly realise – it's a goofyfoot wearing red boardshorts. With a mohawk. Just as you'd appeared on the cover of my last issue of *Surfing* magazine.

'Isn't he your brother?' one of the kids yells.

Turns out Bob Hoskin, a friend of Alan Green's, had gone to Greeny with the brilliant idea of a surfing toy for the masses. Greeny had pointed Bob at you. And the rest, hilariously enough, is history.

Twenty years since the Pro Junior and now there's a Tommy Doll. Hunter and Haley are pretty much in tears.

It's insane how things work out. Not long after the case with Bates was settled, Quiksilver began negotiating to buy back the licences – to bring all these different businesses under one roof. It was a tricky time because John had pretty much had enough of the bullshit. He just wanted to do his job and build the business, and he'd got caught up in the expanding Quiksilver empire. There were head honchos all around the world trying to get things done, and he was having to go through all of them separately whenever he wanted to do a new product line. It was very stressful for him; I could see his health going downhill – probably mine too. I was caught in the crossfire between John and Quiksilver, and the more money that got involved, the wilder the negotiations became.

I was reminded that John's always had a really big heart. He's passionate, direct and at times really abrasive, but then again anyone who's successful in business has to be abrasive at times, and challenge the status quo. John took that to extremes at times. But I've got a lot of respect for him. He tried to help a lot during the dealings that went on between ourselves and Quiksilver. People just weren't talking – there were too many emotions involved. Quiksilver was willing to do a good deal, but it was just how to get us all over the line and agree on prices and values. When there's a partnership involved, the potential is really high for confrontation and holding on. Everyone's got a different expectation, and if they're not communicated the potential is so much greater for conflict. And the lawyers are just hanging on the sidelines – they're very patient and often five stages ahead of everyone else, talking among themselves about what's going to happen.

It was the most intense period I've had in business. I was really sad, really angry, really disillusioned with human behaviour at times. I became really fearful: Is this how business is done? Is this how people have to act? I was really shown how *not* to behave.

But I also saw people with a lot of courage. John and Bruce both showed conviction by staying with the deal when they could have walked out at times. And there was goodwill on Quiksilver's side. They were caught in a situation where they wanted their products to be better and of a higher quality, and they knew they had to get the wetsuits produced some other way. We'd had a lot of quality issues and it was a struggle making a high-end suit the way we were doing it. We were Quiksilver, we were supposed to be leading the market, but we weren't following through and that caused me a lot of esteem issues. I felt caught in between, especially since I was dealing with team guys who were wearing product that was falling apart. I was trying to give feedback but felt like I wasn't being heard, and I didn't have the tools to deal with that. I felt like I'd sink into myself in business dealings, because I lacked the acumen to deal with the detail of the business. I think I had an overall feel for it, but not a detailed feel.

I watch sharp surf industry guys I know, like Chris Athos and Pierre Agnes, who have this great overall picture of where their businesses are going, but they're also into the detail, and I realised I couldn't do it on such a grand scale. I'd have to go enrol in some sort of schooling. Then again, I had no faith in my ability to stay in a classroom. I can actually sit and listen now, I guess, which is a big change.

Eventually, the first part of the sale was finalised in 1999. I look back and think we could have hung on to the business longer and maybe made some more money. But I was really fortunate, although I'd engendered a sort of looking-after-Tom thing with John, and it actually bugged me. At one point during the deal he thought it was all going to fall apart, and he wanted to get me out clean and easy. But it would have meant I'd have ended up with a ten per cent share, not the full third. The proposition was put to me: take this and you're out of this whole mess.

I like to think that John was genuinely looking after his little mate, but I looked at it and thought, *No, I'm sticking this out.* I could have headed for shelter and handed over my share for much less than it was worth.

It was such a relief to get through those years, to have a lot of money, to feel like I'd made it. I'd won Lisa back by then, and we were living it up, having a good time. Everything seemed rosy.

Christmas morning, 1999. We look at each other across a room full of torn gift-wrapping and kids. Madeleine Rose, Jenna Josephine, Amelia Joy, Jack Harvey, all in a room together with toys, while we eat fruit salad and gaze, amused and bemused, at the mess.

Out the window, the Peak is visible – a little nor'-east swell, not quite breaking. Our eyes stray there every now and then.

Frank Hyde was wrong. Pro surfing isn't bigger than Rugby

League. Instead, here in Australia at least, it's in a strange sort of a doldrums. Graham Cassidy has been ousted – that's what they call it in the newspapers, isn't that right, 'ousted'? – from the ASP's top job, and the mainstream Aussie media's lost interest in a sport dominated by a young American. Pro surfing is a sport that happens mostly somewhere else, at remote reefbreaks, and internet start-up companies from the US are beginning to jockey for the rights. Australian surfing culture is already halfway through its slow shift, away from the hard magical dangerous days of our youth toward the gentler days to come, days of midlife sea changes, government-funded coaching programs, recreation, nostalgia.

Friends are scattered. Spyder's in England making babies and millions with Victoria. Twemlow's moved north to Queensland, along with Wyatty, working as a stonemason. Hunter's in town snaring short acting jobs and never quite hitting it. Haley's in Melbourne driving trucks for film companies. Ross is in Hawaii, tuning his skills in the freshly terrifying tow-surfing arena. Dougall's in Queensland being general manager of Billabong. Newling's a sought-after fashion and catalogue photographer and is spending half the year in San Francisco. Martin Daly's got three charter boats running Mentawais trips, and a lot of competition for customers.

The old rivals are scattered too. Steve Wilson's living in Ulladulla. Cheyne is on the Gold Coast running a surf school, happy as a lark. BL's quit the tour and started a surfer management agency.

Joe Engel, the other side of your coin, didn't have your good fortune; after his great win at Bells he struggled with his pro career, went to Bali, took too much acid and slowly slid off the rails into mental illness, while the freshly booming surf industry just steamed right past.

Nobody sees Joe any more. They say he's living up in the Northern Territory, in Katherine, on a disability pension. But then one day I'm on a Gold Coast work trip and his old friend Vince Lawder gives me a call. 'Joe's down,' he says.

I go to meet him with his parents at a Mexican restaurant, the one we all used to go to during the Stubbies contests. He's huge, bald, with the face of somebody who's seen too much.

We have a couple of beers. 'How's Tom?' he asks.

I give him the rundown: nice house, married, two children, surfing a lot, plenty of money, Quiksilver, etc.

Joe nods and says, 'Well, he's got what he wanted.'

I seem to detect an edge, a note of sarcasm or bleakness ... or is it just a remnant of the weird knowledge you once possessed of each other?

Joe repeats it: He's got what he wanted.

Part four

The Wave Breaks

'These days, Carroll is semiretired from the whole professional surfing scene ... Married with two young children, he claims to be surfing more or less as well as ever, with one rider. "Having kids, it's a bit different when you're out on the big stuff. I've just been in Hawaii for three weeks ... and found I was waiting and thinking a bit before I was doing things that I would have done before without hesitation.

"I guess it's something about not jumping straight into risky situations like I used to."

One more thing, Tom. If footballers "hang up their boots", and cricketers "pull up stumps", what do surfers do when they've finally had enough?

"They don't do anything," Carroll says flatly, "because you simply don't retire from surfing. You just keep going and going and going." '

–Peter FitzSimons, *The Sydney Morning Herald*, 1998

Lisa and I were having a bit of a holiday away from the kids. We decided to stay in this nice house down at Teahupo'o for a few days and then go over to Huahine. We arrived there one early summer evening – it was in November, I think. I noticed the wind was different, a different feel, weird and warm. Not a normal trade breeze. We were staying that night in Papeete then getting a car to go down to this little house out along the point near the stream at Teahupo'o. Really quiet.

The Tahitians were throwing ropes over their roofs, tying down their houses. I thought, *They know something we don't.*

The wind was starting to blow uncomfortably strong. We had the kind of jet lag you get when going to Tahiti, where you sleep during the day; we arrived at Teahupo'o in the morning, had a sleep, woke up, and the wind was howling. Gusts were coming down from the north, through the mountains. The swell had started to rise from a direct west angle, and Teahupo'o was unrideable.

The Tahitians were still tying down their houses, stringing ropes from palm tree to palm tree, or wrapping them around big rocks.

The wind wasn't just offshore, it was swirling as it came down onto the coast. It was creating waterspouts in the lagoon, lifting large quantities of water into the air and bringing it over the land, where it'd dissipate and fall, drenching people's gardens and houses. You couldn't go outside because of it. The clouds came in, lower and darker.

That was around midday. I went back to sleep, then Lisa woke me again approaching dark. The wind's stopped, she said. It was super quiet. I went out to have a look and Teahupo'o was twenty-five foot rights, going around the corner the other way. It looked like extended Backdoor, absurd waves. I was stunned. I walked right out to the point.

Then the eye passed and the wind swapped, coming back in at us. The storm moved through fairly quickly and it was beautiful weather again a couple of days later. But people were lucky they'd tied their houses down.

THE NOUGHTIES

The pro surfing project, the great mission of our grommethoods, the wave we've ridden for decades, has paid off, but not in a way we'd ever expected. Instead of elevating surfing to the sporting pantheon along with tennis, golf and professional football, it's given the surf companies the tool they've needed to help pry open new markets, new revenues, new layers of cool.

It's a time of Aspiration, for the surf industry as it is for everyone else in these booming consumer economies where surfing's made its home. Europe's big. So's the US. Quiksilver has a distributor in Turkey and is considering a surf shop in Shanghai. Billabong takes the step into public ownership. The surf photos and splashy articles migrate from the sports pages to the business sections, where they throw around figures. $10 billion? $11 billion? Can surfing really be worth that much money?

Well, it is for now.

The dot-com boom means even journalists get paid ... though that lasts about as long as a tour year.

The surf companies spend their exploding marketing budgets. They buy up the big events and build global promotions around the top surfers.

You play your part. It's an easy part and you play it well, your basic good nature shining through. Tom Carroll, Australian sporting legend. Everyone's mate. Patron of the Disabled Surfers Association. Torchbearer to the 2000 Sydney Olympics. Name engraved on one of the world champion plates inlaid into the paving stones at the new Duke Kahanamoku memorial park at Harbord Diggers Club.

I was contacted by the Olympic Committee to do the torch relay, and that was extraordinary. I'd got to know a guy called Justin McMillan. He was a local Kiama hero, a surf lifesaving champion and was starting up his career as an advertising film guy, a creative director. I had a deal with Volvo at the time and he said, Come down and do this show reel with me.

He organised it so that he would run his leg of the relay and pass me the flame and I would run the last leg of the day. It was about a 400-metre jog. I would take the flame from him and run out to the point at Kiama to light the cauldron, which would then burn all night. All the girls – Lisa, Jenna and Mimi – were down there with me, staying in a house up at Jamberoo. Justin filmed his piece with the Volvo and later pitched it as an ad.

We got our special torch relay outfits and went into security for our briefing. We were taking the footpath around the rim

Lighthearted Gobbo,
tight boardshort days,
Narrabeen, 1977.
[Photo: Aitionn]

Far left: Vic and little Tom, Queensland trip, early 1960s.

Above left: Carroll kids: Nick, Tom and Jo, Bungan backyard.

Left: 'I was the outside chance of getting it.' Tom barred by siblings from the surfoplane.

Above: Pro Junior '77 finals (l/r): TC, Dougall Walker, Jody Perry, Cheyne Horan, Joe Engel and Thornton Fallander.

Right: *Surfing World*'s 'Magic School' cover shot, 1979. (Photo: Aitionn)

Below: First wave at Pipeline, 1978, Shaun Tomson on the shoulder. (Photo: Buddy McCray)

Carroll brothers, Sunset Beach, 1982. (Photo: Peter Simons)

Louis Ferreira, TC and Joe Engel, pinnies on
the Gold Coast, 1979. (Photo: Aitionn)

Post-op resting on the
Chookwagen, 1981.

Barrelled in an early winter swell, Narrabeen, 1983. (Photo: Aitionn)

Nick, Tom and Mike, pissed after another Plus win, 1985. (Photo: Aitionn)

Top: Practice makes perfect. The Snap: (left) Newport '79; (right) Pipeline '91. (Photos: Aitionn and Joli)

Above: Backside version at Winkipop, Victoria, 1992. (Photo: Aitionn)

Right: Big surf is cause for amusement, Waimea Bay, 2011. (Photo: Joli)

Spiritually at home, Quiksilver in Memory of Eddie Aikau ceremony, 2012. (Photo: Joli)

of the bay, along the rocks, and I waited with another young person from the area who was a noted community achiever and would be coming for a run with me as well.

Justin ran up and lit my torch and we did this funny handshake thing, and off we went.

We had two big motorbikes with policemen escorting us, one in front and one behind, and a security crew around us, but there was a relaxed feeling about the scene. It was a beautiful evening, a cloudless sky, the sun had already gone down and there was no wind. People had lit candles all the way around the bay to the cauldron.

It's intoxicating, feeling like you are part of something that big – I couldn't imagine anything bad happening. Everything was up. So I took off jogging in my little white Olympic outfit.

About 50 metres into the run, there was a sandstone wall to my left, about a metre high, where people were sitting and standing, looking on. I noticed out of the corner of my eye this guy jump over the candles and the rim of the sandstone wall, and then he just came and grabbed the top part of the torch. The impact forced me to fall to my right, over the edge of the footpath and onto one knee on the grass. It was a semi-tackle, but all he was going for was the torch; he wanted it so bad. He had the torch down on the ground, both hands on it.

But he wasn't getting it! I felt this moment – I didn't think about it, I just felt it – and I ripped the torch out of his hands, got back up and kept running, like nothing ever happened. I turned around out of curiosity and had a quick glance, and the guy was doing the bolt. He hit the rocks lining the little cliff overlooking the sea and started stumbling, and then he was hit from the side by these two SWAT-looking guys in black overalls. They face-planted him into the rocks; it was horrible. I thought, *Oh my God, something bad just happened!*

I got to the cauldron and I was sweet. The images went round the world. People were calling me from around the world about the hoo-ha. Martin Daly was on the toilet in Jakarta and saw it replayed on TV, reflected in the bathroom mirror, and was thinking, *What's going on here?* He called me immediately in hysterics.

This was after the sale of the wetsuit business. I have some good and bad memories of the period, because it was a very stressful time. At the end of the deal-making there was a big crescendo and I could have taken a lot less money if I hadn't stuck around and held my ground. But I stuck it out.

I was so frightened when I got the money from the sale. It was almost $2 million and I was really frightened about what might happen. I didn't know how to sit still with it. I knew there was a great deal of responsibility handed to me along with that money. At some level I don't think I really deserved it. At some level I didn't see my surfing, or 'Tom Carroll', as something that was a big money-earner. So even though I had all these means, all these things happening around me, I'd be sitting there thinking, *Holy crap.*

Thank God I didn't just go completely crazy, utterly bananas, go off on a whirlwind binge. The girls could have lost their father. Thank God I had some sort of boundary. If I'd thought it was my right to go and party with the money, it would have unleashed some other level of what was lying within.

When I look back it was a real gift Because people don't need to give you money. They can just take things away from you. And people don't always perceive value – the ones in power, that is. They can perceive your value as nothing. They can write you off. It happens all the time in business. It's happening right now. People are being perceived as nothing, people who've put years into some company, and there's a change of hands at the top, and they're nothing. Literally overnight. I was really, really lucky.

I wanted to keep my money in the bank. Dad was saying, Yeah, just keep it for a bit, and I really listened to what he was saying. These people were coming out of nowhere with crazy investment ideas, how I could invest my money and double it in short periods. The influences around me were telling me, You gotta do this, you gotta do that! You're gonna lose out if you don't grab this, grab that! I could see that if you got a certain amount of money, you could never go backwards – unless you were completely stupid. If you got six or seven or maybe ten million dollars, it'd just start multiplying on top of itself. Even if you got six or seven per cent on that money, happy days. The money keeps moving, you keep investing, it builds on top of itself. I was looking at that sum and thinking, *We could take this, triple that* … It started doing all kinds of weird things to my head.

But I did feel it would be right to have a really nice family home to bring the family up in.

Spyder put us onto Mark Cashman, an architect, who came up with the idea for reworking the house. It was either a rebuild or a renovation, and we hadn't really come to grips with the finances. I wasn't quite sure I wanted to do it – I'd looked at the plans and how much it was going to cost, and thought there were probably better ways we could invest money, even though everyone was saying house prices were rising. So I'd got a bit wary. I'm just not a fast mover on that stuff; I wanted to sit for a while and watch what was happening. But we had all these great drawings, and it was in for council approval.

Then the fire happened and forced the issue. It was crazy. We were coming back home in a big bus with all the families from a weekend with Newport Plus when I got the phone call from my neighbour, Al Schomberg: Your house is on fire. But the good thing is, the firies have put it out.

The first thing I looked for at home was my photos, and they were okay, up in a cupboard. But from there we were forced to get the renovation moving. I felt like a refugee that night. All of a sudden you're out of your house and in a hotel round the corner, and you don't have a home to go to. I thought, *This is what it's like: people just get shafted out of their house with no time to get anything.* There was nothing. All we had was the car in the garage.

But the fire brought up the need to change, along with the insurance money. We were with HIH and they were about to go bust, but we scraped in and were one of the last people to get a payout. It helped clean up the house and get the renovation moving to a certain point. Actually completing it cost a lot more money. We rented an apartment in the Squadron apartments on Pittwater, and we had a good time down there. We had a little boat I'd bought, which we called *Mara'amuu*, after the Tahitian word for 'south wind', that was great.

And the world was really flush with funds, compared with now. I watched a lot of people who I'd known for a long time begin to make really good money. Millions and millions of dollars. From people who'd been living in Newport as kids, like Dougall Walker, to others who'd made a lot of money from

Quiksilver, through options and bonuses. The big surf brands were launching into new markets around the world. I had a little feeling of that. But mostly I was watching people getting large, extended sums of money that flowed toward them. It was a very buoyant time. And by now I had a lot of money too, in the bank. I was very liquid.

Your sudden wealth is a bit daunting. It takes you out of my reach and into this other social milieu, full of wealthy, rather sharklike men and their glossy wives, whose kids all go to expensive private schools, who employ Boj the electrician and Squeak the plumber. They're collecting you; Tom Carroll, surf champion, international icon, local hero, training buddy, social ally.

They shake my hand; they have to – I'm Tom Carroll's brother. But they're not inviting me to that party. It's okay, I don't want to go.

But it feels uncomfortable to me, this social distance, and I think you must feel it too, because within months of that Olympic torch craziness, we've embarked on possibly the least expected Carroll Brothers adventure so far.

It starts in an odd way, with the Queensland surfboard maker Dick Van Straalen. DVS, who once shaped boards for Joe Engel, has taken to making these gigantic ocean-going paddleboards. Visiting him for a story, I ask him what the hell they are for.

'Oh, the Molokai race,' he says.

He tells me about this mad race between two Hawaiian islands, in which people paddle for hours barehanded through the open ocean, just about killing themselves in the process. The Queensland lifeguards are into it.

It seems so over the top! It gets me intrigued. Seduced by Dick's surf-wizard vibe, Leroy Moulds and I both order twelve-foot paddleboards. The only trouble is, I can't paddle it.

You've been paddling a surf club racing board in the Rowland Smith torture academy, so you come out with me to demonstrate the correct knee-paddling technique. All this does is convince me that neither of us can knee paddle.

We come back in laughing at how crap we are.

You look at me: 'Let's do it.'

'The race?'

'Yeah!'

'Yeah!'

Here we are at forty, standing on Newport Beach, again, getting ourselves into something we have no idea about whatsoever. Again.

Barrett Tester, the US manager of Quiksilver's adult line, Silver Edition, sends you a fantastic twelve-foot stock racing board made by the paddleboard legend Craig Lockwood, and we start training. We do laps of a buoy moored 250 metres off Newport. We paddle from headland to headland up and down the coast. One day we get a mate with a boat, Martin Cork, and paddle way out to sea to one of the big freighters anchored far offshore, maybe twelve kilometres straight out. The freighter's like a giant buoy. We turn it and a mist descends; the coastline, the freighter, everything vanishes.

Which way are we going to go? What the hell! It sounds silly, but we don't really care. We're at home out here. We set off, Corky in the boat to the side, and power back and find the coastline just off Bungan, about a kilometre south of where we'd started.

Hawaii in summer is flat and hot. Molokai to Oahu is fifty-five kilometres in a straight line. Hornbaker comes with us to Molokai, hugely amused at his little buddies and the situation they've paddled themselves into. He sits in the escort boat and feeds us Gatorade and bananas.

On a rest break, I sit and watch you admiringly: your gaze focused forward into the task of paddling, your stumpy arms whirring. But then, as the board lifts into another downwind run, I sense a change in your posture – some glimmer of an ancient reflex calling to you from a moment long past. Instantly I know what's about to happen ... and sure enough, with the board pushed forward by the rising chop, you just cast it all away and jump to your feet.

We're twenty kilometres offshore in 1000 metres of water, and you're going surfing.

'Paddle!' I scream.

'Do it again!' Hornbaker screams. 'I'll get my camera!'

A colossal flying fish jumps across your bow and the mad moment is over.

We come second in the middle-aged teams division, beaten by Buzzy Kerbox, your old foe from the Stubbies Classic, and limp off to the airport, too crushed to go on any kind of bender. Later I think, *Shit, that's the first time in decades I've seen you compete and just walk away clean.*

But then we get back and you half disappear again, into this other world, the shining house on the hill. Now fully constructed, the Mark Cashman rebuild gazes out across all the spots we'd once dreamed of surfing, the Cove, the Peak, the Pool, the Path.

To me it doesn't fit; I can't square my dreamy preoccupied little brother, his photographs and drawings and his water-focused brain, with the Aspirational Class, the go-getters, the people who have to send their kids to the right school, no matter what the cost.

Whatever else they have or haven't, they've got structures in their lives; things getting them up and driving them through tough work days. I've got structure, of a kind – the mag deadlines that never end. But you? Nothing's ever quite replaced the architecture of the tour, the discipline, training, and heats that must be won.

Between surf trips and R-R-S training sessions, you sit and watch a pair of sea eagles swoop from the southern headland in winter southerlies, reset their wings and climb above the ridge line, then work their way back to their nest, hunting as they go. And the cockatoos who come screeching along the ridge in the mornings and hurdle up on to your railing, their black intelligent eyes watching you, waiting for a feed.

I grew more and more exposed to wealth, and to people who had plenty of it. I'm still exposed to people like that.

The super wealthy live in another world. Lisa and I had a taste of it. We'd travel around, go to Fiji on holiday with other families, booking out whole islands. It was a very free, open, fantasy world. A lot of people at Quik were doing extremely well; there were a lot of driven people, striving for bigger things for the brand – it was all about bigger, bigger, bigger. They had big money, flew first class everywhere, and everyone in the circles I moved in aspired to be like that. Some people in Rob's training group were quite wealthy, some who were clients of Martin Daly. Some were living beyond their means, or planning big moves to get up there. They could see a lot of money in the world – and there *was* a lot of money. Easy money. The dot-com thing. All this hope! We're all going to do amazing things and be amazing! The group I was thrust into was all about living the dream in a big way.

I don't know whether I was really that way inclined. I tasted that world to some degree, but I also knew that I just didn't have the temperament. I'm not a business person in any sense, the way they know the legal side, and the twists and turns everything seems to take. I was held in a bit of a bubble – I held myself there. I was flying around the world, watching people get really rich, and it was a strange feeling. It was actually quite unnerving at times. It didn't always make sense to me, why they were getting so rich, and what wealth did to people, how it changed them. I saw some things that weren't particularly savoury. It's not true of everyone, but there were people who were willing to do things for their career ... well, it seemed that was all there was for them.

People who get rich, or who just want all that money, really *want* it, will do anything to get more, because it's never enough. I can really see that side of human nature. Maybe it was a bit for them like the drugs were for me. It didn't satisfy people. It satisfied me for a little while, but in the end it didn't, really. At some level there was this hole.

I grew uncomfortable because I wasn't a great judge of character in those situations. People's motivations started to become blurry for me – who's hungry like that and who's really not. I'm a lot more perceptive now through experience, but at that point I was still just Tom Carroll the surfer. I thought, *Well, I've been through the business side. I'm happy to have that off my hands.*

Good things were happening, though, like the Quiksilver Crossing. The idea of the Crossing shocked me, it was so bold.

This was way back in 1998 when Quiksilver's event in G-Land had been cancelled due to the political unrest, and we'd come back to Bali on the way home. Bruce and I sat on the stairs of the Kartika Plaza in Bali and he said, I want to have a chat about something really exciting. What do you think about this idea? We'll hire Martin Daly out and do a trip around the world, do all this adventuring. We'll find all these different waves, we'll join it up with all this cultural stuff.

I thought, Wow. I was a deer in the headlights. I said to Bruce, Are you sure about this? It sounds over the top! I was excited but I thought it was a very grand idea. Bruce's thought, from a marketing point of view, was having something to balance Kelly Slater's impact. Kelly was taking up all the light, in the way Kelly can do, and Bruce knew that Quiksilver couldn't rely solely on him as a brand. We needed to build something else, something potentially as strong, with a broad reach – and it needed to be big. Bruce was brilliant, I knew that, but I couldn't see the Crossing coming. It was overwhelming.

The Crossing became really serious. It lasted for six or seven years and travelled through every ocean, along coasts we'd never thought of visiting at the beginning. I know if it had been embraced by the whole of the Quiksilver world, it could have been incredible. A lot of great ideas could have been built off it, especially going directly to schools, to educational programs through UNESCO and Reef Check, and driven through the rise of online media. So many cool things could have been done.

But the Crossing didn't get connected across the company until it was way too late. It was very hard for Bruce to sell the project, the way Quiksilver was structured, which wasn't streamlined then the way it's becoming now. Quiksilver, at the time, was three very strong entities: Asia–Pacific, the US and Europe, all running their own races, trying to fight for their own territories. There were a lot of power plays and everyone was making a lot of money. It was really scary watching it happen, how they were dealing with that growth. It felt unnatural, and staying grounded within the company's surfing roots was always something I thought was important.

But at the same time I was going parallel with it – I was losing my own roots in many ways. Intensive drug use in a lot of the circles I moved in was okay, and that helped me feel like my own use was okay. There were plenty of people who enjoyed their social stuff; it seemed to be widespread. It was pretty acceptable for people to have cocaine, but I'd got tired of the cocaine. It was boring. I wasn't doing that anymore, and I may have seemed like a shiny example of someone who'd stopped using.

But of course underneath I wasn't. I'd become a lot more social, so I'd got into ecstasy, which was a bit more party-oriented. I'd have a drink with a couple of buddies, and one of them would pull something out. You'd have a bit of that, and the next minute you'd be on the phone, and the next minute you'd scored.

I had switched the witch for the bitch, and I knew I was taking a risk. But I was willing to take the risk, and by now I'd learned how to cover up the guilt and shame – put the game face on and work with it. I could put on the mask. It was a masquerade.

It still seemed like it was under control. Everyone else seemed to be doing their stuff – I could have this for myself.

WINGING IT

2002 and 2003 were blurry times. The girls were coming into their high school years. I don't think I was really equipped to deal with all the decisions that were coming along. Where I'd gone with my addiction previously hadn't really set me up to deal with all those responsibilities appropriately, stepping into being a proper father and having a mission in life, getting an eye on what I'd like to be and do.

I was in a La-La Land of sorts. I was scattered. I had all this great stuff around me, but I could also see how quickly it could disappear. I was watching how things were changing in Quiksilver and trying to figure out how I could fit myself into its future. I couldn't see myself heading up any sort of department. I couldn't see myself as a big leader, a person who could drive business in any way other than just through being Tom Carroll. It wasn't in my vision of myself.

I was being carried by a few projects Quik was doing, such

as the Crossing, and was being paid quite well for my image. I was always available. It was all a lot of fun, but there were a lot of changes and challenges going on, and I was privy to a lot of the shifting sands in the upper echelon of the company. I could see how people were behaving, and it didn't inspire me to be involved.

They threw me tasks. I was a contest director for a few WCT events, but it didn't appeal to me. I was already disconnected from competition at a really deep level. I couldn't get passionate about it. As much as I was missing the discipline, I'd really left the tour behind. It'd given me so much and I had all these opportunities, but I wasn't in shape to take that kind of responsibility, get a grip on it and say, This is something I'm gonna take on!

And as time went on I had less and less of an idea of what I wanted to do. I found myself without my feet on the ground, feeling like I should be able to run the family, having all the trappings of success, but I couldn't. I couldn't find a focus. I was just hanging on for the ride.

Surfing somehow held me together. I took real pleasure from the surfboards I was riding and working with the shapers I was close to: Phil Byrne, Pat Rawson and Michael Baron in California. Working with MB again was special, making these lovely, stumpy little boards. It harked back to other boards I'd had over the years, particularly the 5'6" I used against MR at Bells in 1982. We were really connecting and made some beautiful boards through that period. It was really stimulating.

But once you've made a lot of money and you have a highly addictive personality … It cut me off from the beauty of doing small things. I wanted another big hit. Anything I was going to be involved in had to have a big number attached to it. And I knew that big numbers mattered, because I was spending them. The house rebuild. $25,000 or more a year at SCEGGS Redlands for Jenna and Mimi. We borrowed and bought a holiday house up at Wagstaffe Beach, borrowed again and bought an investment property just down the road in Neptune Street, near the Peak.

Then Ross came up with the idea of *Horrorscopes: Cape of Storms*.

He'd done his biographical documentary *The Sixth Element*, with Justin McMillan and Justin's workmate Chris Nelius. I remember him being in Hawaii, doing some interviews with Justin and Chris about that film, and coming up to me afterwards. Ross was just frothing: I just wanna do this thing where we go and find new stuff! I know you wanna do this, Tom! You've been held back all your life! This is bullshit!

I'd been watching Ross and Tony Ray and others get right into the big-wave tow surfing thing, and I had this idea that I'd been restricted from doing it by family obligations. So I was like, Yeah! I'm being held back!

Ross had been carrying on like this for a while. He didn't have a conventional sense of responsibility; he was certainly prepared to do whatever he felt like doing. He was reinventing himself in ways I hadn't been able to figure out for myself. I didn't know it then, but I was an open book to what would eventually come out of our efforts, which was the *Storm Surfers* series. It gave me an avenue for whatever I had left in me as far as surfing and exploring went. It felt like a great adventure, and an opportunity beyond Quiksilver to do something completely different, completely the opposite of what everyone else was looking at in surfing, which was beautiful sunny pristine waves – all the things we'd done the last decade.

Instead, this mission was all about going to really ugly places in the ugliest conditions we could find. That really appealed to me, I thought it was fantastic. One focus of my life I had never pursued was the cinematic, visual side of surfing. I'd done some video production with Quiksilver in the late 1990s, but I'd never felt I had much room to explore it. But that part of me had always been sitting there, saying, *Do something! Do something!*

Leigh Moulds was interested and said, Look, I know Richard Tognetti from the Australian Chamber Orchestra. And I thought, *That's it! We've gotta have chamber music for this! It's the Cape of Good Hope – the Cape of Storms! Dark shit!*

The whole idea was insane; the characters involved were mad. It was a dark trip. We'd talked about it in 2004, and it came about in '05. I knew that Justin and Chris were really serious about what they were doing; they were really serious filmmakers. They'd brought another dimension to *The Sixth Element* that was really nice. They came along with this ambition to create really good things.

The combination of these guys – Justin's and Chris's incredible minds, with Ross's lunatic vision and energy – was really powerful. Justin would just completely go for it. He was used to the bigger budget advertising gigs, and he knew how to work to a budget and understood what was needed to make something happen. So they presented the concept to Quiksilver and Red Bull, and asked guys along like Dave Kalama and Peter Mel, and Jason Ribbink and others who knew the area off Cape Town really well. Anthony Tashnick came down from Santa Cruz, along with Elko.

We had a six-week window marked out to sit and wait, which was a big lesson in itself. It was a house full of misfits. With the cameraman and soundies and everyone, there were sixteen of us in the house at one point. But there were no waves.

We wanted to get a wave that nobody had ever ridden before. That was the idea. We weren't going to just go surf Jaws again. It was ugly Cape Town, middle of winter. We were aiming at this one wave, South-West Reef, which is in the middle of a marine nature reserve, and driving jetskis around in the middle of a marine reserve was just out. Ross and Justin had done a couple of recce trips and got involved with the local mad guys and people who had water safety organisations. Red Bull, who'd been trying to get an event going down there, had set it up. So we were able to get a permit to enter the reserve, but only for one day's shooting.

I was there for about a month, and it was so brutal. We'd go to these clubs in Cape Town to let off steam, because it was so steamed up in the house. We had *Team America: World Police* and *Anchorman* on twenty-four-hour rotation. Justin was pulling his hair out. Chris was in shock at what we were doing. We were wild animals in a cage, really. Literally, a cage. The house's door had iron bars on it, and I kept imagining I was trapped in there. Ross was up one end with me up the other and Elko in the middle. Dave Kalama took one look at us and decided he had to leave. He didn't like leaving Hawaii anyway.

It wasn't a *Storm Surfers* trip *per se*, but it was a really good example for when we did begin the series – where we could and couldn't go, how we should and shouldn't do things. There were lessons learned on that trip that are still marked very clear in our minds today: who to involve, how to involve them and the timeframes we needed to be effective.

But it was exciting, because it was all about tow-in, figuring out the equipment, learning how to tow each other in really ugly conditions and how to deal with those conditions. It really takes a lot out of you in ugly seas. In nice clean conditions you can come out the other side of a day, recover and not feel too bad. But a big ugly day takes a week to recover. And it took a while to recover from that trip. We were in the cage for too long.

It turned out that we had to extend the trip by one day to get a swell. Six weeks … then one day. This is how surf trips are. That's the way nature plays with us. It's so cool the way it fucks with our minds! We want it all, now! But nooo, we have to wait. And everyone was calling their partners, telling them what we were doing amid the mayhem. Then we got to this last day, and it was ugly.

There was a little launch ramp area called Miller's Point that we'd planned to use to gain jetski access to South-West Reef, just inside a little breakwall where people would go scuba diving nearby. The Sunday before we went out to the reef a medical student was eaten alive at the spot. Taken whole, right in front of his mate, by a great white shark. I'll never forget looking at the Sunday paper and realising, *Crikey, that's Miller's Point! That's where we're gonna take off from!* Crazy thoughts. We knew how dangerous the place was.

But somehow we got that one day. It was horrendously ugly out there, but we got a couple of waves – Kong was involved – and there was just enough craziness in the water for us to pull it off. Eventually the helicopter pilot pulled out on us and we had to pull the mission. It took us forty-five minutes to jetski out there from Miller's Point, and we had to make sure we had enough gas to get back – and we only just made it. That mission taught us: Don't get stuck sitting around.

Tai-Fu, taking on the typhoon swell in Japan, was the second mission. That's when we started to get the *Storm Surfers* team together. We'd learned by then that it wasn't about staying at a location. Instead, it was all about setting everything up, then flying in when the forecast told us to. That was our first trip with a real surf forecaster, Ben Matson, from Swellnet. You should have seen the meetings with the meteorologist in South Africa. The tension was radical. I thought someone was going to strangle him. The insanity in the house was running hot. He was thinking, *I'd better come up with something good*, and every time he'd forecast something, nothing happened. So when Ben made the call about the super typhoon, and it paid off, it was a big call.

When we were doing missions like that, I could bring a different kind of focus into play. Even though there'd be madness around me, I wasn't using. There were times when we'd party afterwards, but I wasn't using all the time. I wasn't hiding. I was out, with the guys, right there with 'em. It was full-on, intense, and it had nothing to do with my girls, nothing to do with my family. I didn't have to be responsible for them, at least not directly. I could bring myself into full play.

And there were my commitments with Quiksilver, which I was still pursuing. I can see now that I was trying to make the money I needed in order to keep afloat all the things that were going on at home. But I was going backwards anyway. A lot of money was going in, but I was juggling assets to try to figure out how to make it all work. Eventually I started borrowing money. I was having to spend more than I was making, and not really wanting to look at it, just winging it. Both Lisa and I were winging it.

You're not the only Carroll who's out on a limb. Dad wasn't uncrackable, but he didn't crack. But I'm not the man he is. I turn forty-two years of age and crack like a dry branch. The big strong older brother, the adult male provider, becomes a parody: the midlife crisis, the affair, the humiliation, the farce, the cliché.

Sensibly kicked out of home, I end up renting the top floor of your investment property in Neptune Street, six houses up from the Peak, and set up an office. Lisa, being in charge of the finances, checks on the rent every now and then. It shifts our brotherhood slightly, yet rather nicely, or at least in a novel manner. 'It's interesting,' you tell me one day. 'It's like I'm the older brother now.'

It occurs to me in a black-comedy moment that I'm supporting you in an entirely ironic new fashion: helping pay the mortgage.

My eyes are off you for a while, so I only get hints of what is going on. Little hints about it. They come obliquely.

The boys, shaking their heads after a long weekend. 'Your brother,' they say, 'ho ho ho.'

Never seeing any of you just … around. Nobody ever just bumps into Tom or Lisa or the girls down the shops; just hurried glimpses of one or the other of you with the girls off to SCEGGS or off to the airport – always somewhere else.

Craig Stevenson, head of Quiksilver Australia, emails to ask me if I can help them with a career review of your performance and direction. Craig has employed a consultant for the purpose. The consultant knows his stuff; he contacts me, talks at length, sends me questionnaires cloaked in the faintly threatening garb of Human Resources. I know Craig is a straight shooter, but ... things are shifting in the new surfing century. Brilliant young Hawaiian Andy Irons is taking Kelly's world titles, and the surf companies are looking to the next generation, hunting them with millions.

What are they thinking? I wonder. Is this how they ease ageing top-gun surfers out of companies these days – via an accumulation of paperwork?

That wave we've ridden since we were kids, is this how it breaks? Not with a boom, but a dribble.

As I clamber up out of the mess I've made and begin to pay attention to the rest of the world again, I see something else occurring. Your face is more lined than it was. I can tell you're worried about how much it's costing to keep up with the Joneses, but this is something else. A kind of heavy cynicism has wormed its way into your essential grommetty light heart, your Sir Thomas Tom-ness. Something is being eroded, or you're growing resigned to something. Maybe you're feeling that wave dribble out, I think; maybe it's just age.

Then I hear about the ice.

THE HEAVENLY VAPOUR

There was a time in 2001 when I began to feel again that I had a big issue with the substances. I wasn't doing it every day, but I was doing it pretty much every weekend. I'd feel like crap Monday and Tuesday, then come back around, and by the weekend I'd be searching it out, raring to go. It was really hard to focus on anything, and I was going up and down like a yo-yo emotionally. I'm sure it was really bleeding out into my relationships at the time. There were all kinds of little bits of denial, just to survive.

My response to the outside world was creating a lot of discomfort for me. I became more fearful about external circumstances. Then September 11, 2001, happened, and this whole other level of fear came up. I was in France at the time. I remember walking into the Quiksilver offices and everyone standing in front of the TVs in the foyer, watching the Towers going down: *This is happening in New York right now.* It was freaky.

I'll never forget sitting with Pierre Agnes at his house that night, and we shared our feelings that there was some sort of larger balancing act happening in the world. Forces way beyond our control. That things like the Towers happen when there's that much money here, and that much greed there. It gave me some sort of comfort to know that someone else was feeling the same way. I was scared for the girls; I just wanted to get home and be with them. All these conspiracy theories were going on in my head, and it didn't auger well – I get overstimulated really easily. But I got home, and it was good to be home.

Then in 2002 Lisa fell pregnant with Grace.

It was really strange; I reckon we conceived on Anzac Day weekend. Anzac night was on a Saturday. I got up in the morning, a little bit hungover, and said, I'm going surfing out the Wedge.

There's not many people around on a Sunday morning after Anzac Day. I got down to Whale Beach and it was a beautiful morning. There were a few surfers out in the middle of the beach but just one guy out at the Wedge. So I started meandering up that way, walked out on the point, paddled off the rocks, and the one guy out was Michael Kay, the doctor who'd delivered Jenna and Mimi. And his first words to me were: You haven't got another baby to wake me up on New Year's Day again, have ya?

I said, Nah, we're done, we're not having any more. We had a bit of a chuckle about how we'd had to get him off his boat for the birth of Jenna.

Six weeks later we were in his office, having the same conversation we'd had in the surf.

That was a tough time because I certainly wasn't ready to

be a father again. I found that each time I had a daughter, there was a period of overwhelming resistance, or fear. Really deep fear of bearing the responsibility for another human. I made it way over-complicated. I don't even know where that reaction comes from. So my response to the news was to plunge into another layer of fear – and one way to cope is to use. So I was using stuff again, fairly regularly, to escape the reality of that fear. I was still working for Quiksilver and doing my Crossing trips, and people were still making a lot of money.

But I was starting to lose my surfing. I lost my feel, my performance. I'd given up on working out with Rob or doing my own work-outs. I was paddling sometimes and swimming, but nothing like I'd been used to, nothing with a routine. I was all over the place with it. So I'd lost myself.

When Grace came along in early 2003, it was beautiful and it was the other end of the spectrum too. She came equipped with every colour in the rainbow of emotions. I've often compared it to being hit over the head with a baseball bat, because that's what it felt like. She was a bold character; she wasn't going to sit back and not be heard. In order to get attention in this full-on household, with these two older sisters already budding into young women, she had to be loud. So she was *very* loud. She didn't cry much, but she would yell. And she'd kick the walls in through her cot. If she wanted us to get up, she'd just start kicking the walls. And the house had an echo, and she liked the sound of that echo. So the house was *very* loud.

It was like, Okay! We hear you!

We were toasted. It was quite a disorienting time. Jenna was about to go to high school, and she was on a dance program.

We had all this stuff going on, trying to figure out how Jenna was going to get into her dancing career. Lisa was doing a lot of work in that area, and getting high schools organised. I kinda just let her do that. I had no idea.

But the amount of money it was going to cost was frightening. All of it was frightening, and I had no idea how I was going to do it, I really didn't.

My response was to get outta there and try to figure myself out.

About that time I started to switch again. I hated the feeling of ecstasy and its aftermath. It was really depressing. I'd try to manage the supply, and it was really hard to get a good one. It was also really dangerous. A lot of e had a cocktail of other stuff mixed into it – it coulda had heroin in it, that sort of stuff. It became a really nasty experience, and really dicey mentally. I felt up and down, not knowing if I would feel happy or sad or really angry. I was hanging on by a thin thread.

I'll quit it, I thought. *I'm not going to be involved in this.*

My ecstasy dealer wasn't using e; he was just putting a little amphetamine in water and drinking it. So one day I said, Just give us a bit of that. I thought I wasn't into the idea of speed or anything of that nature. But in fact it was a perfect combo for where I was at in my hectic life. It sharpened my mind and kept me going. It felt like it lifted my capacity to deal with reality.

So it wasn't long before I was totally addicted to it. I never liked alcohol – it didn't fit my pathology. I'd probably have a couple of drinks with Lisa at night and that was about it. Even that wasn't where I wanted to be. I didn't like smoking pot anymore – it was really confusing and mentally damaging at that point. I could really feel the effects and was scared, because I was already hanging by a thread. I can imagine people who smoke a lot of that and are on the dicey edge … I've seen people coming out of that state, and it's horrible.

At the time I felt like I had to lift my capacity to pull my end of the bargain somehow. My perception was that I didn't have the energy. My perception was that I needed to be able to do more.

I thought, *How am I going to keep up with all this?* It takes so much energy with a young family, to try to hold it together. And amphetamine is perfect. It's like an extended cup of coffee. It can sharpen your concentration like caffeine. And this discovery seemed to sit with my pathology better than anything else. I was able to pull the amphetamines off for a while without too much damage.

I don't know what the Newport crew saw in me at the time. They probably just thought I was full of energy. That's what I told myself, at least. I was probably quite sporadic and they thought I was a little crazy, maybe. When I look at my behaviour it was no doubt a really powerful addiction, but I hadn't completely lost my mind yet. I still had a family and a home, and I still had money coming in, and I still wasn't ready to be revealed.

I became more and more covert, more underground, and I considered myself better at doing it. I'd use fairly regularly, but I wasn't using too much. I was a functional user. It was the kind of drug where I couldn't use huge amounts. I was on a downhill spiral though, slowly going deeper and deeper. And eventually you end up wanting to inject it, because the effects start to back off and you have to use more.

Three weeks into the New Year I was doing laps around the buoy off Newport. I started getting into a bit of a fitness routine again, the way I had so often in the past, running myself down and building myself up again. I came in after doing a couple of laps one day, and some of the guys who I'd scored ecstasy from in the past were hanging on the platform near the Peak.

I told 'em, Look, I'm off the eccys now. I'm laying low, taking it easy, feeling pretty good about myself.

One of them said, Look, I've got some really, really good stuff. You might want to try it.

And because I had no gap between the thought and the action, as soon as I had that feeling, I couldn't stop the train of thought – before I knew it I was tasting the crystal meth. And the feeling I got from it was a lot more pure.

At first it's a very crystal clear, sharp mental state. No fuzzy edges at all. Really clear concentration. Sharp responses to everything. Efficient, sustained, concentrated efforts. Clear responses from the body. Heightened senses. But not high, so you're out of control – just a high that senses everything. The world around you becomes much sharper.

So instantly I was like, *This is where I need to be.*

It wasn't just ten minutes, or twenty minutes, or an hour or two hours – it was ten hours at a stint. It was on for a long period of time. From using just a little bit. That was because I was fresh and ready for it.

I started taking it orally. I'd get a little bit, thinking, *I'll just take that.* But because it was so insidious, because it fit in so perfectly with my pathology, I was gone. I was a goner. Everything was set up in place in my nature and what had been developing over the years and – *boom!* – it ignited a very strong addiction.

In the beginning it seemed like it helped me. It seemed like it backed me up with everything. I was there for people, I was getting stuff done, I was engaging. But then you *need* it to do things, and then it wears off, and you're left with yourself.

It was scary. Really scary. Another level of fear that you can't express to anybody. Then I started studying the drug I was taking, started reading the horror stories and started seeing it all going on for myself. It was scary. But I kept going to it because I had set up that compulsive obsession with the drug. When it wasn't around, maybe one-eighth of me would be thinking about what was in front of me, and the rest was consumed thinking about it: *How am I gonna get it? Gotta get on the phone.* I already had the covert behaviour pattern in operation.

I did all sorts of things to try to score, because it was pretty scarce. It brought me into contact with some really seedy people. People who died doing it. A guy I knew committed suicide. That was a really frightening thing, because I realised that was where it leads, that was the end point. But understanding what happened to that person still didn't stop me. It wasn't me, after all. It didn't happen to me. The nature of the beast is to keep going until it stops.

I'd try to go surfing, take a couple of paddles and I'd be buggered. I couldn't get outside without feeling sore. My muscles would say, *What the hell's that?* Quite often I'd sleep for long periods of time. I read further about the meth and thought, *Ah, that's exactly what's happening to me.* What I was reading scared the living shit out of me. I thought, *I can't keep doing this*, but I couldn't stop.

The ritual of smoking it becomes so addictive. Just like smoking. I'd never tasted smoke like that. It was a totally different kind of smoke. It was just all white. It was like a vapour. The smoke became a heavenly thing. I still like the thought of it. Such a cool smoke, such a beautiful thing. So I'd end up doing more than I'd think because I liked the ritual so much. And all of a sudden you've got more in you than you need, and then you go on for longer. And eventually your body needs more. The spiral becomes quicker, downward, a steeper gradient, falling deeper, steeper and deeper. It's brutal at that point, because you'll have lost so much sleep, and you've got to regain it. I might even sleep for twelve to sixteen hours at a stretch.

There's a certain amount of life force given to you from the beginning – a number of heartbeats, the amount of energy it takes to give you those heartbeats, what the Chinese would call the *chi* energy. The Hawaiian *mana*. I really felt that I was taking a big chunk of my *mana* and throwing it down the drain. Literally burning it on the spot – *whoosh*, gone. *Oh my god, this is what I'm doing. I won't have any life force left.* I would sleep for sixteen hours, Lisa wondering what the hell was going on with me. I just wanted to get my normal energy back, but I knew as soon as I did that, my mind would be straight off again.

It was a vicious, vicious cycle. And I had no say anymore. By the time Grace was two years old I was in the full grip of it.

I thought I was really covert, really clever and secret. It would be my secret, a whole other life, all for me, no-one else. It's still really appealing to me. Fuck! And you don't pick up what people are seeing. You can't hear anyone anyway. There's too much going on in your head. Your thoughts are too loud. Only the dealer, maybe. There was always that weird connection with the dealer. A conspiracy to escape and make this deal and get high. Often it's done behind the back of someone he's involved with. So it's a very secretive enticing space.

Fuck everyone else. The dealer would understand.

My ice dealer, in Mona Vale, I remember getting some from him and we were having a pipe together, and he looks at me as he's lighting the pipe, and says, No-one understands, do they, Tom? No-one understands.

I can't protect you from this. I don't even know what to protect you from. This part of you is as big a secret to me as it is to everyone else. The ice dealer is invisible. I ask around; nobody knows who he is, or if they do, they're not telling me. They're doing me a favour, I realise later; ice dealers aren't surf industry fluffers to be threatened on the phone.

Who or what have I been protecting all these years, editing out the drugs from your life and my so-called journalism? Careers, hell. We'll paddle out in waves of any dimensions, but we can't even face our families. We love surfing, but God help the people who love us. Gobbo and Woggo, I think wryly. The Newport hell grommets. The legend surf hero and the top surf writer. The adulterer and the ice addict.

Years earlier, Dad has written a short memoir of Mum, he says in order to preserve her memory in our minds. Scrabbling for ways to understand – to do something – I come across the memoir. I read it over and over, obsessively, trying to form a picture from the words. The memoir is full of observations both loving and sad, but they're Dad's memories, not mine.

I forget about protecting and start digging. I'm enough of a journalist to do that, at least. I find Syer Barrington White's childhood home, The Poplars, in Horsmonden, Kent, first built around 1750 and now a grade two listed heritage building with six bedrooms and the recent addition of a swimming pool – a bargain today at around 1.35 million pounds. I find Nam's childhood home in the village of Stalybridge near Manchester, and read her father's self-description on her birth and marriage certificates; when she's born he's a 'farmer', when she's married he's a 'gentleman'.

I read about Syer White's war record as a medical officer in the useless terrible enclave of Salonika, and his death, of pancreatic cancer. I read Janet's school reports, nursing records and postcards from her trips to Europe and India, and chase old friends of hers from the days in the South London maternity service. I picture her, a twenty-four-year-old young woman enveloped in the fifty-six-hour working weeks at St Bartholomews, her Left-leaning politics taking her to post-war Czechoslovakia and Italy, exchanging envious letters with friends who've visited Moscow.

A cryptic note marked 'T' leads me to an ex-lover from those days, a Tony Barnett, who turns out to be a professor living in Canberra, and who on visiting turns out to have been married at the time he and Janet knew each other. Professor Barnett recalls Janet as being modest, quiet and good company. I think she must have hidden a lot of herself from him.

Dad's memoir mentions an episode of anorexia nervosa in Janet's teenage years. I read about anorexia and its terrible relentlessness, and wonder more and more about what happened when we were kids wandering around in the hospital grounds. I call the Royal Prince Alfred, where the staff are in the process of throwing out all the pre-1990s paper records. They confirm that Janet's file is still there; it's due to be destroyed in a week.

They post it to me, all 212 pages. I sit down on the floor of your investment property in Neptune Street and start reading, and the mysterious clouds of our childhood grow dark and split apart.

She contracts hepatitis in 1955 after visiting India, suffering no relapses. Then has a small benign tumour removed from the head of the pancreas in 1962.

In September 1964, she develops leg rashes and is admitted to RPA for almost three weeks to deal with the dermatitis and chronic anaemia.

She is readmitted almost two years later, on May 23, 1966. A note on the records reads NOT TO HAVE BARBITURATES. The doctors and nursing staff must have read this note, but in late June they start sedating her in the evenings with Pentobarb and Amytal. On discharge, in early August, they give her a note recommending 200mg pentobarbitone each evening.

She has a short stay at RPA for a blood transfusion in November that year. In April 1967 she is readmitted for six weeks for further treatment. Now she has developed mild diabetes mellitus 'which may have been unmasked by steroids', and her eyesight is beginning to fail. *These long hospital stays*, I think, *they'd never happen today.*

The dermatitis flares up on her left foot, and Janet spends another two weeks in hospital. Reading this I have a vague memory of oatmeal baths, supposed to be beneficial to skin complaints, and of Mum smoking, the cigarettes hidden in a cupboard somewhere we couldn't reach them.

Almost a year passes before she is admitted again. It must be the year of anger. On October 30, 1968, she comes into RPA via emergency with progressive severe weight loss, pneumonia and a pancreatic cyst. Janet is weak, tired, not eating well, and complaining of pain in the epigastric area around the pancreas. Surgeon Mr Mills feels that surgery on the pancreas is too risky given her state.

She is discharged on December 21, 1968, just in time for Christmas. The Christmas of the Coolite under the bed.

Three weeks later she is readmitted for a small bowel biopsy. At this stage Janet is described as an 'extremely emaciated pale woman looking older than forty-eight years, in no distress, giving a wealth of details observed by herself with her typical introspective attitude'. Conditions listed: pancreatic tumour, malnutrition, psychiatric imbalance, malabsorption. Adult anorexia nervosa diagnosed. Undergoes surgery in mid-February for a blood clot in the left femoral artery.

On March 11 she is admitted to the psychiatric ward for treatment of anorexia nervosa. 'Present episode prob. of 3yrs duration', says the merciless medical record. 'Grossly emaciated.' The doctor's notes say the goal of admission was to 'get her into a fit state for operation' on the pancreatic mass. The psychiatrist's notes summarise the taut desperate conversations of a dying woman trying to account for her life. Janet grows more 'demanding and anxious' over the next two months, gains some weight, then becomes drowsy, withdrawn and confused.

She finally dies in the psych ward at the age of forty-nine, around 7 am on May 11, 1969, the doctors never having quite dealt with the actual cause of death: cancer of the pancreas, metastasising to the liver, the same disease that killed her father, with anorexia nervosa and dermatoses listed as secondary causes.

Not until the second reading do I find this: Janet 'has a past history of multiple drug intake ... there was a strong suspicion that she was an amphetamine addict'.

Amphetamine addict.

The pieces falling into place, *click, click, click.*

You don't know your parents, not really, and they don't know you, not until you're revealed to each other by time and experience. Mum could never have known what would happen, the kinds of lives we would live and how we'd turn out. I feel sure that she would never have wanted what happened to you.

But I also know now why she'd been so furious – the reason behind those screaming matches of our childhood. Because she knew what she'd be missing. All this, all the waves we rode, and Mum never even saw one of them.

I stood to lose my sanity. I stood to lose my family out of my life. I stood to lose my home. I stood to lose my job, my career, who I was. But I hadn't lost everything yet, and that's what the disease is going for – everything. I was going downhill very fast.

I knew that I needed help. Group help. I needed people around me. But I was super super scared of that too.

THROUGH THE WINDOW

To come clean. To be humble and come clean. When I look at my life, I kinda define myself as before and after that decision.

There's a cycle, it seems. It's a cyclical thing. The window opens and it closes, and you go back into rationalising and denial and discomfort. You go deeper and deeper into that state, then all of a sudden reality intervenes again. That window opens. And if you don't dive through, you fall back in. And God knows how long it's gonna be before the window opens again. You might go so far up your own arse you never come back.

I'd already made up my mind that I needed to do something. What made it really unnerving is that I didn't know whether I wanted to stop. There was a big part of me that didn't want to. There are a lot of people out there right now who don't want to do what they're doing, but a part of them says, *Well, you can just keep going, you're getting away with it.*

But I wasn't getting away with it.

Lisa had thought I was clean for years, more or less. Then, while I was out of the country on one of my trips, she came across all the ice gear, the pipes and the rest of it. She waited until I got back and confronted me with it. She was incredibly upset, incredibly angry and confused. I was just crushed, to be revealed to her and myself as the junkie I actually was.

Right then the decision was made, somewhere in me, but I couldn't get there. I'd put on too many masks that I'd needed in order to operate in the world. I couldn't get them off. The light outside was too fucken bright.

I went to Narcotics Anonymous meetings for months, getting two weeks clean, then using and lying, and trying to cover it up, then going back to NA, then lying again – it was just a horrible, confusing time. I'd get a few days clean and then use again and have to go back to the dealer. Spending more money, more secretiveness, more lying. Anything could happen. It was a moment when something dies and something is born. It was a fine edge.

So when I had the opportunity to do some rehab time, I didn't know if that's what I wanted. I certainly didn't *want* to do it. A lot of me was cringing, terrified of the consequences. Everyone's gonna find out! The drama playing out in my head was horrendous.

Home was really hectic. I was trying to be a father to three daughters and something of a husband. And when the prospect of rehab came up, it got more hectic and painful. Lisa was saying maybe we should put it off until the New Year because it was so daunting for her to face Christmas on her own with the kids. It seemed so ridiculous to her, and maybe there was some fear in it for her as well. There was a lot of emotion in the house, the girls didn't know what was going on, and I had to come clean with them. There was all this stuff that'd been shoved down for years. So that's when I knew I couldn't put it off until after Christmas.

I didn't know it was my window at the time, but I knew this was the time to move – to put myself somewhere where I wasn't exposed, so I could get some space. That was the advice from people who were working in recovery programs, because you can't recover on the street.

Murray Close got me over the line. It was Martin Cork's idea that we talk to Muz. Corky was good friends with Lisa, and while she'd tried to keep my addiction a secret, more and more she'd needed to talk to someone about what was happening. That's how Corky heard what was going on with me – and he knew Muz had been involved in NA and group addiction treatment. It seemed he might be able to help.

Murray Close. Northern Beaches boy. One of the many faces from our youth, here and there, Narrabeen, Dee Why, keen surfer, competitor, judge. Around 1998 I start bumping into him again on surf checks. It's part of the warmth of coming home after the California years – bumping into mates from those times.

One day he pulls me up outside Newport Post Office and explains he's having trouble getting the cashier to recognise his credit card; can he borrow $150 to cover off his phone bill?

Trusting my feeling about a fellow surfer, I say yeah, of course, hand over the money.

Murray says he'll drop it around the next day. He never shows. Not that week, not the next. Then someone tells me: 'You gave him money? Didn't you know about him? Murray! He's on the hammer. He's gone, mate.'

I think back to our youth again, remembering the smack zombies, Cookie on the nod outside the bank. The thing we rejected with everything we had. Now it's back in town, and I've just been scorched by it. I write off Murray Close and try to forget what's happened.

Eighteen months later, I find an envelope in the mailbox at home. Inside is $150 in cash and a letter from Murray. An extraordinary letter. Without a shred of confusion or self-pity or bullshit of any kind – just a clean admission and accounting of his behaviour in our exchange outside the post office that day, of the associated drug addiction, of his desire to make reparations, and here is the money I stole.

He puts nothing on me whatsoever, but I write back anyway, expressing my admiration. It's not enough. What he's done entirely erases the bad feeling I'd had, not just toward him, but surrounding the entire incident. It almost seems like an act of magic – a private sort of magic that only he, Wendy and I know anything about.

Murray Close, jeez. Now he steps in where Lisa can't go, where I don't know to go.

Murray was crucial in my getting clean. He was always calm. I'd be wigging out: trying to be a parent, going to meetings, lying, using, being 'Tom Carroll'. And Muz would be calm. He'd say, You can't have one foot in and one foot out on this, Tom, because it will drive you *insane*. You have to go somewhere you can get some space.

And he was right: I was insane. I remember in the middle of it all, heading up to my office, in secret, and having a pipe – taking a long, deep hit – and it had almost no effect. I couldn't take it. I screamed in frustration: God, help me with this! God, help me!

I thought I'd have to go to church. Instead I went into recovery – South Pacific Private Hospital, Curl Curl. Luckily we'd switched our health plan around to prepare for it.

I had to be assessed before I was admitted, and I was able to get to another level of honesty with the assessor, Lisa Chapman, who was great, I still see her. I knew then that I was going into the right place. I broke down, finally started breaking down, and went in on a Monday morning after a weekend when I can remember using, but not hell for leather, not desperate.

When I did go in I was in a surrendered state. It was December 18, 2006. I can't remember what it was like that day moment to moment, but I was going in for five weeks. They put me straight into detox. They put me into this bed. There were two beds in each room; I was the only one in my room and in the next room was a guy who'd got in the day before me. His name was Murray – a different Murray – and he had a problem with speed and smoking dope. A really nice guy.

They offered me valium, and Murray said, Don't have anything. Don't take any of that. I listened to that, because I didn't need it. I could see how people would come in after barbiturate or alcohol poisoning and valium might help soften the blow, but then you've got to get off that. You've swapped the witch for the bitch.

South Pacific had decided to renovate the place and started work the day after I went in. And the renovation began outside my front door. The workers would get in there at 6.30 am and start ripping down the hallway, and I thought, Hang on! This place is costing big money! After the first two days of noise I just accepted my space and it wasn't too bad. I started to sleep better almost instantly. I was just open to spending time away from the mess that I'd got myself into. Like, Who am I? And I was really open to see where I could go with the rehab. I'd already dived through the window of opportunity.

I had heard all these stories of people walking out of rehab and using the first day. And three days into that detox, this guy turned up. He was a panelbeater from Parramatta. Abdul his name was. He had burns all over his lap and wrists and forearms from six months before, when his speed lab had blown up on him. He'd come to the place via the court; it had given him the option of rehab. He was talking away, carrying on. At night he'd have his curtain drawn and he'd be up all night, doing shit. You're not supposed to have a mobile phone, but I'd wake up and he'd be there tapping away.

Next morning, I looked at him and he was sooo high. He was super high. He couldn't look at me while he was talking; his eyes were all over the room.

I talked to Murray and said, Fuck, that guy's using. I was wondering what he was on. Part of me was thinking I could score something off him. It was a crazy time: three days in and there's this renovation going on and this guy is using across the room. He was using speed and heroin combos and I was thinking, *Maybe I could try some.* Anything could have happened, because my brain was set up to act without thinking. My brain was so sketchy. I had no defence from that first thought, no tools to redirect it or share what was going on. Well, just a little bit from the NA meetings I'd been to – just enough to stop myself.

Anyway we dobbed in Abdul, and they came and grabbed all his gear and called his family to get him out of there. And his brothers came down to get him. You shoulda seen his brothers. They were in this top-of-the-line HSV, everything on it, they just pulled up and came in and got him. I dunno where that guy is now. But there it was, in my face, in this place where I thought I'd be safe. It was a challenge from the get-go.

I finally got out of detox after a week and I was joining in the group therapy sessions in the mornings. I was allowed out for a walk in the morning and a walk in the afternoon.

But they wouldn't allow me in the ocean.

Residents used to be able to go for a swim in the South Curly pool, but it became a safety thing, because people could get sucked out in those currents. Curly's a dangerous beach.

We were working on these things called 'levels', levelling with people, just being honest about how you feel, instead of crawling up into yourself and being quiet or out of control. Rehab is all about personal integrity and honesty and working through the twelve steps. And first and foremost, being authentic. Learning how to be yourself and getting a relationship with yourself. Learning how to speak with integrity. When you've come from a very secretive and dishonest place, and lost a lot of self-esteem, you have to build that back up.

There was a way of addressing people in rehab: we learned a new language about how to voice our feelings to others. Without being judgemental – You're to blame! Why don't you change? – you might say, This is what I make up about this situation, owning whatever was going on inside you. This is how I feel, and either I'm going to keep myself safe from you, or see how you respond. Then you start working forward.

So I put in a formal complaint. I wrote a level to the top and I was very stern. I wrote that I understand this is a safety issue, but you're always talking about bringing in a higher power, a connection with a source that's greater than you. And it's plain and clear that all my life I've been living in it. The ocean. So what do you mean I can't go swimming? It's the middle of summer and you're taking my connection away from me.

Every day I had to walk up and down this beach and come back and say I hadn't been for a swim up the north end. I had to actually practise that. A couple of times it didn't quite work out. I got up the north end and jumped in for a swim and made out that I was still dry. I eventually pulled up and realised it was about my integrity.

They responded to my letter and told me it was an insurance issue: We can't endanger people just for you, Mr Carroll. So I wore it. But there were quite a few people behind me in it. I rallied quite a bit of support.

It was funny. I felt like I was on some sort of TV show. There was quite a bit of reality TV going on at the time, and I thought, *Fuck, I'm in* Big Brother. But eventually I made a real commitment in that rehab; I realised I didn't want to come back out and use again. I wanted to feel myself again. I knew that I had a lot of determination on my side, from prior experiences in my life.

I don't think I would have been open to this kind of recovery had I been twenty-five, or even in my thirties. I was just so full of myself, you know. Still am to some degree. But it was really obvious that what worked for me when I was young worked against me later – turned into a weapon against me.

It reminded me of being in hospital after my stomach rupture way back, that no matter what the situation, I could survive. In the hospital that time, even after not eating for two weeks and being emaciated, I could still laugh with people, I could still enjoy the environment. My spirit is pretty much a fun-loving spirit, and it could still move around in that space. I've never suffered from that feeling of being confined. Rehab and recovery is not for everyone – at first it does feel very confining – but I started making friends and was able to open up to recovery and empathise with other people. I opened up to certain people's way of life and their characters, and it was cool, I thought it was pretty amazing. And you could see the value of other people being in there, and I had stuff about myself painfully pointed out in group that I didn't see. You just don't see it.

We weren't allowed to have caffeine or sugar, so of course as soon as we went to meetings outside rehab we just hit the coffee, stole some tea bags and wolfed into the biscuits, if they were there. When we were allowed to go to the shop between Christmas and New Year, we could only get flowers, water, other drinks. Hardly anything. Even the person over the counter knew we weren't allowed to buy certain things.

But it was Christmas, so I said, Right guys, we're gonna go out and get a whole lot of those lolly party mixes.

The person who knew wasn't behind the counter so I loaded up with a whole lot of natural confectionaries. The lady who was on shift that night, I'd been getting on with, she was really nice, really cool, and when I got there she had to check out all the bags and I got busted! I felt like such an idiot. She had to take them off me. I said, Come on, they're just lollies!

She said, No you'll have to pick them up on your way out of here in three weeks.

I was going, You're killing me. My integrity was shattered. She said, Look, you're not the only one. It wasn't pretty at the time.

I did notice that South Pacific allowed smoking in rehab. It was the one addiction that was permitted. I could see people going outside to have a cigarette, and I started getting jealous. I could see the effect it was having on them – this moment of relief from whatever they were dealing with, from the reality of rehab.

Then one day they said, We're gonna ban smoking. *What?* Just about everyone in the place smoked! The whole place went mad for a day. A couple of people were packing their bags, saying, Fuck them, I'm not staying!

I said to one guy who'd packed his bags, You can't go now, man, you've been here for two and half weeks, you're gonna use for sure!

He said, Fucken oath! Fuck them, they're not taking my cigarettes away! They had to pull it back and make a special little smoking area out the back. It was this little enclave the size of an outdoor dunny with a little seat in it. And the place was like a chimney, smoke billowing out of it all day. It was heavy.

The week before you go into South Pacific, I take off on a relatively small wave at Rocky Point in Hawaii, mistime a turn, and have the whole wave land directly on me. The wave drives my right leg through the board and breaks the ankle and both bones of the lower leg.

The day you go in, I'm flat out in surgery being pinned and screwed back together.

You call me a couple of times in the following week, tell me little bits and pieces about how things are going, about something called Family Week, where family members enter the process for five days. Your voice isn't exactly joyful, but it's not hesitant, and you don't disappear mid-conversation. You ask if I can do the Family Week process with you and Lisa, and of course I say yeah, as long as I can use crutches.

I drive up there and hobble to the front door, and note it's about 100 metres away from where they'd operated on your knee twenty-five years ago.

The place is a house on a hill, but any resemblance to your house on the hill ends right there. It's cramped, dark and smells of cooked lunch and new paint. There are no straight lines in that building; to get anywhere you have to walk around looking at room numbers and following signs.

It's soon clear that rehab is imitating life: everyone loves Tom. It drives Lisa a bit crazy. She wants something else from you; some sort of suffering, perhaps. She is alternately angry, happy and blinking back tears.

I am amazed at how angry I am. At silly things; how you drop out on the phone. The way you say, 'I'm with ya!' when you're not. At how you drive your car, for fuck's sake. 'Our sister died in a fucken car accident,' I say, 'do you *know* that? I've only got you now, do you think I want to lose you like that too?'

You hear it all, calm as the midsummer Tasman Sea.

We are in a circle one morning late in the week when Brian, the psychologist in charge of the session, introduces the subject of motherhood.

One of us says something. I can't remember which of us says it, but whatever is said rips the room open.

We look at each other for a long moment, the air crackling.

The facilitator, Brian, says, 'Look, this is not what we'd ordinarily do, but I think you need a half hour by yourselves, so you've got it. Go wherever you want, just be back here in half an hour.'

What, like anywhere?

We walk out into the fresh air. A light nor'-easter's blowing. It's almost midday. We drive in my car around the headlands, looking at the little waves. You tell me the ridiculous story about trying to sneak lollies into rehab, and that sort of squashes any thoughts about going to the shops for a soft drink.

Somehow we find ourselves driving up past the Duke Kahanamoku memorial on top of Freshwater, pull in and stop near the statue of Duke, both thinking the same thing: of how we'd come up here a couple of years before on a Saturday morning to check Queenscliff Bombie in a big swell, and some wit had tied a tutu on Duke overnight. A lovely silvery tutu, shimmering in the morning offshore.

We clamber out, me wrestling with the crutches, and walk and hop our way along the path through the bushes, looking at the names here and there on the world champ inlays: BL, Dooma, Midget, Nat, Pam, Layne, you. Nobody else in there, just us, and these plaques.

And out of nowhere, we're crying. Sitting and crouching now, under cover of the bushes, holding on to each other and crying like babies. Like the little boys we were and still are.

That Family Week helped another level of honesty to come up, with the support of the rehab, especially between Lisa and me. Stuff that'd been underneath everything. The start of healing from co-dependency and from that enmeshed situation we'd been in, where neither of us felt heard at all.

And our connection with our mum and Jo. I really felt Mum in there. She really made her presence felt. She really did. A lot of strong, clear messages: I was in the right place, I needed to stick it out, it was really valuable to be there and I was doing well. A lot of confirmation from her.

Did I mention an eagle feather?

We were talking about a higher power in there, and I was learning my meditation practice, which I stick to today. I dunno how or why, I'd never have thought it, but I was doing fifteen minutes of meditation before our walk each morning, and I got into a routine of doing this practice called Blue Door Meditation, which is a guided meditation. You imagine going into a room and sitting down in a chair, and feeling what that's like, then opening a blue door in front of you.

And in my version of the meditation what I would do was walk through the door and climb into the palm of a hand, and lie down. This was me being really creative. And the palm of the hand, for some reason, would be coming out of a valley, like one of the valleys between the plateaus in the Blue Mountains. There would be a tree growing from the side of the valley, right on the cliff, and to walk through the blue door, I would have to walk through the tree, into a room inside the tree, then open the blue door and step onto the hand, and then lie down and begin breathing.

The breathing would then last about twelve minutes. While I was in there, I'd be breathing, suspended in this hand overlooking this beautiful valley, quite deep, all natural bushland.

One day while in this meditation I sensed an eagle flying. It flew around in a circle and came right up to me so that its eye was looking directly at me, very clear, really powerful. It really struck me – very emotional.

And then it said: Attention. Bring your attention to this. Then it flew off, and the meditation ended.

Then I went for my walk on the beach. Only a couple of people came along. I went off by myself because I was still quite stunned by the vision of the eagle in the meditation.

I got to the estuary at the north end of Curl Curl. I wouldn't normally have wandered up toward the lagoon; normally I would walk right along the shoreline, so at least the waves could wash up around my feet, at least I was touching the water. But what struck me was that the lagoon was fairly full, super glassy and a really bright blue sky, and the reflection of the sky off the surface of the lagoon was really beautiful. So I was drawn to it.

I began walking toward the lagoon, watching my own reflection appear as I did, and there was a big sea eagle feather, in front of me, a big thick feather, with one side slightly kinked out, so it wasn't quite perfect.

And I felt that what it said to me was, Nothing's perfect.

And that was the message from Mum: Nothing's perfect, Tom, and it's okay to be that way.

Those few little moments connected a few dots for me. I couldn't have got the message in any other way. It couldn't have been more perfect, in its imperfection. And it did feel like I was in the presence of Mum. The message is there with me today, it doesn't just go.

I kept the feather. It showed me there was more going on than meets the eye. I'd always tried to be right for everyone else, never quite right for myself. But I wouldn't have been able to get that message anywhere else, if I hadn't spent that time in rehab, thawing out long enough to listen. And the fact that I was drawn there to my reflection, and found that feather, just after receiving that strong message: Pay attention. Pay attention. Have a look.

It would mean absolutely nothing to anyone else. But it opened the door for me.

And maybe in all that crying out for help, in the darker moments, when caught in the bonds of addiction, when the spirit is so sucked dry that it's just this emaciated thing on the ground, choking and drained – it requires a spiritual path to walk its way out.

LIKE A RAW NERVE

I got out on January 21. I was scared. Scared of using. Scared that I'd take a left turn and try to connect with my dealer. Over time I'd narrowed it down to one guy, one dealer. I'd had to be as secretive as possible, so I only had one person who I'd got anything from. There'd been a couple of other options, but I'd shut them down a few months before. The whole situation reeked of the shit you go through to do it.

And I had an encounter with him.

I was about six months clean. For months on end my energy was really weird. I couldn't surf, I couldn't really spark physically. I'd lost some connection with myself. For the past three years I'd tried to find or use my drug of choice on a daily basis, and for many years before that I'd used something. I'd always enjoyed the feeling of being out of myself, it's fucken awesome, I love it! But getting clean, for a good six months my energy wasn't right.

I was actually working for Quiksilver – thankfully they were supportive and they'd given me a job with an office. An office job, it was brutal! I was meditating every day, going to meetings, sharing my situation, getting into my twelve step work, doing all the things it was suggested I do in recovery. It was difficult at home, too, trying to live in the same house with Lisa – a lot of emotional stuff coming up, not knowing what we were doing or where we were going.

Well … anyway. I hadn't come across my dealer. I'd got rid of his phone number. I normally wouldn't run into him, but I'd see him driving around, he had a very bloody obvious car, and when I'd see it, all the thoughts and associations of using would come up. I was driving around the back of Warriewood, going from the store at Mona Vale towards Manly. It was eleven o'clock in the morning, a beautiful, crisp day. The last thing I was thinking of was using. I was really content.

I came up to a roundabout T-intersection; it had a left-hand turn in it but I was going straight ahead. And as I approached the intersection, no-one else on the road, my dealer pulled down into the roundabout and came around toward me.

He saw me and I saw him, and we stopped, right there.

I'd heard about what happens if we don't have a good idea of our boundaries and where we want to be with people: we just go back to the way we talked to them the last time, right back to that moment. And the last time I saw him I'd scored drugs. So I went straight to that.

He said, Haven't seen ya, mate.

I could feel myself returning to that same space, thinking, *Wow, this is crazy*.

He said, Where ya been? Everything's good.

I said, I don't have your number. I'd better get your number.

He said, No worries, let's do it.

Yeah, let's do it this afternoon.

No worries, I've got it. It's all ready to go.

This was all still in the roundabout.

I punched his number into my phone. I hadn't saved it yet. I was looking at myself thinking, *Holy shit.* I could feel a surge of adrenalin going through me. When you're an addict, you start feeling it before you do it, and I was starting to feel that surge, just by looking at the phone number.

I said, Okay, I'll give you a call, he said Okay, four o'clock this afternoon, it's on.

So I'd made the deal, and the dealer was back in my phone.

I drove off through the roundabout in this surreal state, thinking, *Look what you've just done.* I could see it really clearly: I had the option to save the number or delete it, and without even thinking, I just deleted it, *boom.* Within a few seconds I was already looking in the rear-view mirror, thinking, *I gotta go chase him down.* All these insane thoughts. Luckily someone in recovery was available and we talked it through. All I needed was to talk on the phone and start to unravel the episode with someone who would listen and had been in that situation before.

We need that. Someone who doesn't know addiction would have said, What the fuck are you doing? They'd be in automatic judgement, and that's a place where we don't get to heal.

I haven't seen the dealer since. I've forgotten his name. Haven't thought of trying to track him down. I'd heard he got into a bad situation where there were guns involved, but when I saw him he didn't look too bad. The encounter with him was a warning sign, a shot across the bow, because the drugs are always there, the alcohol is always there – but it's not the drugs, it's me.

You know, it's baffling. It's so fucken baffling what can happen, but there's always that opportunity. I always have a choice to be in either recovery or relapse. There's always an opportunity to work on a spiritual path, one moment to the next. That's all we have.

It was really frightening. It was like a raw nerve. I wasn't too bad because I had a fair amount of surrender on board toward the path of recovery. But coming back home and dealing with the stuff there. And all the people. Everything that I was running from within myself started to appear, the anxiety of who I was without these substances. Within that first six months I felt a lot of anxiety. My hands and arms would literally tingle with anxiety. Like a crawling under the skin.

Immediately I wanted to say sorry to the kids. I immediately felt a lot of shame, and addressing the shame was difficult. It takes a long time to address shame, or it does for me. It's not instantly gone. I had to work on my recovery program daily, and I did a step-down relapse prevention program about twelve weeks in. I went back to the rehab centre three times a week and eventually knocked it back to once a week. I also joined a twelve-step fellowship, and that in itself opened me up to various messages. As the saying goes within the program: principles not personalities.

If we're not prepared to look at how we judge ourselves, we'll start judging others.

All that time and energy I'd spent using or chasing drugs now had to be spent on recovery. It was extremely uncomfortable, because there was still a lot of anger aimed at me. And I had to figure out what anger was real and what anger was masquerading as something else. Deciphering that difference is difficult.

We could really feel that this huge load of emotion had built up in the house, and there was no longer enough room – a big fricken house, but you've got such an emotional charge over this person that you can't be anywhere near them. For us, everything was really covert – until it exploded.

You really need to be apart for a while, to figure yourselves out, to become yourself again. But that decision was very scary. It was initiated by Lisa. She decided to leave home; she'd made her mind up to go and get her own space in order to understand herself. She could see that I was committed to recovery, but she still didn't trust me at all. A lot of people didn't trust me at that point. I sensed that. Why would they want to? This guy's been gypping us.

At some point Lisa and I had become spiritually divorced. That's what addiction had done to us. I'd destroyed her ability to know who *she* was – I'd done that much damage. For her to discount her intuition, undo her voice and muzzle it … In the end she didn't know what she was thinking. It must have been a relief for her once she figured it out, because I'd played so many games at such a subtle level.

It was so abusive and a really horrible thing to do. But that's what happens when you forget you're human, and you forget the other person is human too. It was really sad to recognise that.

So our marriage could not survive in the light of recovery. And I didn't know who I wanted to be with in any case. I'd lost myself.

It took us a while to work through it, and even through this apparent dysfunction we had enough respect for each other – we'd been through enough in our lives together – to know we had beautiful children and we needed to work for them here, not for us. Take care of ourselves in order to take care of them. (I don't like to say things are dysfunctional, because I think things are pretty much where they are, and sometimes things have to get to really tough in order for you to heal, so nothing's out of place.)

But things were really nasty there for a bit and it was difficult for Jenna, Mimi and Grace; they didn't know what was going on for Mum. It was hard for Lisa to express how she was feeling, and I didn't know how to do it – we were like young kids ourselves.

There were so many times that I felt like getting in my car and driving off. *See ya, you can have the lot. See ya.* That was my normal way of behaving. But I stuck with the program and worked through it, doing the suggested things, and listening. I started to really listen in rehab and in the meetings, and around that six-month mark there was a kind of a crescendo.

I was travelling still and trying to manage all this new stuff with the kids. I was cooking, doing all the domestic chores. Lisa just said, You do it. I've had enough of this. I'm out of here. You deal with what I've had to deal with. It was a hard time, fronting up each day, learning how to take care of my duties at home, learning how to back up in an office, doing it sometimes under a lot of anger and bitterness and sadness.

I was given a couple of tasks to do at work that were completely out of my league. I didn't know how to put together things. I was asked to help with the company's surfboard program, which I still find completely baffling. I haven't got any square answer about it. Chris Athos was running retail and he was my point person. We'd already known each other for a while and had a good relationship going. Because he'd had experience with people in addiction and recovery, he was good to talk to, and we became friends through it. Rob Brown was working in retail as well, and he was another good companion.

Going to an office every day, trying to give my input into the surfboard program and working from a desk proved to be a gift at the time, and I was excited to get out of the house and into the rhythm of something completely new. But a lot of the time my anxiety built up inside the office, and I struggled to understand what I was doing, what sort of difference I was making. I was still caught up in the notion of instant gratification. Why wasn't anyone taking notice? It takes a while to balance out. I'm still pretty unbalanced, actually, running hot in those corporate environments with people.

There were other commitments. I started doing market research, going out to stores all around Sydney. That was interesting; going out west, going into stores, talking about the product, getting feedback for the marketing department, things like that. I did that through the winter of 2008 and filed a number of reports. It meant some very uncomfortable trips out west, driving around Sydney and getting lost, being reminded the whole time of using. I'd get lost in thoughts of running away: that this might be a good time to escape. But at the same time I humbled myself to the task, approaching sales staff, being told the manager's not here, come back in half an hour. Talking to managers who were just not interested and developing other relationships, which I could see was very important for me in rekindling my ability to make connections with people.

A ha ha ha. I can't help it. You. Working in an office. It's too good. The rest of the Newport boys are a bit baffled by what's happened. But they love this, just the incongruity of it – Tom, the golden god, finally stuck doing the same shit everyone else has been doing for ever. Working for a living.

In the end, I suppose, we laugh about it because we can. There is space to laugh about you again. There's been nothing to laugh about for a while.

Not long after you get out of rehab – you clean and me still on crutches – we take a drive together up to the Northern Suburbs Crematorium and visit our mother and sister. Janet and Jo are both there, their ashes behind plaques in the curving brick walls of the crematorium's big garden.

The day is sunny, but the seasons are changing already, toward the epic autumn of 2007, when the surf will rip away at the beaches of Sydney in a way it hasn't since we were little kids back in 1974.

We sit on the grass near Janet and Jo, and talk about things, and don't talk about much really – just sit there, with the knowledge of what's happened, and with the novel sensation of it being knowledge easily held. The heat and secrecy gone from it. Of our lives at last being spoken openly between us.

I'm not sure if I'll ever surf again, or if your career will survive, but for the first time in nearly forty years, it almost doesn't matter.

People sometimes ask how I'm going, which is nice. But I don't think people in a busy world really want to go there. It's dealing with the emotional and spiritual in a physical world, and it's a confronting place to go. It's brushed aside a bit, like, Well he *looks* like he's doing well. It's good to see him doing well.

But the fact is not many people are approaching themselves in the way I have to approach myself in order to keep my recovery going. Sometimes I want to share it. And because I'm more engaging now, because I can just be right there with people more, rather than flying all over the place like I used to, I think people just come to me naturally. The recognition is subtle, but it's there. Quite often it doesn't need to be said.

The people who really supported me – Craig Stevenson, Pierre Agnes – they'll ask me how I'm doing, how I'm getting along, and however hardcore they are in their own pursuits, they've got that human understanding and can hear my honest answer. For that I'm really grateful. Because they all could have just completely written me off. And I'm sure under the strain of relapse, they might. People relapse all the time and there's no guarantee about anything, and they've all seen it, the vulnerability of the spirit when it comes to addiction – we're fickle.

I came out of all this by the hair on my chinny chin chin. I had no fucken say in it, really, other than that I dove through the window when I did. I dove through it because I knew it was passing. I watched my first sponsor go out and try and neck himself. I know how close that can be.

But that life force is there in us, and it wants to keep going. It's relentless yet so fragile at the same time.

It's like our bodies. Our bodies are constantly trying to heal. We're always trying to be alive. Try to kill yourself now.

Try to drown yourself in the bath. Try to get a knife and start hacking at your aorta. Everything in you will resist it. There's so much resistance to death. It's all about life and rebuilding. And however pessimistic we want to get, the underlying truth is that it's all about maintaining and growing and helping and nurturing. All of this going on underneath and there's so much power to it. Where there's an opportunity, even through all the shit, there's life.

Part five

A Way Back Out

'I think sincerity, most importantly. Being who you are, and what you are … It's a much stronger thing than to try and be someone else. Bugger the vocabulary, bugger everything … If it comes from the heart it doesn't matter.'

–TC, *Surfing Life*, 1994

It's pretty easy for me to put a travel bag together. I've got a little formula. It's just my backpack, with my camera and my computer and passport and wallet and diary. I pack a jumper for the plane so I don't freeze my arse off. A pair of comfy long pants, comfy shoes, a T-shirt. And one small bag with one or two changes of gear – that's it. And my toiletry bag. That's not minimal, but I can go for a while on that. I can go for a long time. Weeks. I can really collect stuff when I travel, so off-loading as I go is really important, but I always like to bring a couple of bits and pieces back, especially for Grace. It's nice for her to get something that feels like it's from another planet, which it does to her. It creates a dream in her to move. It's cool to see that in her. She's got an eye to travel.

December, 2011. North Shore surf season. You and Ross Clarke-Jones have acquired a rental house at Mokuleia, just off the Farrington Highway on the quiet coastline west of Haleiwa, out of the way of the scene. A week or so after you two have settled in, I fly over to join you, to begin the conversations that will eventually result in this book.

Around midmorning I drive down the snake road from the airport, vaguely recalling the story about your first trip here as a sixteen-year-old, trying to drive a third-hand rental wagon down this road alone in the dark, and how unsurprising it seemed at the time. Crazy days, long past.

The house is down a dusty beachfront street and a long driveway that leads out onto a lawn with a view of a lagoon – more Tahitian than Hawaiian.

I can see Ross out surfing a playful small right not far down the lagoon. You're off somewhere; getting new surfboards, probably. That's something that hasn't deserted you in the new era of recovery: the TC luck with surfboards. The pure good fortune of having people throw new boards at you constantly.

Ross comes up the beach, shaking off water and carrying one of your latest acquisitions, one of two from a Rhode Island-based architect named Kevin Cunningham, who in his spare time hand-makes chambered wood craft with these extraordinary intricate internal wood frames, laminated within thin hardwood sheets and fine-glassed into place. The work involved in these two boards I can't even imagine, yet Kevin's just … sent them to you, after a chance meeting at a California surfboard show.

The wood boards join the Barons, two new hand-shaped and light-glassed performance stand-up paddleboards from Blane Chambers, and two new guns from Hawaii's master shaper Pat

Rawson, including a massive super-gun for the next Eddie event and a beautiful 8'1" thing for Sunset Beach.

Ross is giving up cigarettes – well, to be precise, he is reading about giving up cigarettes. He tells me, 'Tom reckons you thank god you don't smoke anymore.' He's right.

I watch you both, this strange pair, wildly different yet very alike. You very neat, a precise packer of bags, rolling your T-shirts up into tight cylinders so as to fit them into the backpack more cleanly, thriving on a certain evenness and precision in your daily affairs. Ross, however, scatters things in his wake uncaringly; a few days later, when he decides to head back home to Australia, nothing interferes with the urge – boardshorts are left behind on washing lines, food in the refrigerator, rental car receipts on tables, all at the mercy of his impulses.

You, left behind once again in the RCJ whirlwind, mutter to yourself, shaking your head as you check through the receipts, fold the shorts neatly and leave them as a surprise gift for the next tenant, wonder what to do with the food. 'He's always like this,' you say.

So different yet so alike: both younger brothers, both lost your mothers early in life, both bound together inextricably by the mad circumstances of your friendship.

Something about Ross reminds me of Twemlow. There's no transaction here, no expectations. He's just your mate.

One morning we go down to Sunset and surf solid ten- to twelve-foot waves all morning, more or less by ourselves, just in a spirit of play. You take the new Rawson 8'1" and promptly snap it in two almost exactly similar pieces.

On the way back to Mokuleia we stop for a while to watch the second round of the Pipeline Masters. Kelly is surfing, along with several others. We spend a couple of hours in the front yard of Quiksilver's primo front-row house directly in front of Pipeline, where an eclectic band of characters is gathered. The Quik elite: Bob and Annette McKnight, Mark and Helen Warren, Bruce and Janice Raymond, plus some top gun surfers, Reef Macintosh, Mark Healey and others. Herbie Fletcher and his New York artist/filmmaker mate Julian Schnabel, who is wearing yellow-tinted sunglasses because, he says, everything here in mid-Pacific is just too blue. And in a corner of the yard a small collection of fourteen-year-old super grommets mill around, breathing the rarefied air.

It is all costing hundreds of thousands of dollars a week, yet it is oddly grungy and low-key, the way surfing likes to see itself even today, even here in the epicentre, in the house of the Beast itself, the Pipeline.

The surfing is critical, messy, dramatic – everything one would expect. But you're the first to say, 'Had enough?' You're shaken by the imminence of the situation, and by the aura of this place where your biggest moments, the best expressions of your long narrowly focused engagement with surfing, have occurred.

As we drive away, you say to me, 'I don't know when I won't feel that way.'

Maybe next year, I think.

Maybe when you're sixty.

Maybe never.

RESET

At the end of 2007 I was cut in half financially. My compensation at Quiksilver went down and it was a reality check, like everything else I was doing. But it was important to change – to have something structured to do that was new, something I hadn't done before. It caused a lot of anxiety for me at first, especially the first six to twelve months. My mind was running hot.

I was driving off to work, not knowing what to do, not knowing how to structure my day, not knowing who to communicate with or the resources I had to get the job done. There was a lot of help available to me within the company, but I didn't know it at the time. I'd find myself stuck at my desk, very anxious, not knowing what to do.

I was given the task of working on the Quiksilver surfboard brand; looking at ways of developing that for the wholesale departments. Chris Athos, who was heading up the retail program at the time, was working out of the same office, and he also happened to be quite close to me in regard to my recovery. He was keeping an eye on me; he knew what was going on for me and he was awesome support. He had no illusions about what could happen. He gave me a list of things to do to get structure in my day – things I needed to do. All this stuff, this structured work. I felt quite bad about it; I thought, *Am I getting in his way here?*

My mind was still in the Big Things mode – believing that whatever I did had to be big, had to bring big results. I found it extraordinarily frustrating, not getting the big results I expected of myself and other people. My ideas about the surfboard program didn't quite fit the reality, and I didn't know how to voice that clearly, so I'd just run along with what was going on. I wanted to see certain boardmakers involved and get things happening, but there's not a big profit margin in surfboards; for a company like Quiksilver the board program is really a marketing thing, getting the brand closer to actual surfing. As long as I kept it there and didn't get too ambitious about it, it would work, but I was thinking all sorts of things, how to do this and that.

Doing the market research was a bit different. I'd give weekly reports on the marketplace for head office, and it was interesting. Once I relaxed into the job I got a focus and it was a nice feeling getting a job done, completed and handed in, even though I wasn't quite sure how it was actually being used. But the real big thing was that work structure allowed me to get a rhythm at home. For the most part, the girls and I got it together. It was good for me to have all this stuff going on. It was a massive change of lifestyle and helped me understand what other people do in the world.

I just let myself go physically. For a good year or two I had to allow myself to physically fall apart. I didn't have time for it, and I don't think it's very good in the first part of recovery to disappear into physical things; you can use physical training as a kind of addiction.

My body was really haywire. A couple of things were going on for me. The first was that my body was rewiring itself for a clean life. And that takes a while. The body's copped a battering, not only from the drugs but just from responding to life with fear. That doesn't go away quickly. The body's quite tense. Before, I was running on the drugs and adrenalin – either intensely connected or not connected. I hadn't been surfing consciously; it had been super-intense, crazy surfing. I'd have this illusion of connection; I might think I was killing it on the drugs, but in reality, at a moment's notice, my head would be somewhere else. I didn't know if I was Arthur or Martha.

So when I started rewiring both my brain and body, surfing just seemed dull. Timing waves felt hard, and the enjoyment level wasn't up because my brain was trying to come back to its normal endorphin production levels. I'd just fucked up the whole serotonin–dopamine loop. That takes a while to reset. So all of a sudden I was paddling out, feeling engaged again, and my body changed the way it moved: it was stiffer and sore. I was feeling everything. It felt slow and I felt tired out after surfing.

One thing I could do was get a really good, gut-deep laugh going over stuff again, which was really good to feel.

Eventually my body started to respond; surfing began to make it feel good. The surf, the ocean was clearly where I loved to be; it answered me back all the time in a really positive way. That relationship had always been there and it came back.

I still couldn't spend more than an hour or so in the water at a time. Even then, the business of life in general was pretty hectic because I was taking on the responsibilities of life again, which didn't leave much time. But I still had this big idea of my surfing, and I knew I had to change a lot of things. They say in recovery, You're going to have to change everything, and my idea of my surfing had to change too.

Then stand-up paddling came along, and it was a gift; it was perfect for me at that point. I may have struggled getting further into my surfing, but the stand-up paddle surfing was such a challenge. I was a kook! Suddenly I'm on a surfboard and getting knocked over by bits of chop. Me! I can't catch waves anymore, I'm fumbling and falling over the thing, I don't know how to use the paddle, the boards suck ... everything about it sucked!

But I knew there was something in there that I really wanted to get hold of and gain an understanding of. I was okay with being humbled – I'd already been humbled – and that's a perfect place to learn.

I went to Hawaii and there were guys stand-up paddling. I hooked up with Dave Parmenter at Makaha, and Brian Keaulana and Blane Chambers, and Bruce Raymond was starting to do it too. And it was *new*; it had an element of excitement about it and people were genuinely buzzed, whereas surfing kinda seemed like something you do, like breathing or walking down the street. I mustn't have been getting much fulfilment out of it. But this was a whole new way of engaging. All of a sudden I had a new view of the ocean, standing up and looking out at it, trying to time a wave. Because of the new movements involved, because it was a whole new way of surfing, it ignited that insane intensity, the intensity you need in order to learn something at a certain skill level, and I was back in this very enthusiastic space.

It was perfectly, subtly new and in its own nasty way a real challenge to the body. It was the right time for me – physically, mentally, spiritually. It woke me up and got me more engaged with the ocean again. I was driving around with all these big boards and paddles, trying to paddle out on big days, surfing out on the edge of the Path, and I'd come in euphoric, physically spent. It took a while for my body to gain the stamina to deal with it and follow through with technique and style.

The early winter of that year explodes into huge storm surf, tearing at the beaches, exposing sand layers buried for over thirty years – before Newport Plus, before the Pro Junior, world titles, fame and glory, drugs, marriages, kids, the lot.

It forces us into the ocean, me wrestling strength back into my healing leg, you, well, just wrestling. You've got hold of this huge three-and-a-half-metre tandem board designed by Laird Hamilton – Laird! The comic book Superman of surfing – and a single paddle on a long stick, and you're trying to bash your way out through the shorebreak at every opportunity.

The board's so big it barely fits on the roof of your car. You can't even get your arm around it. You hoist it onto your shoulder and walk down to the Peak from the platform, a small muscly figure dwarfed by the magnificence of the Laird.

But the bashing slowly becomes something else. I watch you, on a rare smaller, early springish sort of day, paddling just to the side of the Peak, then dropping your knee and swinging in the paddle somehow, and the Laird turns 180 degrees almost on the spot. With two or three quick strokes you're into a wave and away, standing square and poised, something curiously ancient in your stance, like some petroglyph carved into Hawaiian rock. The paddle trails behind, its blade flittering along the surface.

Paddling out, I laugh and yell something at you. You laugh back, and carefully lift the Laird onto another trim line.

Lisa has moved down to Neptune Road, leaving you up there in the house on the hill, and the girls flit back and forth: Jenna pursuing her dance career here and overseas, Mimi tracking along through high school and getting into snowboarding, Grace at Newport Primary, where we once went forty years ago, running on her tough spindly legs around the playground.

The Newport boys aren't sure what to make of this new, drug-free Tom. They like it – they recognise those bits and pieces of you returning, the Gobbo Resurfacing – but it challenges their perception of who you'd become. The egotistical super grommet; the humble surf star; the distant furtive character in his car; the weary gentle-eyed stranger who never drinks at parties. What's he gonna turn into now? they wonder. What's next? They settle for bagging the shit out of the stand-up paddling at every opportunity.

Life goes on, oddly enough.

In mid-2007 you get a cold call from a journalist, Annette Sharp, from the Sun-Herald's celebrity gossip page. Somebody's leaked to her about your time in rehab.

And there it is, in the next edition: 'Surfer Tom Carroll In Private Clinic'.

Oh shit, I think, *here we go*.

Yet even more oddly, nothing much happens. Yeah, you're not some chintzy reality TV star; surfing isn't striving for the mainstream, the way we'd tried to do in the 80s. But beneath that, within surfing itself, I begin to understand the strength of the goodwill toward you – the surfing world throwing a cloak around its champion in a time of need. Payback in a way, for all the years being Little Tommy, for the Snap Heard Round the World and all it's cost you.

~~

I'd completely tuned out the media. I'd quit looking at newspapers, quit looking at TV, kept to my routine during the day and really practised it. It was a big thing for me to do and gave me a lot of relief, and when I got stuck I could refocus my mind more easily. I didn't look at surf media, I didn't look at anything.

Then the call came. I remember being on the phone to her, thinking, *I can't talk to this girl again.* Thank God I didn't.

It was a really fragile time. I had to accept that the news would get out one way or another, but I was on a steep learning curve, six months in, about how to deal with recovery in the outside world. It's fricken frightening. It's such a dicey process and chances of recovery are slim at best. In treatment I'd heard that early recovery takes two and a half years, and I just shit myself; I couldn't imagine that I'd ever get there.

When you're in that fragile space, you either want to tell everyone everything, or sink into yourself, backward into your darkness. You can't get a gauge on your energy. You'll either overdo it or underdo it. The sickness will try to find you again.

My first reaction was to tell the world, but all my close contacts who were helping me in recovery just said, Say nothing. We're here. And Nick and Dad were saying, Don't give this journalist any oxygen at all, because she'll just blow on it.

In the end it was all just part of the learning curve. It wasn't like I'd had press outside the rehab room, knocking down the doors. And the surf media was really, really good, and I appreciate that. There was respect given to me during a really difficult time. I said to them, I want to keep it private for now, and they allowed me to do that. They didn't need to. They could have gone to town on me.

Once that article came out, I started to see people at another level, for who they really are. But I didn't lose anyone who I'd regarded as a friend. Some friendships have deepened as a result of me coming home. If I decided to go back into those ways, all that would go. It takes a long time to get that trust back, and you don't truly get it back.

I remember one time, being a few months clean, when I was down in Victoria and walked into the Quiksilver surf shop, and Tony Ray was working there. I was feeling really present and in myself, in my body. T-Ray saying, Hi, Tom, I haven't seen you in a while.

He had an inkling of something, wasn't sure what, and I told him all of what had happened, and he said, Wow, Tom, it feels like I've met you for the first time. I'll never forget it. I was really touched by that, because it was a real, sincere acknowledgement of where I'd come to at that time. It was a subtle message that I was in the right spot and to keep doing it, keep being who I am.

Genuine feedback like that is really lovely. I've had to learn how to give that same feedback to people myself. I used to not be able to, wondering, *Ooo, am I saying the right thing here?* But now, I see it's just simple. Being present with people. Being here.

THE STEPS

The meetings are everywhere, if you choose to attend them. They're in Avalon, Dee Why, Maroubra, Mona Vale, Los Angeles, Honolulu, and you're at one every couple of days. You go off to them, sometimes happily, sometimes a bit grimly, like someone off to a job they don't like very much at all.

I'm not sure what's occurring in this other world you're embracing, where I haven't gone. I sense it's good for you, but it doesn't seem to be bringing you much in the way of joy.

Not willing to invite myself to one of these meetings, I read, look and listen instead. Plenty of people have attended, it seems. Many of our mutual acquaintances. Some people are openly contemptuous of the Steps. Others are dismissive. Still others write it off as religion lite. Hunter, who's been to some AA meetings, says he can't stand the self-righteousness.

Underneath it, I get the feeling they're all shit-scared. And looking at the Steps, I can see why. Admit we're powerless.

Surrender our will. God as we understand him. Searching and fearless moral inventory of ourselves. Admit the nature of our wrongs. Become willing to make amends. Who does that stuff? By choice?

A lot of people, as it turns out. Murray Close did; that's how he performed the magic with me. You do.

When I first read the twelve steps on the wall of a meeting, I thought I could do them just by reading them. You know: I've got that, no worries, I've got that bit, I don't understand this bit so I'll ignore it, but I've got this other bit nailed.

In the twelve-step process we're posed questions that we wouldn't normally ask ourselves. I call it a program but basically it's a path, of questioning and answering, and sharing the process with someone who's done it. They say the first three steps are about getting a relationship with a higher power, the second three are about getting a relationship back with yourself, the third three are about getting relationships with others right, and the fourth three are about maintenance, and carrying the message to others so the cycle completes.

Going through the first three steps, it's really about looking beyond ourselves. It's a bloody big ask for a self-centred addict who's been running completely on their own ideas, or who's been using someone, or gauging everything on this one way we want to feel, lacking any faith whatsoever in reality. You're very narrow and self-centred at that point.

In those steps we work through honesty, open-mindedness and then willingness. Honesty in the first step, then open-mindedness to the possibility that something can restore my sanity, because my addiction had certainly driven me insane. And third, we're asked to become willing to hand our life over to the god of our understanding.

At that point I rejected God. The idea of God just didn't work. My idea of God was not particularly healthy.

But it doesn't have to be a person: it's a god as I understand him.

And every step starts with a 'we'. It's everyone working through the steps together. It's not I, me, mine. So once we get to the third step, the last thing you want to do is hand over your will. It's like, Fuck you! I'll do what I want! It's a tricky one and it's asking you to make a decision, and we're not great at making decisions, addicts. We'd rather someone make the decision for us, or do something that manipulates some co-dependent person to make the decision for us. You don't get to stand on your own two feet too much.

But here we have to, to relieve us of our obsessions and compulsive behaviours.

Writing the third step and sharing it with my sponsor at the time was a really strong step. That's where I understood where my will is.

It was my will, my strong will. Back when I was using, I would ask myself, Why are you so weak? You're weak as piss. You keep saying you don't want to do it, but you keep going back. Why are you so piss-weak? But it's our strength of will that keeps us going back. Your strength of will becomes a weapon against you, as opposed to a tool to live life. And you can't see it.

That space where I was able to delete that dealer's number out of my phone? In a really hardened addict, the brain chemistry has changed so much that they've lost any ability to connect with that space. You get an urge and you follow it.

You think about it and you do it. You go back to the animal centre of your brain, the hypothalamus. All day, every thought is a direct response to that. Even if you desperately don't want to do something, you'll do it.

But with the dealer and the phone, there was a momentary gap. And gaining a gap between your thoughts and actions is basically the crux of recovery: rewiring that stuff, reconnecting a few of those things. It's been shown that meditation and reflection, sitting through emotional pain and watching it pass, changes the brain chemistry – it allows that gap for choice to develop. And you can do it, it's evident that you can do it. And there was evidence along the way of that happening for me.

At that point I learned to use prayer regularly with my meditation; the third step prayer, the 'Serenity Prayer', became kind of like a plea from the heart to the universe. That's what it is, for me. Once I had some faith around the recovery process, I could get enough faith to do what we're asked in the fourth and fifth steps, which is to begin a relationship with myself again, making peace with the past and all the shit and the damage, the shame and the guilt.

I noticed in step four, when you write down your resentments, at first you think, *I don't have any resentments! I'm sweet.* Then you start writing them down, and you just think: *Good God, look at how many I have!*

To think that I resented my mother was a really uncomfortable idea. At some level I did. I never wrote it down in the fourth step, but I did see it there. I'll be able to work through it when I'm more prepared. But I can see that it's there.

Making a fearless moral inventory of myself, that's a hard one. That took me a year and a half or so. That level of self-honesty isn't always easy to come by. But it happened, just by sharing and writing stuff down about it, posing those questions that I wouldn't have questioned myself about, in areas I wouldn't have challenged myself.

I've just finished the sixth step, which goes through all the defects and examines the ones that stand out: complacency, avoidance, self-judgement. Things that are just a part of everyone's life but may be more pronounced in some parts of an addict's life. Formally writing down my defects and shortcomings … It took me about two years. Because it's such a long, gruelling step, I put it down for quite a while.

In step seven I'm asked to pray for my defects of character to be removed. The defects have run for many years, and they'll come up in times of stress, when our minds narrow down to only a few options and there's no gap between thought and action. Under stress, our behaviour becomes more acute, more impulsive. For me it can be avoidance, harsh self-judgement, an inability to forgive myself or others. It takes a lot of courage to say, Okay, maybe we can do something different here.

There's been a lot of writing, something which I don't particularly like doing; sitting down and having the patience with myself, for a start. Answering questions I would never think of asking myself, on paper, is a cathartic sort of experience for the soul – talking back to yourself and getting it out. It's completely the opposite of what we do in the outside world. But it's ancient, whatever's going on there.

A fearless moral inventory! Lists of the damages and defects. I picture you, carefully writing things in a book, looking, reading and writing again, enduring the waves of shame and fear and sadness, talking to Murray and others about it, holding on to that hard place in your head.

How far it seems from the ocean, the salt water on skin, the fear and adrenalin, the swift animal responses to movement, the eye cast across light and shadow, the wind, the rhythm of a swell, the moment-to-moment sense of flight across the face of a wave. The ocean, where there is no gap between the thought and the action, where error or fault is eliminated by wipeout, boom! Simple! And then you paddle back out.

I think of the surfers, so many great surfers, who were never able to reconcile the two; for whom the sea was too much and the land never enough. They felt the magic of one place and the dry reality of the other and could never find a balance.

Many of them are past choice now. But how many would choose to go where you're going?

There's no fame in this, no money, no Big Thing; almost nobody even knows you're doing it. You do it anyway, you grind it out, building a foundation for yourself, one day at a time, as they say. But it is all on a fine edge. In October 2010, news breaks of the worst thing ever to happen in professional surfing: Andy Irons, thirty-two years of age, big, strong and the only surfer to have Kelly's true measure, is found dead in a Dallas/Fort Worth airport hotel room by a cleaner.

The medical examiner finds two causes of death: one, heart failure; two, cocaine overuse.

It could've been you, I think. Then the next thought: *Well, people relapse. It* still *could be you*.

I put that aside. I'm not up for that thought.

It was just really really sad for me. I'll never forget how it impacted me and the sadness that's still with me. That humanness and vulnerability was so much on display with Andy. It was so close to things with me at the time, but I didn't expect it to have that impact.

I knew that things were running rough for him. After he won the Teahupo'o event that year, I remember seeing interviews about how he'd just like to win one last event, and I thought, *Huh?* He's only young, he's possibly in the middle of a great comeback if he wants it. He'd made this choice that he'd be happy if he won just one more contest, and when he did, it showed his potential on all those different angles: to either kill himself or become great in his own way.

I was in Hawaii at the time of the ceremony on Kauai, and I had a chance to jump on a plane and go over for it, which I did. I'd been in recovery for a while at that point, sitting in those rooms and hearing all those stories and what goes on, how drug addiction can take us down, and when I heard what was going on for Andy, I was just praying for him. Because that's all you can do.

And I knew that Andy didn't muck around. He did what all hardened addicts do: they use. By whatever means possible. And everyone else get out of the way. You use people and surround yourself with those who let you do it. And there you go, a life just lost. What was a great surfer like him doing dying in a hotel room in Texas? It's just whacked, it doesn't make sense. But that's disease untreated: we find ourselves in places we never ever wanted to go.

After being on Kauai, I was submerged in sadness for about a week, and sometimes despair. But I also had a lot of people close to me. If I didn't have that connection with people, those are the sorts of things can take you down, and there's no telling where you'll go.

I've gotta keep talking about it all. As soon as I go getting quiet about it, shutting up and holding onto my thoughts and ideas, that's the danger.

I know a guy who was fifteen years clean. His drug of choice was heroin. Then he started taking painkillers. He did it for six years, all the way up to twenty-one years, saying he was clean. Taking oxycontin, all that kind of stuff. He moved out of his home, renting it to a guy for a load of money and – *boom* – over the edge. He started using heroin again. I saw him in the middle of it. Holy shit. It took him a while to come back. And he'd helped me a lot.

That's the disease. It's never done.

Then again, I went to this meeting in Waikiki one wet morning. It's called the Twelve Coconuts. It's a really good meeting. The crew, they just come out of the bushes. They don't have our social safety net over there, so some of the crew are nuts. Crazy. It can get pretty wild at times.

There was this local brudda, big guy, hanging in the middle of the room, an umbrella over him. I think he just wanted to be different. He went up front toward the end of the meeting, decided it was his time to share. He had a big Hawaiian voice, full-on local talk, but I could recognise the accent as from the North Shore, aggressive and strong. He'd been sober for many years and he was really solid, right into his baseball and coaching. Stoked! He'd say, At least now I can travel! I can get out of this dump. I've got a whole world to see.

Then I got up and had a share, and I saw his eyes light up. Shit, it's him!

After the meeting he came up and gave me a big, Ho brah! Remember da North Shore! Wild fucken West! Remember all the guys? Mickey Neilsen and Marvin and Junior and all of them!

He was one of those guys, a full survivor, and he was just stoked. He's like, Fuck, we're lucky, brah, we made it.

INDICATIONS OF GROWTH

Lisa and Corky are soon enough an item, but you stay single for a good while. Wary of women, is the real TC; and in any case, it's what your recovery crew has suggested. A relationship may not be a good idea for some time after this process has begun, they say. It can become a way of avoiding yourself.

I have a moment of amusement, remembering Monty tearing his hair out over Elizabeth, when he thought she might get in the way of a world title.

But then a little surprise. Back in 2007, trying to pay for my broken leg, I'd advertised one of my prized Van Straalen ocean racing boards for sale. The buyer is one Mary Graham, part of the small Northern Beaches ocean paddling community. I like Mary. She's graceful and she's tough. She meets me in Newport car park, pays full price for the board and drives off with it on the roof of her neatly kept black Mazda.

Now, two years later, it turns out you've taken her on a date!

Mary Graham, the red-headed New Zealander who can paddle almost quicker than you. That feels like it fits.

December 5, 2009. Near dusk, we sit in a rental car overlooking Waimea Bay from the west, watching a rising swell. It's a calm evening; fluffy light clouds hang suspended between the trade wind and a light sea breeze. The air is warm and humid, softening the dying light so the sands of the Bay look like an Impressionist painting, half in shadow and half aglow.

Very late, after the last surfer has come in, a single line of swell comes in – a line that stretches outside the Bay on both sides.

Then another. The swell angle north of west. We count the period: twenty-one seconds.

The North Shore is buzzing. There's a strange electric energy in the air, clashing with that warm calm sky and the ominous ocean. The Quiksilver in Memory of Eddie Aikau, surfing's greatest event, is on hold for the next day, and the only real question is how big it'll get.

The Eddie. Just the invitation is on any champion surfer's life list. It's run only seven times in twenty-five years. Ross has won it, Kelly, Clyde Aikau, Noah Johnson, Keone Downing, Bruce Irons, and young Denton Miyamura the first year. Never a goofy-footer.

You've been invited every year since 1990 and missed it three times, when family obligations in Newport got the better of last-minute flights to Honolulu. You tried and failed to shake off the resentment at the time. (*I'm being held back!*) Now the resentment's long past, back there in the world before recovery, but the memory of it is still there.

Now you're preoccupied, vague, your mind far away in some place only you truly know, imagining the day ahead. You call people on your mobile phone, then forget you've done so and call them again. I imagine the people on the other end, laughing it off. Typical Tom.

They say Eddie chooses the winner, sends a set wave at the right time to the right person, whoever it is – the person who needs it in his life. I feel a half-forgotten tingle of anticipation from pro tour days long gone. *You've been good*, I think. You've walked the walk. Maybe Eddie will choose you.

The ocean roars through the night with a sound that visits no other coast, a deep *basso profundo* note underneath all the house-shaking booms and crashes. By 6 am it's a grey drizzly morning with a light sideshore wind, and on the main road heading toward Waimea there are cars. Everywhere. The sides of the Kamehameha Highway are clogged from Log Cabins on down, a distance of two miles from the Bay. People are trudging through the drizzle, backpacks on, folding chairs under arms, heading for the Bay.

Traffic is locked down. It's madness.

As light filters through the cloud, I meet you in the Waimea parking lot and we walk and jog with giant boards down to the keyhole end of the Bay, watching huge grey set waves explode far off the back of the ledge.

Thinking to get some crazy scoop interviews in the world's heaviest line-up, I stick a waterproof camera in my back pocket. The camera's survived big Teahupo'o, but it doesn't even survive the trip through the Bay shorebreak.

Putting a size on the surf seems a bit silly. It's big enough to close out on the real set waves. That means twenty-five feet plus, but it's jagged and thick, the coast reverberating with its impact, clouds of spray rising between the line-up and the land. Out there in that incredible surf zone, you, Ross, Shane Dorian, Kelly, Sunny Garcia and a few others – the surfers inured to adrenalin – separate from the pack and hunt these jagged colossal waves, that tell-tale glitter in your eyes.

It's easy to lose track of each other on days like this, so after a couple of hours I'm only vaguely surprised to realise I haven't seen you for forty minutes.

An innocuous fifteen-footer has heaved unexpectedly, landed clean on top of you and driven your left leg sideways against the board. Your ankle bends until it can't.

Tom Carroll Injury Number – what is it? – Five.

Injuries happen when you're not listening. But that day at Waimea, I can't remember hearing anything. I really wanted to attack it, and I was starting to gain some ground. Then that wave. BAM! Get out of here, little *haole*!

That injury came at a crucial time, when I was feeling pretty good about my surfing. I felt really within myself, more ready to calculate my way through that surf without getting out of my body like I might have done once.

So it was such a shock when it happened. But at the same time I was more prepared for an injury like that than at any other time in my life. From the moment it happened, I was able to surrender and get myself back to the shore and out of danger in a very focused manner. The deltoid ligaments, three ligaments on the inside of the ankle joint, were cleanly severed – a really violent impact, a perfect hit. The ligament in between the bones, the syndesmosis, was also popped clean, and then there was the broken fibula. So it was all flopping around.

The injury was so severe that I couldn't walk. I was sitting up there on the ridge of sand above the shorebreak in the corner of the Bay, looking at my foot, and when I moved a muscle in my calf, the foot would just fall off the bottom of the leg. I must have gone into shock because there was no pain. It allowed me this really clear realisation that I was completely and utterly stuffed.

The lifeguards came over with the ATV, and straightaway I felt incredibly supported. I still didn't have any pain, however they asked me many times if I wanted to stick painkillers into me. I never felt like I wanted any. Any time I've had that stuff it hasn't really taken the pain away; it's just distracted me and taken my mind off into this fuzzy, blurry space, which is not what I enjoy.

But I felt supported, even down to the uncanny phone call I got in the emergency ward at Wahiawa from Dr Steve Nolan in Sydney, who had direct connections with Kim Slater, the ankle surgeon in Australia, to advise the doctor in Wahiawa what to do.

I got to watch the Eddie next day, and by then I had enough surrender on board that I wasn't cursing. I was happy to watch the event and calmly go through it.

Back in Australia, there were bits and pieces floating around in the joint, but Dr Slater cleaned everything up. He said the cleaning process in between the joint during surgery is key to a quick recovery. Any debris or excess blood can be sucked out at the time and cleaned up. Then he stuck one big screw through the bones to pull the syndesmosis together.

One good thing about recovery was that I'd learned how to sit still, so I could sit down and allow the thing to heal, give it time. I don't think back in the day I'd have been able to do that – all hell could have broken loose.

The doctor said to me, Well, this is healing up really well; you don't drink any alcohol, do you?

I said, No, I don't drink.

And he goes, That makes such a big difference to what I see in the healing process.

The fact was, there were other things going on in my life that I needed to slow down and take note of, and the injury was a gentle way of saying, Sit down, Tom, shut up and look at this. It was gentle compared to what could have happened. And it was also about learning how to reach out for help. I was on crutches, I had no driver's licence for six months – all my old speeding fines had caught up with me – and it was all about sitting down, asking for help and allowing people to help me. I had to let people drive me around. I found it so uncomfortable then, and I still don't find it easy now at all.

An injury like that could be viewed as a curse, or it could be seen as a series of little gifts nudging me in a certain way to learn a lesson, and I chose to take that route.

But it would have been a great Eddie to surf in. It was the best Eddie ever.

I think *Storm Surfers* was something that kept me in touch with the side of me that I can't kill off.

About a year after I got clean, there was a chance to do an episode, and I was honestly thinking about pulling out of the whole thing because I thought it was potentially very dangerous for me and my recovery to keep engaging in this shit. Encouraging that adrenalin-based life. I remember talking to Kelly Slater about it, telling him, I don't know if I should do this adrenalin stuff with Ross, going crazy. Is this really what I should be doing?

I knew that now there would be no escaping my feelings, because I'd been focusing so strongly on feelings in recovery – identifying them, naming them – and that's different to the way you view things like surfing crazy waves.

I almost quit. I was so close to saying no. But something must have shifted in me. Instead I went, Nah, I'm going back out for more.

I know it's dangerous with Ross – life's dangerous with Ross. But I really did feel that it might be okay because I'd been so trained in engaging with the ocean every which way and being with Ross in those conditions. We'd done it for many years and we'd never used drugs in that heavy surf. We weren't like the Santa Cruz boys, getting on the gear and going out at Mavericks. We'd do it clean and clear, we were just mad. We both loved being in those situations and sharing it between us.

For a while I stayed worried about re-engaging that adrenalin. But Lisa Chapman, my therapist, helped me understand something about it. She said, Tom, you can't afford NOT to engage in these circumstances. You HAVE to. It's gonna save your arse. She helped me see it's a little like Dr Jekyll and Mr Hyde; there's a distinction between being Mr Hyde 24/7 and choosing it, saying, Okay, it's appropriate now to be Mr Hyde for a while.

That's the distinction I started to make. I started to understand the energy involved. What I was dealing with was essentially an energy question: how much energy was I going to give to this thing as opposed to that thing? I take Kelly as an example. What I love watching in him, what I'm inspired by in him, is his masterful ability to use energy: what he gives and what he holds back, where he puts it and where he doesn't, where he concentrates. I think that's the mark of a very successful person, the choices they make about where they put their energies. I see that in myself. When I'm not sure who I am in a situation, my energy's all over the place. I give too much or I give too little, or I sink inside myself. It's a tricky thing.

But that choice to keep on with *Storm Surfers* was a real marker to me. How much energy do I want to give to this? I can actually be aware of how much I give to this, and that was part of the awareness that came with being clean and clear. I had to be aware that there'd be ups and downs, there'd be fuck-ups, and it can be really intense with all the crew. I thought, *Well, I'm up for the lessons again.*

And it was Ross's show anyway. I was just along for the ride. I discovered that it didn't have to be a Big Thing. I didn't want to take some big deal role in it. I just wanted to go out there and explore myself.

So we took the opportunity to do *Storm Surfers* for the Discovery Channel. We did Shipsterns and Dangerous Banks, and one session at really clean Cow Bombie, and New Zealand. It was really nice to work again with Ross, Justin and Chris, and the whole crew, walking in with a totally different mindset but also re-engaging with that old part of me. Justin and Chris really supported me, and they were there to create, whatever happened. I mean here we were at the most ridiculous surf spots in the world, where nobody else would ever want to go, and getting amongst some of the most mad people you'll ever meet.

It was super uncomfortable at times. I was physically strong enough to do it, I wouldn't say I was in perfect physical shape, but I was in shape to make decisions, and I started making better ones. I was in front of a camera, where I'd normally have done whatever came up, but this time I was able to say, I'm not going to do this. I'm not going to go.

Whatever I was learning in recovery was coming out in the world.

The way *Storm Surfers* eventually played out was completely and utterly honest. Yeah, there's some silly stuff in there, but it's quite lighthearted and genuine. It's just us. It's pretty simple.

Ross has always been interested in my recovery, watching me go through all these changes, thinking, *What the hell is going on here?* Though I think it really frustrates him, my slowness on land, and my apparent airy-fairyness. For him it's really super frustrating when I take my time getting things ready, or sit and meditate. Ross is my biggest lesson. It's the perfect relationship for me to be able to draw the line and say who I am, because it becomes dangerous otherwise. We're out there doing ridiculous stuff, and sometimes it's a real challenge and frustrating. It's not always awesome, by any means. I frustrate him no end.

We did five weeks straight of promotion for *Storm Surfers 3D*. Forty-four screen presentations – sometimes three times a night. Ross and I could not have got through that together in the past. There's no way! We wouldn't have had the capacity to deal with it.

I think a lot of my energy was misguided when I was world champ, trying to be someone other people wanted me to be. I was in front of so much media that I was overwhelmed. I'd be so sensitive to it! I used to get up in front of audiences to collect my trophy, on a podium or whatever, and they'd give me the microphone: Say something, Tom! And I'd go … *guck!*

I literally didn't know what to say. And what I did say would come out so opposite to what I was thinking. Even I'd be wondering, *What the fuck was THAT?*

I still say really stupid things. I start thinking I'm supposed to weigh in on something I'm not qualified to talk about. It just comes up. It's ridiculous. Absurd shit. But I've learned now – you're only qualified to talk about *this*, Tom. You don't have to be big. You don't have to be someone else.

When I'm sitting on stage with Ross, and Ross is going *yahh yahh yahh*, I don't have to dive in and be something in that situation. I can play around, but something's guiding me now. I don't have to be anything more than I am. I don't have to *do* anything. And I've got more energy to give as a result. I'm a lot more available.

And we got through the five weeks. I got through it and I was breathing at the end of it! I was breathing, I was alive, and I could still talk to people. That was cool. I'm so glad I followed through with *Storm Surfers*. If I'd shied away from it at the beginning for fear of it, I may not have found out I could do it. If I sit in a comfort zone – which I can – and feel safe, I'm not challenged, and I don't think there's much growth in that. It's another way of becoming more brittle, more sensitive, instead of loosening up and allowing stuff to flow. The more I'm exposed to those challenges the better.

VARIOUS PAGES TURNING

The last time I was with all the world champs was during a Legends heat at a Quiky Pro in Queensland a year ago. We had a fairly gentlemanly kind of surf, but it still came out, the froth. The boys were rabid, keen to get the inside. I bit into it – I'm guilty as anyone.

Then Cheyne accused me of taking his wave! I guess I did. I paddled up the inside of him and took the wave. He was very serious – Cheyne can be very serious – and he was very serious about it in the changing rooms. It was all time. I really didn't notice it; I thought I was just getting a wave.

That was the first time I had a little bite at surf competition when it felt stupid; it didn't feel like me anymore. It felt teenage.

But I noticed the urge was still very strong for Cheyne. And Rabbit. And Pottz! Pottz is very competitive. He loves it, gets right into it. He could actually probably still compete.

There's a bit of a showman in me. I think to become a

world champion you have to have some showman in you. Just to start off with, to ride that many waves, to get that damn good at riding waves, to get to know the ocean that well, to actually win that many times over a specific period, to win against every other surfer who's chosen to compete for the world title – you've got to have something happen in order to be driven in that way. It's not an average thing to do, to go out and develop this skill. And it is a skill. You can have all the talent in the world and you won't become a world champion. That's why there's so much conjecture around it.

There's so-called enigmas like Tom Curren, but it's all bullshit because Tom loves putting on a show. Look at him now – he still wants to compete. It's fantastic. Michael Peterson, he loved it, being on stage. He made out he didn't, and of course it would have been uncomfortable for him, but each of us has got that showman in us. Damien Hardman, you'll never get an answer out of him, but he loves it too. At some level, if you dig around long enough, you'll find that little chuckle in him. It's there, he loves it, even though he'll do everything he can in his Narrabeen sort of way to tell you it isn't. He can't get away from it.

But to become an incredible competitor you need to have something occur to focus the mind. The people I share most with in that respect are probably Kelly and Barton Lynch. I've shared a little bit with others but those two have been the closest ones. They've been really supportive and I've felt fully understood.

With Barton it was really cool because we've been good mates through a mad time in our lives. We weren't good mates at all during competition – he disliked me intensely, thought I was on steroids once – but he's been really respectful of what I've passed through. It's been cool watching him shift in his way. He really changed himself after he stopped competing, letting go of the competitive bitterness and opening up to new things. I'm glad he got a world title. The world benefited from that, and from what he does now with his coaching and consultancy work.

Pottz has been good. Everyone understands at their own level what's going on with it and with me.

Kelly's been really cool. He's had his own stuff going on, of course, he's had more world titles than anyone, and he's done an incredible job of getting the highest performance out of himself. He's so self-absorbed because of the path he's taken, but it's been a big thing for him to be able to reinvent himself and apply himself as an athlete. A person who's not as emotionally aware and willing to grow would have fallen apart a long time ago. He's constantly challenging everybody who comes up to him, and he loves it, thrives on it. It's exhausting to think about, but he makes it look almost easy. It's awesome to see that level of mastery. I'd be distracted and want to do other things, but he seems to be able to stop surfing for months then come back and win contests.

For me, it was always a struggle to sort the bullshit out. But it's been good to share with Kelly what's been going on in my life. He's got a lot of awareness around it, his father being an alcoholic. And he's always looking for growth.

My old Newport friends are still there. I can talk to them about stuff and we get to share surfing from time to time. We've been sharing that gratitude we have for being able to surf and enjoy our lives, and we often say that surfing has helped us stay healthy and connected. Me and Squeak talk about that, and Kev and Boj. There's no doubt we have a lot of respect for each other, but it's not suffocatingly close. We're not in each others' face.

And we know each other really well. We're past the

judgements; the judgements are there and set in stone. To dissolve them now would be nearly impossible. They'll have a chuckle about me, then we'll have a chuckle about someone else … you know, funny old men's stuff. We know how Boj is gonna respond to this; we know how Squeak's gonna respond to that; Kev does the other thing; I do things – there's a great common thread. They know me better than anyone.

You don't just 'get to know' people like that. Everyone shifts and moves around in our culture, but we've lived in the area, had families and handled all these big changes in our lives, yet we still get to have an opportunity to reignite those relationships as we go. Like, Kev's gonna come round in half an hour and help me with a bit of house maintenance, and Boj did the electricity, and Squeak did the plumbing, and I can help them out with surfboards and equipment.

Or I can just drop in on them to stoke the flame of the relationship. That's a quick way of doing it.

When I was in a bad place, in the pit, I was particularly dislocated from them. I wanted to be. I didn't want them to see me that way. I couldn't get honest with those guys. I needed to go to a place where I could be with people who had suffered the same disease. I couldn't gain recovery around my old friends. It doesn't work that way. You can't start that inner journey in those familiar situations and have some kind of success without turning back to addiction of some sort.

But they didn't know what was going on because I was completely distant and acting really weird. It must have been frightening for them at some level. I really get a lot out of hearing what they see now, compared to what they saw or felt from me before. It really helps. Just little things, the smallest comment, can ignite that warm feeling and appreciation for a friendship.

You know your friends; you've lived through their bad behaviour. It's like brother stuff. Nick and I, we know each other so fucken well. We're gonna be the harshest and most acute judges of each other till the day we die.

With my old business partners, it's actually matured into a very respectful space for me. Bruce Raymond's retired now and pretty much does what he wants – he's been getting into painting a bit. I really enjoy going for a surf with Bruce; he and I have had a nice connection through Hawaii for many years. Over the past few years we've spent time together over there and reconnected after all the stuff he had to go through, stepping away from Quiksilver. That was his life's work.

I see John all the time, and he's still the same guy – just as intense but much healthier. Bruce and John both look a lot fitter physically and they seem more at peace with themselves. John doesn't have a big company to deal with anymore and he's a one-man show, and to some degree Bruce is too. It was quite interesting being in between such high-powered human beings.

John still has that thing where he wants to see me okay. I engender that in some guys – I dunno what it is. Maybe it goes back to him selling sausages to Nam, and seeing me as this little freckly kid, and me and the boys down the Peak, and letting us drive his Mini up and down the car park as fast as we could. I wouldn't change any of that shit at all.

I've grown curious again about Mum. I thought it was amazing from Nick's research that she'd had some issues with amphetamines – amazing to find that her pathology reached for the same expression. So it was in me. When I heard that, it helped me a lot in my recovery. I knew then that I had a disease that was in me and I'd woken it up. It was something I could pinpoint, and I could commit to my recovery then.

I think about it. In the Bible they talk about eternal life, and that's what it is – that's eternal life, right there. The memories in the body passing on, the carried behaviours, the carried shame, the carried joy, carried from generation to generation through contact, and it lived through me. It's eternal. It'll keep going through the girls and through their kids, on and on. I imagine people who don't understand who their parents are, or who don't know their parents, must find the world a very confusing place.

But I didn't go prying into it. I didn't want to know all the details. Maybe it wouldn't be a bad idea, one day. To some degree, I might understand my relationships with women.

There's some underlying thing that stops me from connecting with women, from coming out from behind the wall and saying, Here I am! It's a real struggle for me to be fully there for a woman. You can't just say, Oh, *that's* it! and fix everything. You can only take slow sure steps in coming forth and being present in a relationship. That's the only way I get to learn about myself, rather than running back behind the wall. Like anything to do with the heart, there's nothing practical about it.

To some degree I'm still that seven-year-old kid who hides behind the wall, not quite sure what that woman's gonna do. Is she gonna scream at someone? Is she gonna have a crazy argument with her mother? Is she gonna *die*?

I certainly don't want to go back to the emptiness that I felt back then. That long, elongated emptiness. It seemed to stretch out forever.

That space that was created especially for surfing, especially for the ocean. Custom-cut for the ocean, wallowing in it, being pounded by it, getting spun around and cracked open.

Three or four months after I got that first Coolite, Mum died. So instantly a space was created for that intense relationship with the ocean. It would have been a real sketchy business having someone like me growing up without the hand of Mother Ocean.

Even today it's tricky getting a hug out of Dad. He'll try to push you away. Last year he gave me an elbow! It was all time! But then he'll grab you round the shoulders. He's just not touchy; he didn't grow up with the value of a warm embrace. But I was naturally touchy and cried out for a warm embrace, and he finally came around.

I dunno what goes on for Dad when I do that sort of thing. I think it must rock his logical, practical mind. But it's been really lovely being able to be clear and honest and see how, even at his age, he moves and grows. It's nice seeing his heart open up and say things like, I'm really pleased for you, it's so good this has happened, you've done really well. It really confirms what I've done and affirms my journey, which I'd say from a father to his son, is probably the strongest message that underlies our existence. Having that affirmation: you're on a good path. And you're doing well. You're a man now. I need that sort of thing from my father at times when things are shaky.

When Dad has those little open moments, he really lets me have it, and it's really beautiful. We can sit there in a fair bit of silence, Dad and me, and it's really comfortable.

He's in a good space, Dad. He's not embittered. The only thing he worries about is someone intruding on his space or treating him like an old age pensioner. He's got a really strong will in that respect. I see that Dad likes his quiet space, and I notice I really strive toward that now, where I might not have recognised that part of myself before. It's become more important.

The older I get, the more I'm like Dad. By the time I'm eighty-seven I'll be completely over the drama I get with all my girls. I'm frozen like a deer in headlights with fatherhood sometimes – I want go upstairs and be in my own space and not deal with it, because a lot of it doesn't make sense to me. I try to make sense of it, but sometimes it's an incredible struggle and I get nowhere.

So I see myself going quiet, giving two- or three-word answers that are really practical. I can hear Dad's voice; he always has practical answers to situations. And when the girls are wigging out around me, I hear Dad's voice inside. It's not mine.

And it is more like his old message, these days: slow and steady wins the race. It's more like that all the time.

It's probably tricky for the girls. I had a lot of masks on; I didn't show them much of myself. It was all covert. They didn't really see the real Dad until probably a year or so into recovery. It was a tricky time for them, coming into teenagers. I think ultimately it's been quite scary at times, frightening that Dad's really here – I liked it when he was a bit silly. But there's also some comfort knowing that Dad's really here. I'm imagining this, but this is what I read in them. I sense that it's been a conflicted mix of those two things: fear and comfort. *I can actually ring Dad up, he's there.*

But this disease runs through the family, so there's a tricky underlying tone.

I think they see the potential for themselves to go down this path toward addiction. I look for it too much, because I have this awareness, and it's not always a comfortable awareness to have – that's why we stay in denial. But I know I can't go back, and I've got to be right there with it.

I can't fix anyone. I have to have a lot of patience. Being there with Jenna, especially, through her big changes with the ballet. I know that was a big expression of control for her, an ultimate expression of control – and control is the underlying mechanism of addiction. She and Mimi seem to be pretty good at the moment, they're on their own discovery tour right now, and they know they can come and hang with Dad and talk to Dad about other stuff.

My relationship with Lisa took on new dimensions. It required a lot of patience on both of our parts, and willingness. She's the mother of our children, and she knows that I'm here. We haven't gone too deep. One big element of recovery is making amends to those around us who we may have damaged in some way, and that doesn't necessarily mean making direct amends – I'm yet to step all the way into that.

But I can put that into my life, partly by being here, being present, and being a contributing member of society, not just pillaging.

Grace has been an extraordinary example for me of pure love. Love is something I've made real complicated. I've been fearful of allowing people to love me and fearful of allowing myself to love people. That's shocked me in the past and created a lot of pain, caused me to step away and shrink into a corner. And it's such an important part of our lives – it's one of our basic needs – so when I deny myself it, and cut myself off, active addiction takes all that away. It tears up the relationship with the heart. Grace was my first – and I don't want to pin it on Grace, it's more like my own response to seeing what was available to me in the world. And I think she was a great person to do that with, because she was so bold. She didn't back off. And I was like, Shit I've gotta do something about this.

In essence, I was doing it for my kids at first. I didn't know if I wanted to do it for myself. It takes a long time to regain the connection to the heart; it's a real big journey back to love, the giving and receiving of it. I didn't know what it was. I'd lost it years ago.

Jo. Yeah. That's really sad. Still really sad for me. I've still got quite a bit to deal with, with Jo. It's amazing that it can still have such an impact after all this time. The last time I saw her, when she came and visited me and was really concerned about her situation at work and wanted to have a family, she'd just come out of nowhere. I recalled then that she had a concerned look on her face, because she was concerned about me too at some level. And somehow, through it all, my experience of losing Jo in such an instant, she has stayed with me. It was such an instant parting I feel like she hasn't really gone. She didn't go anywhere.

I remember her being down at the beach the day I first stood up on my Coolite. I remember her laughing. She was cracking up.

I was saying, I stood up for about a minute, Dad!

He said, No you weren't, Tom. You weren't up that long. I was devastated, I thought I'd done better than that. I thought I was up for ages.

She's around. I can't explain it. It's unexplainable. It doesn't make any sense at all. I feel her.

AGE

Things I notice about my little brother at fifty:

He takes photographs of everything. He would almost rather take photos of things than just look at them.

He still drives fast, just not quite as fast.

He appears to be growing, but only sideways; his waist is stouter and his face creased, as if his head has been compressed from above and below in some sort of clamp.

He has a highly refined sense of how to cope with public onsets, and never rebuffs strangers who approach him outright, instead deflecting their attention as suits him with remarkable subtlety. He will nevertheless deliberately avoid public exposure if he feels it may result in inordinate layers of stranger-conversation.

He doesn't like TV.

He drinks coffee but no other thing that might be considered mood-altering. In the parlance of recovery, he is four years clean.

He has a tattoo of a turtle, the wise animal of the Pacific, on the inside of his right biceps.

He has a scar above his right eye from bumping his board while surfing Pipeline in 2007. The cut featured in the girls' surfploitation movie *Blue Crush*. It's his only injury from surfing Pipeline.

He wears fairly strong reading glasses.

Your 50th birthday falls on a Saturday. You've had that big party house on the hill for all that time, and there's hardly ever been a party thrown. So Mary recruits us all to do just that.

You're a bit uncomfortable with the fuss. All these people coming to celebrate you! I think to myself: *He's got no idea, does he.* You're like Dad – you don't know how important you are.

The Saturday is warm and clear, a perfect spring evening. Light nor'-easter, small south swell. The house fills with voices and music. Gifts, plates of food, glasses scattered across tables, people hugging.

I think of the people who are here and who aren't: Mum. Jo. Joe Engel, died of a heart attack in Katherine. Wilbur Fowler, who once knighted us in the order of Newport Locals and who now lies in Mona Vale Cemetery, having taken his own life years ago, run aground on those perilous shoals you're navigating today.

Charlie Ryan, said to be in the Philippines. Dougall and Twemlow, in Queensland. Alan French, the kid who ended up not travelling, up in Scott's Head fishing.

Haley and Hunter and Newling and Boj and Squeak and Kev and Phelpsy are here. Leroy. Bruce. John the Butcher. Lisa, who wasn't too sure about coming, until Mary talked her up. Wendy, and Maddie and Jack, both now taller than both of us. Phil Byrne, who has carried his surfboard label through all the years. Julia, who'd dared to surf with us, the terrible Newport Boys of yore. David Jones, the local legend whose stories of surfing the Path we so badly needed to believe. Billy Wawn, once Josephine's

Wee Willie Winkie, whose youngest daughter, Holly, is now under-16 Australian girls' surfing champ.

Dad, who lives by himself now in a small flat overlooking Sydney Harbour, a little bit frail yet still calm and sharp of eye, still completely our father. Valerie and Annie the wonderful dancer turned writer, and powerful elegant Lucy, and her soon-to-be fiancé Moshe, who has sensibly done the driving from the city.

What they don't know is that soon you'll have to sell this house. It will become part of the divorce settlement with Lisa; you will pay back the bank, clear the debts of the past decade, set the girls up in a flat of their own and, day by day, prepare for a time when you – when both of us, all of us – will finally grow up. Grow old.

You can see surfers disappearing into themselves as they grow older. You see them wandering off to Indonesia or elsewhere around the globe, these Australian male surfers. It's a place where we can disappear, make it number one in our lives, into such an obsession that it starts to rule out any human contact. The ocean can seem a much more friendly place, and your surfboards are there, or your surfing status: *I was the one who first rode the wave around the corner from G-Land*, or whatever. There'll be Brazilian men like that and European ones. There are Japanese ones – I've met them. They travel to Indonesia or Hawaii and then go home to their spots. We met a couple of them when we did the Tai-Fu project. There were a couple of old guys who were looking at us sideways, like, *What are you doing here?* We asked them for an interview and one of them wouldn't do it; he made his son do it instead. It was the same thing; that was the ground they'd pissed on.

For me, too, surfing has been a way of not growing up. I've had a big part in my own choice not to grow up, getting other people to do things for me and manipulating situations so I didn't have to engage on some level. I've found it really convenient to not grow up. And now, taking on the role of growth, at a time when a lot of men my age are grown up, emotionally well adjusted, having had a good solid growth period. They know themselves in risk and they're strong in themselves and so they're able to make specific moves and back themselves in life ... I think as a surfer I escaped those things so often; it was kind of convenient to use surfing as a way to not engage.

Growth is there for me still. But changing those mental pathways after fifty years is my big challenge now, I reckon.

I was talking to Barton Lynch, the other day, up at his house. I gave him Tim Winton's book, *Breath*. He's not a big reader, BL. It's gonna shock him. Jack Entwistle was up there too. He's eighteen years old. And I thought there's no way known that I'd have been hanging around with a couple of fifty-year-old surfers when I was his age, talking about things. It's really cool. If you're a young surfer now you've got this connection to this older group as a much broader part of the community. The results of what we've done are there and the guidance is there. Jack was genuinely interested. He has issues with his body; he's young and he's physically stiff, super rigid. I was too at eighteen, just from lazing about, sleeping for as long as I possibly could, trying to be cool. There's probably about three years like that when you're around that age.

But there were no fifty-year-olds around when we were young. Older guys were like twenty-four, twenty-five. Charlie was twenty-four, and I remember asking him, Your mum and dad, were they alive in the horse-and-cart days? He was, You cheeky little bastard! That's one memory I have of Charlie, in the Ocean Shores shop one day, sucking on a Marlboro.

My surfing is pretty restricted. It's not really where I'd like it to be. It's suffered, the whole scope of it – the vertical, the round turns, the constant on-edge, the critical edge has gone. There are little bits and pieces, little moments, but it's not where I think it could have been if those injuries hadn't taken place, if my body wasn't so damaged.

A lot happens physically between forty-five and fifty, I believe.

Wayne Lynch once told me that when I was forty. He said, You wait till you're fifty! Something happens when you're forty-five.

I wrote it off, but he was right on the mark. I think those particular changes – physically, mentally, spiritually – happen at different rates. I've still got that young surfer in me, I've still got that mind, I watch the young guys surf and rip, yet I just have to surf within whatever's on offer for me at the time. I watch someone like Occy, and then I go and surf and things just don't fall into place. I go, Wow, I've just got to accept that.

My knee is a big player in my ageing. I feel like a disabled surfer a lot of the time, because it's not even a real knee anymore. It's a one-hundred-year-old knee in a fifty-year-old body. It's like a coconut. And it's grown in the last five years. It's got bigger. I can't disregard it the way I used to. I tried to get it replaced when I was forty, and they said, You're not getting that done for thirty years. It doesn't have the power. Coming out of the top and down the face is a lot of front leg, leaning into it and powering out, and that's really diminished. I've gotta use my body differently, in a smarter way.

I know how to bring it back. By focusing on one piece of equipment. Focusing on a board I enjoy and spending time with it on all sorts of waves. Keep going out, keep doing it. Stretching the body, opening it up. I have to stick to a good routine on the same piece of equipment and keep to that formula, then the performance starts to emerge. Surf a wide range of conditions. If I did that for a month or two, I could get myself up to an okay standard. Bring in some yoga and swimming – real repetitive type of stuff. Then I could start to gauge where I'm at.

I've surfed so many different types of equipment over the past five years or so – SUPs, four fins, towboards, alaias, everything. It'd be bloody interesting to see what I would come up with.

It's not sad, having the fame drift away. It's another kind of awakening, really, as you come out of it. You can choose to live in the past, and that's the danger of *Storm Surfers*, that I make another journey back into that Thing I call Tom Carroll, into that character. But it's not necessarily who I am.

It's an awakening to step into ourselves gracefully as we move on from fame. And you've got to move on. It sounds easy, you know – just move on! – but it's not easy. Not when the fame has been so exciting. From the moment we come out of the womb, we're looking for recognition. You look into your mother's eyes and there it is. It's like, Y*eah, I want more of that.* You'll cry or make gestures – you'll do anything to get that recognition again from your mother or your father or whoever's close to you.

So when you're recognised at such a high level – when you've got thousands of people looking at you, thousands of people stroking that needy part inside you – and then all of a sudden it begins to fade away, your sense of mortality is really powerful. It is a birth-and-death situation.

It's sad sometimes. When I see myself diving for the fame through some sort of ambitious fantasy – I won't say I don't do it anymore because I do, it's been such a large part of me – it's a heavy dive, my whole body's in. But there is something in me that stands back and observes that urge these days. And it says, Oh Tom, look at that! You're still like that. You know it's gonna hurt! But I do have a chance to observe it now.

Being around the surfing world, being around all the top surfers, the memories, being able to go to Hawaii, just to get that hit, that last hit of it – it's sad in a way, but there it is! I can still walk around and get stroked. People feel good about it, and about me. It's nice to be there with people feeling good about me.

But it's slowly drifting away. A lot of things could have dropped away really fast. My place in the world could have altered very quickly to something different. I don't want to be self-conscious, or holed up in my own monastery of shit. I like people! I don't want to distance myself from the world. I like the idea of having a sphere of influence. That's much more subtle, which I welcome.

I hope I'm not one of those people hanging on to old ideas, and I hope people will tell me if I am. I don't want people saying, God, what's he *doing*? He's so bad we can't say anything! We can't tell him. He won't listen. Scary! I've seen people like that, and it's not pretty. But my relationships are close enough today that I'm sure I'd be reminded of it.

I'm a brand ambassador for Quiksilver now. Still. And I'm in a transition period within the company. I'm an icon for the brand, which I've been pretty much since I was 13, with a small gap. What that means in the marketplace, I don't know. I have no idea whatsoever. I know I represent the brand in numerous areas, all the way from the kids to the middle-aged surfer, so there's a pretty broad area of the market that I can communicate with. That can happen in all kinds of different ways.

But Quiksilver's changed. It's going through a massive shift right now. It's stripping back and streamlining. Whether I'm part of that down the track, I don't know. I'm open to suggestions from them about how it moves and how I'll fit in, but I dunno how I'm going to respond. I'm trying to keep my mind as open as possible.

It's scary thinking about how it's all gonna look. I don't know where I'll be in six months. I'd like to be able to sell my house, but I might not be able to. I might be stuck with a massive mortgage, trying to deal with that and having absolutely no money. I might have to move out of the area for a while. Then again, I'm not trying to force anything because it's all happening naturally. The only thing I've gotta force is packing up this house. I've got the tenant downstairs moving out, and I'm getting bits and pieces of maintenance done on the house, ready for sale.

It's symbolic in a way: cleaning up the wreckage of the past, staying with that cleaning-up process, whatever it takes, and not having to be perfect about it all. I would have seen it as being absolutely insurmountable before; I still struggle with my emotional sobriety. That may become easier with time.

Trying to grow at this age is a pretty bizarre thought, but it's all I've got to work with. It's amazing that I can do it, that I've got this choice. It's really, really clear to me now: I have a choice. I never really had that before. It kind of excites me, and scares me again. There's a lot of freedom in it for me. There's an opening. I can give something of myself that I feel worthy about. There's another deeper value in my being here.

Sir Thomas Tom of Appledore.
No other Knight in all the land
Could do the things which he could do.

It doesn't come into my mind the night of the party, or the next, or even after the meeting in the Waimea church where I watch you begin to tell this story; but somewhere in the telling an idea forms, a sort of hope, or at least an understanding.

All the pieces of your life – our circumstances, the times, the way surfing was and what it turned itself into, your gifts and flaws, your short strong body and artistic mind, your freakish ability to exist in the moment, your actual DNA – fell together to make you a world champion, a Pipeline master, one of the greatest surfers who've ever been or ever will be.

And all those same pieces then fell together to make the addict, the chaos, the secrecy and shame that nearly brought you down. *Click, click, click.*

But maybe neither of those things was really you.

You're still special. You're still lucky. That'll never change. People still give you things, they always will. They can't help themselves. How many surfboards were there when you counted them, under the house and in the garage, trying to think about moving? Two hundred? You don't even know what to do with them all.

And me, the supposed journalist. I don't even know what kind of story this is. You were perfect and now you're not. I was supposed to protect you and I couldn't. What the hell is that?

Some hero's journey! Break a leg. Turn fifty. Lose your hair and half your money. Sell your dream house. Can't surf the way you want. Fail!

Become happy.

POSTSCRIPT

(From a small booklet of stories contributed to by various of Tom's mates and family members and handed out at his fiftieth birthday party.)

To Tom, my dearest little freckled buddy. Have so many different and fantastic memories together and I'm going to give you 50 of the finest in word form only. Each of the following words should provoke a memory for you. Good exercise for preventing Alzheimer's apparently!

Eighties Nineties Naughties Nowra Alfa Madwax Ke Iki Jenna Mimi Gracie Lisa Marvin Haleiwa Rockpiles Angourie Hotham Jakarta Sao Paulo cafe Foto Floripa Rio Mentawai Capetown Queenstown Paris Capbreton Chiba Osaka Amsterdam Forries Shippies Margarets TurtleDove Metropolis PorscheTurbosideways brother sister father Utah Rockies

Pyrenees Maui FightingChickensWaltz Jaws Hunter Valley
Girth WAIMEAWIPEOUTTOGETHER.

Love you like a brother. Happy 50 winters.

Ross Clarke-Jones

～

Feliz Aniversário, Thomas Victor! I am so happy to be able to
celebrate your 50th birthday with you. Thank you for helping
me conquer the waves of Waikiki beach on a longboard (circa
1991), for taking Moshe for his first surfing lesson in the rain
and for being an incredibly supportive brother who is able
to light up the room with your infectious energy. You always
make other people feel so special. The longboard moment is
one of my first memories of you, although one of your first
memories of me might be holding a 'little grommet' (aka – me
as a newborn) as seen in a '83 copy of a surfing magazine!

Hope you have a wonderful, happy birthday filled with joy.
Looking forward to celebrating many more with you.

Lucy Carroll

～

My first memory of Tom is that of a blond, curly-haired cherub
in bare feet with freckles and a big smile. When I married his
father in Mosman in 1978, did he come to the wedding in
bare feet? I like to think that he did, but if he didn't, his feet
were bare in spirit.

Valerie Lawson

～

I was staying in an apartment with Tom during the 2009 Quiksilver Pro at Greenmount. We both got caught up in our own little routine each day, before and after the comp. The morning routine sticks out and still rings loud to this day.

Thomas was always a step ahead of me in the morning, preparing himself for another long ten-hour day at the comp site. I was doing my best to stay present and organised, but lagged badly. His routine was morning meditation and mine was yoga. I was mindful of his space and solitude and he mindful of mine.

Tom would gather his things quickly after meditation and proceed to the front door. He would hold the door open slightly, take a deep breath and call out, 'LET'S GO!!!' It would be said with an intensity and authority that I would just jump and start to run to catch up as he was stepping in the elevator.

He never added anymore to this and never judged me for dragging my sorry arse. But he

was relentless with this little routine – day in, day out he worked me with the 'LET'S GO!!!' He knew he had me and took great delight in letting me have it every morning.

The 'LET'S GO!!!' has been psychologically damaging to this present day. It still rings in my head when I'm slow off the mark, especially early in the day and/or at work. Who'd have thought two small words said with passion and volume could have such impact.

Thanks, Gobbo. Love ya mate.

Murray Close

Landing in Cow Bay, Nova Scotia, in an antique seaplane and we land on the middle of a bombie field and do this huge bounce in the air. Water everywhere, everyone's shitting themselves, and Tom is howling in excitement at the back of the plane. He's just not well and never will be.

Martin Daly

~

Tom crashing Stretch's motorbike, circa '78–'79.

This was a highlight for many an onlooker.

In the car park just before going surfing, Tom in his wetsuit, Stretch with his new-to-him Honda 750.

'Can I have a go?' asks Tom.

'Can you ride?' asks Stretch.

'Sure!'

Tom gets on looking like a stunt rider in tight rubber. Going up the car park, looking good. Coming back going very quick. Really quite quick. We don't think he can pull up in time before the log fence at the end of the car park. We're right. Tom crashes into a log pole just before reaching the fence and inertia does its thing, and Tom continues over the handlebars in a backflip, and somehow lands on his feet beyond the fence in the safety zone.

The cops come but Tom has grabbed his board and run into the surf. Stretch's bike was never the same, and I don't know if Tom was either.

And we all learned a valuable lesson: never lend Tom anything with an engine and wheels.

Paul 'Squeak' Lindley

~

A silly time …

My first trip to Hawaii in the mid-80s and the assorted pack included Robert who had just won the lottery and had taken to leaving $5 notes on the windscreen as his calling card, Mike Newling who was travelling on a shoestring, Nick who was under the influence of est and TC.

We had hired a rent-a-wreck and on one of those days when the surf was blown out we made a journey to Makaha. Peter Crawford was in tow as I think Mike was growing mung beans and looking for coconuts to supplement his diet as he had spent all his money on a new Don Johnson board. TC, who was the most experienced driver at negotiating the wrong side of the road, took the wheel and we headed off. Or maybe Tom just took the wheel as he liked driving more than anything else.

I am not sure who pulled out the *pakalolo* but it appeared and we all had a puff except PC who was either waiting for his turn or passed.

Before the smoke could even get out of the car, we were pulled over for speeding – I know that is hard to imagine, Tom speeding, but it happened and that he had a puff was an incredible coincidence. The odds on that – more chance of winning the lottery!

So the cop walks up to the window, which TC winds down, and the smoke billows out. He reels back and snarls, 'You boys been smoking dope!'

Of course we all thought of witty responses but were not about to reel out, 'Yeah book us, Danno.' Tom is told to get out of the car and the cop then asks who else could drive and he expressly demands that they can't have partaken. He looks at me and I look away, as I am sure Nick and Robert do the same.

Up steps PC to the rescue: 'Officer, I haven't touched any and I will drive.'

I know the cop didn't say look into my eyes but PC looks him straight in the eye, holds his gaze, and it was his majestic presence which allowed the cop to look him up and down, say ok, and hand TC a fine. We drove off having witnessed another 'what do you reckon' moment in the life and times of Thomas Carroll.

Love,

Spyder xxx

We were all just as competitive on our pushbikes as in anything else, so when Tom came out with his statement that he felt he was the best pushbike rider in Newport, a tremendous jousting began. In particular it was greeted with absolute ferocity by Haley, who felt HE was in fact the best.

Anyway, there was heaps of mockery and a savage tussle with Robert and Tom in particular trying to prove who was who. Nick and I joined in but I don't think we really cared too much, it was more that Tom had made the claim.

It all came to a head one day when the four of us were riding down Robertson Road with Tom out ahead doing all sorts of re-entries and cutbacks and us all trying to stay out of his way. We were all wearing Beachcomber Bills – big, thick, black thongs that were the fad at the time. Tom is sticking the edge of the thong on the front wheel spokes to make this 'tick-tick-tick' noise. And the thong suddenly got itself wedged in the spokes and he catapulted forward over the handlebars onto his head. Bang.

The self-declared best pushbike rider in Newport was prostrate on the ground with us screeching to a halt all round him, and we didn't know whether to panic or laugh ourselves stupid, you can guess which course we chose.

Andrew Hunter

~~~~~

This happened when we were living in a house at Bungan overlooking the south end in the mid-80s.

Tom came round and we went surfing and got washed in – the surf jumped from three foot to fifteen foot in about an hour, madness. So home we went, up the hill, and found ourselves standing around in the lounge room in our wetsuits. That was the sort of thing that happened in that house, you just hung around in your wetsuit.

Anyway, there we were ... and out of nowhere I suddenly began to hear this very faint voice saying, 'Help! Help!'

'Can you hear that, Tom?' I asked. No, he couldn't, but the voice persisted, very faintly off in the distance somewhere.

I went out on the front balcony where the voice seemed stronger, took a look up Bungan Head Road, and about three houses down from the Eyrie, not far from where Myola Road goes up and over the hill, there was a man stuck under an F100 truck. He'd left it in a driveway and it'd started rolling; he'd run after it to try to stop it and it'd rolled over him and trapped him. He's yelling, 'Help! Get this off me!'

'Look at this!' I say to Tom, we both do a double-take and say to each other, 'Let's go!' and take off running up the hill in our wetsuits to where this weird scene is unfolding. Tigger

Newling appeared out of nowhere as well to help, but it's winter and there is nobody else around, very odd.

We rang the police and the ambulance people, and they came and got the guy out. I think he had a broken leg but was okay. So that was a good ending. But what happened next was hilarious.

The next day the *Manly Daily* had it all over the front page: 'Tom Carroll To The Rescue!' 'Tom Carroll Saves Man!'

Tom was so famous that his fame had actually overwhelmed the situation. It was as if the newspaper had morphed Tom into Superman – lifted the truck up with one hand, applied first aid with the other, then lifted the man up and with fist clenched skyward yelled, 'Tom Carroll! Awayyy!' and actually flown him directly to Mona Vale Hospital.

When in fact we'd just got washed in from a surf and were standing round in our wetsuits.

Robert Hale

In April 1991, Tom's buck's night was held at my nightclub, Metropolis. For those who attended, it was an outrageous night. Many funny incidents occurred that night, in no special order: Pottz jousting with faux roman columns, wetting the large terrazzo floor and having a nude swimming race, my staff were concerned that we were destroying my nightclub, Jamie Brisick crouched in a corner looking like a gargoyle stunned by the events ... Who could forget 'Get Down Saturday Night', a song we played endlessly into the night ... grown men doing some primitive head-tapping stomp led mindlessly by RCJ!

The night finished early the next morning at Newport Beach with Tom being carried in the nude across Barrenjoey Road to the surf, only to be greeted by Mr and Mrs Walker doing their morning walk. As if nothing was out of place, Tom perks up: 'Morning Mr Walker, Morning Mrs Walker ...'

'Good morning Tom,' they replied.

But it wasn't over. The night before Tom's wedding day I was at Metropolis when Mike and Tom cruised through the door. Mike thought it would be a good idea to bring in TC for a quiet drink to calm his nerves. Mike was wrong. Unfortunately for TC and Mike, upon arriving at Metropolis they were greeted by Steve Lidbury (Libbo to his friends). Well, Libbo seized the opportunity with both enormous hands and led us all on a merry adventure. He had Tom under his spell. We left Metropolis and headed to Oxford Street to some gay nightclub ... don't ask me why. TC, Mike, Libbo and Leigh ... OMG, the gay boys were in heaven. However Libbo didn't appreciate the attention, and we soon left, only to proceed further in the night, arriving at the infamous Bourbon and Beefsteak bar, only to be greeted by the NSW State of Origin team, who upon seeing Tom started chanting, 'Tommy Carroll ... Tommy Carroll ...'

We left around daylight. Tom was getting married that afternoon in the Hunter Valley. I drove Tom's Alfa home, only to be greeted by a stern and pissed-off Nick. Apart from the incredulous look he gave us, the first thing he asked Tom was, 'Where is your tie!!'

Leigh Moulds

The surf trip that will stay with me as the best time was a year in Hawaii staying on Sunset Beach.

As the storms raged that year and trees and power poles were down, we bobbed along each day out to the east or west coast of Oahu. Passing the modest but neat houses and appreciating the humility about them. As we'd arrive the sky would open, the wind would drop and we'd enjoy a solitude surf in an amphitheatre of nature, more Tahiti-like than our usual Hawaii visuals.

To and from those surfs we'd review our thoughts about looking at the world in a broader and non-judgemental perspective. A couple of weeks passed and we started to notice other people and their gripes about it being a 'bad winter'. We'd missed the bad part and had a time more metaphysical than usual.

Tom, you are a great friend and congratulations on reaching a milestone turning fifty as an awakened human being.

Bruce Raymond

I'll never forget riding skis out to Shipsterns Bluff in Tasmania with Tom for a *Storm Surfers* mission, episode one. It was minus-eight degrees wind chill factor, snow down to the boat ramp, and onshore squalls that suggested we'd made a big mistake going down there. I remember sitting on the ski under the giant cliffs on the way out to the Bluff as the huge ocean swells rolled up the face of the rocks and thinking, *This is the best thing I've ever been a part of.*

Tom looked at me as if he knew what I was thinking and said, 'How awesome is this … I swear I was a seal or penguin in a past life ... this is awesome.' I agreed wholeheartedly but I was so cold I could hardly raise a smile.

Tom's taught me people can do things they never thought they were capable of, and I'll always love him for that.

Justin McMillan

~&~

To Thomas,

I could think of a hundred silly stories, and even more incredible experiences we have shared. It would be easy to pick any one to add to your birthday wish.

But I will take the time to do what is usually put aside until some time off in the distance when the past is only faint memory.

I will take this time to say what an incredible friend you have been to me in this life. Many of the richest moments I have experienced have been with you by my side.

I do not have any brothers by blood, but you and your brother Nick are what they would have been just like, it just took a travel far across the ocean to find my brothers in life. It is an honour to be called your friend.

Jeff Hornbaker

~&~

Tom is such a classic!

He's a man who has much compassion and empathy for all, including the least fortunate. On the other hand, he might run circles around you at your home surfing break as well. He has been a loyal friend and an extremely honest team rider with many new ideas and the ability to take that new idea out in the water and hit home runs with it.

I can't express my thanks for his involvement in my surfboard business here in Hawaii, as well as my immediate family. (They absolutely love Tom!)

As you know, Tom is a very accident-prone individual and has had more injury recovery time in his lifetime than most. I can only remember the injuries and the very worst incident, when he heard the news of your sister's passing just before a perfect contest performance. I hurt so much for him at that time. I hope his next half is less traumatic. I doubt it, though. Tom will push the physical limits on anything he embraces.

I can only express that Tom will continue to use his valuable gifts and empathy to teach and help others as he ages gracefully, and I truly believe he will continue to be one of the world's best mature surfer/athletes, along with Kelly and a few others in our surfing world. Thank you, Tom, for everything you have shared with me over the years.

Sincerely,

Pat Rawson

Tommy gives 110% effort in everything he does!

I'm so bad with years but Nick will remember because it was their first year doing Molokai team on a prone board. They asked to come out paddling with me on the North Shore, and I was honoured to be asked – I had known the boys for years but didn't know if they knew me.

So they came out with the North Shore crew, including 10-time world champ Jamie Mitchell, still waiting for that first win mind you at the time, so it was over 10 years ago. Anyway, to the FROTH of Tommy.

So he was just spinning his arms and chasing everything in the ocean and not really going anywhere much at all.

I said, Hey Tom slow down and get in sync with the ocean and when the nose dips down paddle hard and when the nose raises up back off. And the reply was something like, Back off?! Nick won't stand for that!

But it was the way he said it. And then, just like anything with one of the greatest watermen of all time, Tommy was frothing and catching everything with ease and hooting and looking back to see where Nick was and just going off.

You had to be there but me and Jamie still laugh about that day whenever we take a new guy out on the North Shore for the first time. Great memories to me anyways. Say happy 50 to him for me.

Mick Dibetta

Here's one thing that stands out to me. It's something many of his newer friends may not know about.

What Tom did by boycotting the South African leg of the world tour in 1985 seems to go by without much comment these days. And that's understandable; the world moves on, and South Africa is the new South Africa, and all that … but back then it was a bad time in that country. It's easy when you're 20 years old and travelling round the world to just skip over things, it's their reality and not yours, you're there to go surfing and you're oblivious to politics really. As surfers we were insulated from the worst, but you could tell there was something terribly wrong with the society, and the fact that we were allowed to surf and have fun sort of made it even worse.

It was huge for Tom to make the move he did. I was one of his best friends and travelling with him a lot, and he gave no indication that he was going to do it. He had to be so mature and strong to deal with it the way he did; it showed so much backbone and integrity. Surfing's a conformist sort of sport and nobody else was even thinking about stepping up like that, which just made his actions more individual and strong. There's not many other people in Australian sport who've done anything like that.

Plus he's so lovable! I don't know what it is. People just seem compelled to look after him, not because he projects as a victim but – I don't know! I recall him going to stay with my relatives in England at one stage, and they looked after him better than they looked after me! It's fascinating.

Mike Newling

The thing I think of is the 'you and me DJ!' syndrome, which has been going on now for forty years, since the first Plussie days. Usually he takes off in front of me on the wave and whips his board around my ears while I struggle to stay on my feet.

I never had any say in it. When he was young it was interesting because he was so precise and accurate so there was no danger, but as we've got older it's got a bit dangerous – you never know who might make a mistake. But it's the fondest memory I have from our personal time in the water together over those years: the trust in skills and the confidence it showed that Tom had in our friendship, that it wouldn't go wrong but just grow as a result. And it has.

David Jones

You may be aware that a couple of years ago our good friend Tom added to his impressive list of surfing feats by fearlessly facing and conquering the power and glory of the huge Southern Ocean swells breaking at Pedra Branca, a remote reef far off the southern tip of Tasmania.

I bet you didn't know that thirty-three years earlier and 180 kilometres to the north-east Tom had faced raw, terrifying Tasmanian power during his first trip to the Southern Isle, but this time there was no casual bravado, no elegant disregard for common sense, oh no.

On that day the trembling little bastard shat himself and begged for mercy, and I should know because I was trembling and begging alongside him in a shabby room on the sixth floor of a cheap hotel in Hobart.

It was Easter of 1976 and we had flown to Tassie as members of Newport Surf Club to compete in the Malibu Board Display at the national titles being held at Clifton Beach.

Some of the memories that linger are: 'It was bloody cold.' It was fucking cold in the water because the wetsuits we'd smugly brought from home were banned as they were deemed to be an unfair advantage, so it was sluggos, a heavy canvas singlet and the maroon and gold cap.

Despite this – or maybe because of it – our Tommy blitzed the field and won the National gold. That was his biggest victory up to that point.

The Newport clubbie hierarchy were beside themselves with joy and snuck us into the pub and plied us with beer and let us witness the rowers' homoerotic ritual of the Dance of the Flaming Arseholes. The image of Bickies running naked through lunchtime Hobart with a flaming roll of toilet paper streaming out of his anus remains with me.

By 10.30 we were back in our hotel feeling like kings of the world except for the presence of our chaperone, the nasty and ambiguous Alastair Walker.

To amuse ourselves we threw things out of the sixth floor window onto hapless Tasmanians below.

Apples are cheap in Tassie, so we threw the whole bag. The last one was one of those throws that the moment it leaves your hand you know exactly where it's going to land; part of you wanted to look away but it was mesmerising in its plummet straight into the meaty head of a neckless beast wearing a jacket with 'Tasmanian Devils MC' emblazoned across its broad back.

FAAARK!

We looked at each other, stunned, then burst out laughing as he yelped and swore. We ducked back in just before he saw us (or so we thought). Ten minutes passed, nothing – sweet, we got away with it, then just outside the door: 'I RECKON THIS IS THE ROOM, MICK! OPEN THE FUCKEN DOOR OR WE'LL KICK IT IN.'

The trembling started, the pupils dilated, the heart rate exploded, the Golden Boy put a finger to his mouth and shook his head. We were now both very scared.

Seeing this, Big Al leapt to his feet and swung open the door, laughing that weird Scottish cackle. 'Here they are. I told them not to do it,' he shrilled as two of the heaviest looking bikies burst through the door, ready for trouble.

I can still see the puzzled looks on their faces when their bulging eyes focused on two freckly 45 kilo, 14-year-old boys. *We can't smash them*, they thought disappointedly.

'Sorry,' we blurted.

'Don't do it again, you cheeky little pricks.' We wouldn't and haven't.

So Tom got braver, Al found God, and I've never been back to Tassie.

Kevin Long

I remember the time I'd just moved to the northern beaches and was asked to join the Newport Plus Boardriders club. Part of my initiation into the club was to co-pilot Tom Carroll to the Gold Coast in an Alfa GTV 6-cylinder beast.

Remembering back then there was no freeway to the Goldy, it was mainly the back roads. With no help from me driving, he managed to make it from Newport to Snapper Rocks in a record seven and a half hours! Don't think I said a word the entire drive, white knuckles the whole way! On the return trip after winning the event, Tom managed to write the car off in Coffs Harbour … I remember spinning in a circle in the middle of the intersection for what seemed like forever. Have been reluctant to get back in a car with him ever since!

Happy Birthday, mate, love you.

Pottz

It was Newport Plus's last win after fifteen years of dominance. The Gold Coast was the setting, the event was tag team with the best clubs in Australia. We bombed badly in the heats, and it was up to Pottz to get us through. He had not lost in three WCT events and went up against Kerrbox and flogged him, only to lose on some very dubious judging.

We weren't going to take it lightly, so with my mouth, Mike's brawn and Dougall's power (Billabong was the sponsor), we got the Bondi judge to admit he had cheated.

So we were back in it. TC and Pottz pulled the boys together and said, 'Right, we are going to show these guys.' We drew Bondi, of all clubs, and TC destroyed their main man to lead us on a roll to the final with a team of Stuart Bedford-Brown, Joel Jones, TC, Pottz and Daff. We were up against Merewether in the final: Nick Wood, MR, Shane Powell, Luke Egan and Matt Hoy. I was torn as to who should be the double-whammy surfer, TC or Pottz? They both wanted the other to have the honour – no ego, just plain mateship.

TC took it on and schooled a young Luke to set up an epic victory, the last of the empire.

During a long night of celebrations, three small nude men ran into a resort and boxed every plastic bubble light off their posts. After a struggle to escape, they disappeared into the night, only to leave one damning piece of evidence: a pair of black sluggos.

The next day, I hatched a plan. We had a grommet Matt Hoy hanging with us, who'd heard about the bubble light incident. I told him the police had been to the hotel and had the sluggos and wanted to talk. 'So Hoyo,' I said, 'go wake Tom up.'

Matt came back a half hour later and said, 'He's packing his stuff and getting out of here.'

I called him on the phone to ask what he thought he was

doing, his words were: 'I can't be seen to have done stuff like that!' Yeah, thanks Tom, it's okay, we'll cop the rap.

We told Hoyo it was a set-up and the police were never involved. He couldn't believe it and exclaimed, 'But that's Tom Carroll. You can't do that to Tom Carroll!'

Yes, you can. He can take it as good as he gives it. That's why we love him.

Glenn 'Boj' Stokes and family

Acknowledgements

Thank you to all our family and friends, everywhere, who've put up with us to varying degrees over the years.

And to the surf communities in Australia and around the world, thank you for giving us a home.

For a long time both of us thought we could go it alone, in our different ways. It took us many years to realise that's not just irrational, it's impossible.

This book is for everyone who helped us to see that.

Thanks also to Alison Urquhart at Random House, who kept the pressure on; to Brandon VanOver, whose meticulous and elegant editing was immensely appreciated by Nick; and to Kevin Hudson, Tom's sponsor, who gave TC confidence when it was needed.

– Tom and Nick Carroll

About the Author

Photo: Wendy Carroll

Nick Carroll is the world's best known surf writer. He grew up surfing with his little brother, Tom, on Sydney's north side, won two Australian surfing titles, then turned to journalism, editing Australia's *Tracks* magazine and spending several years in California as editor-in-chief of Western Empire, publishers of the internationally distributed *Surfing Magazine*. More recently he has turned his hand to television, co-writing the ABC popular culture documentaries *Bombora* and *Wide Open Road*.

Nick lives in Sydney with his wife, Wendy, and two children, Madeleine and Jack.